To Robert Marcus, my father,
and Mary Weisstein, my grandmother,
for both nurturing and challenging me

AKNOWLEDGMENTS

First and foremost I would like to acknowledge the anthropology program of the Graduate School and University Center of the City University of New York. As an anthropologist, I am purely a product of this rigorous and stimulating program. I would like to thank the following people without whom this project would not have been possible: Ida Susser, Edward Hansen, Michael Blim, Gerald Sider, and Marc Edelman.

I owe the biggest debt of gratitude to Dave Burner and Robert Marcus for editorial work, far above and beyond the call of duty. Elizabeth Marcus helped to edit this book and I am grateful to her for all the love and work that she lavished on this project. A special thanks to Susan Masayda Senter of Brandywine Press for copyediting and proofreading the manuscript.

Thanks to my many colleagues in the program who encouraged and challenged me: Eric McGuckin, Charles Menzies, Katherine McCaffrey, Molly Doane, Jonathan Hearn, Yvonne Lassalle, and Belkis Necos. Thanks also to Deborah Pellow, Michael Weinstein, and Tracy Morgan.

Finally I want to thank all the authors. Without their professionalism and tolerance of my demands and quirks this book never would have seen the light of day. Thanks guys.

TABLE OF CONTENTS

I
RACE AND NATIONALITY

II
GENDER, SEXUALITY, AND KINSHIP

III
IDENTITY AND CONSUMER CULTURE

INTRODUCTION

A SMALL PLANET

Everyone knows that we live in a global world. Today, children with inexpensive personal computers send and receive messages across the globe in seconds using technology that was once only available to scientists and statesmen. Native peoples in the most remote villages in the high mountains of South America gather around a village television set to watch Baywatch and the X-Files. Colombian peasants without running water in their homes watch CNBC financial news to decide when to sell their coffee harvest, while high school janitors in Little Rock, Arkansas, keep track of the Singapore stock market to decide when they can retire. The defeat of industrial strikes and protests in Korea in 1980 and the collapse of the Mexican peso in 1982 by lowering wages in Korea and Mexico lead companies to shift factories around the world and decrease workers' living standards in the United States. The actions of people we will never meet on the other side of the planet change our everyday lives.

Anthropology has always taken all of humankind as its subject and the whole world as its laboratory to study what it means to be human and live in groups with other humans. For anthropologists, the "new globalism" is but one new chapter in a much longer story of human development, part of the epic tale of one species, *Homo sapiens*, which has been engaging in long-distance travel and trade, war, intermarriage, and cross-cultural contact since the dawn of modern humans nearly 100,000 years ago. These external connections and outside influences that transform local lives have been the rule of human history rather than the exception.

On this small planet where the actions of people across the globe have a profound influence on our daily lives and our futures, we must understand something about the lives of people across oceans and the way they view the world, if we are to successfully interact with them. This is the mission of anthropology: to understand the differences and similarities, the understandings, expectations, and desires of peoples living in a wide variety of conditions, circumstances, and environments.

This introductory essay underscores why anthropology is well-suited to make sense of the crazy quilt of human existence. It looks at the discipline's origins as "world anthropology" and the way in which contemporary political and economic processes, in particular the events and aftermath of World War II, have reinforced this mission. It considers the volume's articles, written from fieldsites as different as Taiwan and Cuba; covering actors as varied as Brazilian shoppers, Tibetan refugees, and Canadian fishers; and shows how they are informed by a recognition of the broader forces of politics and economics that bind humans together in a complex weave.

ANTHROPOLOGY CONFRONTS GLOBALISM: EARLY TRENDS

Anthropology, as a social science, developed in nineteenth-century Europe as it was being fundamentally transformed by the rise of capitalism and the industrial revolution. Anthropology and the other modern social sciences such as sociology, economics, and political science, developed in response to the sense of uncertainty and social dislocation caused by these profound political and economic changes. Anthropology, however, more than any other social science, was global in its vision. Its very name identified it as the "science of humanity." It set out to explain the world that capitalism had made smaller, trying to bring some sense of order to the chaos that is human existence (see Wolf 1982).

At its origin, anthropology was concerned mainly with the study of non-Western peoples. Since the days of Columbus, Western travelers and missionaries encountered people vastly different from those of European extraction. Westerners told wide-eyed stories of two-headed beings, flesh-eating savages, and naked wildmen running in the bush. At the moment of anthropology's birth in the nineteenth century, however, European nations were expanding across the globe, establishing colonial empires in which they could secure resources and establish new markets. This required Westerners to develop new relationships—however unequal—with these peoples often described as so exotic.

Early anthropologists, responding to Europeans' need to understand their colonies, first sought to explain the evolution of culture on a worldwide scale. Edward Burnett Tylor (1832–1917) and Lewis Henry Morgan (1818–1881), the key thinkers on this topic, theorized that all of the varying peoples of the world belonged to one race, humanity, and that social and cultural differences could be explained by charting human development into different sequential stages: savagery, barbarism, and civilization. There were gross limitations to their theorizing: they viewed human history as a linear path of progress, in which European social organization represented the pinnacle of progress and all other societies were just underdeveloped versions of Victorian England. But unlike other thinkers who searched for racial explanations of cultural difference, Morgan and Tylor established the mainstream of anthropology: the idea that all people, however different and seemingly strange, nonetheless belonged to one race: humanity. The next generation of anthropologists soon made a name for themselves by going out into the world and describing life as they actually saw it. Ethnography, the art of describing culture, became the hallmark and distinguishing feature of the discipline. Often but not always studying colonial subjects of the anthropologist's home country, they went to small villages in distant lands, learned new languages, and recorded the lifeways of peoples vastly different from themselves. Working on a local level, with a commitment to seeing life holistically through the eyes of the people they studied, anthropologists gained intimate understandings of individual cultures and rich descriptions of local life. But theorists often had a hard time relating these community studies to a broader schema, to an understanding of how this one village or society, was part of a larger picture—a region, a nation, the world.

Furthermore, ethnographers too often neglected history. Even though many of the places anthropologists studied were colonies, enmeshed in a complex and changing relationship with imperial powers, these small villages were often depicted as outside the currents of human history. This depiction of cultures as essentially isolated and static became increasingly difficult to maintain in the aftermath of World War II.

WORLD WAR TWO AND BEYOND: TOWARDS A SMALL PLANET

World War II fundamentally reoriented anthropology towards its origins as a world science. The war moved people around the globe on an unprecedented scale. Fought on every continent, the war linked previously ignored sections of the globe through new military communications networks, supply lines, and political interdependencies. The seemingly timeless and isolated tribes and village communities that anthropologists had studied before the war were now permanently transformed. After the war, when anthropologists returned to the fieldsites of the colonial world, they found everywhere the direct effects of outside forces: whole villages wiped away by advancing armies, abandoned military hardware, electric generators for field stations, children of long gone soldiers bearing their father's names, international bankers and U.S. and U.N. advisers attempting to organize the reconstruction and still unresolved conflicts generated by the war.

As the pre–World War II colonial world disappeared, former colonial peoples sought to rule themselves in their own nations. In places like China, Africa, Korea, and Vietnam locally-based militias composed of ordinary citizens found themselves victorious over fascism and asked why they should continue to allow colonial powers like France and England to dominate them. Often liberation from the colonial powers meant overthrowing their own indigenous rulers, tied to the colonial system. Worker and peasant militias, led by popular local leaders like Mao Ze-dong in China, Kim Il Sung in Korea, Ho Chi Minh in Vietnam, and Marshal Tito in Yugoslavia fought civil wars against the traditional rulers of their countries.

On every continent people confronted a bipolar world divided between the communist camp of the Soviet Union and a capitalist camp led by the United States. They struggled over what kind of a society they would build and which camp they would join. Nations in both camps suffered with the changing position of their "superpower" patron—as the Lee article on Taiwan and the Marcus article on Cuba demonstrate. Groups unable to consolidate strong nation-states with the direct support of one of the two "superpowers" were likely to be left out in the cold, fleeing their homes as refugees or living as foreigners in their own nations as the Palestinians and Tibetans discussed in Sawalha and McGuckin's articles.

In sum, out of the global cataclysm that was World War II came our present world: a much smaller, more interdependent planet where events in one place profoundly influence people's lives many thousands of miles away. Anthropologists now had to study individual cultures and societies as part of a political and economic system that was constantly creating and re-creating people's very sense of themselves.

ANTHROPOLOGY IN A GLOBAL ENVIRONMENT: THEORETICAL APPROACHES

Anthropology in the postwar United States increasingly focused on issues of cultural change and "modernization." (Vincent 1990:225–307). Robert Redfield studied how modern processes of conquest, urbanization, and migration transformed peasant society into urban society (see Redfield 1960). Another example, Anthony Wallace treated the Ghost Dance of the Plains Indians as a cultural response to a colonial encounter (Wallace 1956). Julian Steward's People of Puerto Rico project represented an effort to move from studying small cultures and microcosms to the study of complex, class-structured colonial society (Steward 1956). Anthropologists, once identified solely with the study of "traditional" peoples and ways of life took up the study of rural proletarians and the urban poor (Mintz 1960, Lewis 1966).

The most significant development in anthropological thinking of the postwar period, however, occurred in the context of anti-colonial revolt in what came to be called the Third World, particularly the revolutions in China and Cuba. Marxism entered the academy. Like anthropology, Marxism was holistic and global in its approach. It brought a focus on power, history, and worldwide political and economic process to anthropological theory and practice.

As a result of the focus on power, anthropology confronted its own complicity in the spread and maintenance of imperialism and revamped both its methods and theories (see Hymes 1969). Marxism brought a focus on history to the discipline. Anthropologists were encouraged to contextualize societies, individuals, and behavior in light of historical events and processes (Smith 1984). Wars and acts of resistance and the contemporary politics of Third-World peasantry became important topics of inquiry (Wolf 1969, Scott 1976). The poverty and quaintness that was often depicted as part of the traditional way of life was shown often to be the result of exploitation by and resistance to the West (Worseley 1957, Wolf 1982, Wilmsen 1989).

Significantly, Marxism also functioned on the practical level. A key element of Marxist theory was its belief in the unity of theory and practice. Marxism encouraged anthropologists to address issues that would not just remain in the academy, but contribute to the achievement of a more just world. Thus Marxist anthropologists took up issues such as the subordination of women (Etienne and Leacock 1980, Nash and Safa 1974), racial and ethnic conflict and inequality (Mencher 1974), and colonialism (Wessman 1981) as part of a vision of not just describing the world, but changing it.

CULTURE AND COMMUNITY IN A GLOBAL ENVIRONMENT

The collapse of the Soviet Union in 1989–1991 and the triumph of capitalism have forced anthropologists to ask new questions about human life and culture as they grapple with the social and cultural implications of the rapidly accelerated pace of globalization. More and more, anthropologists feel uneasy about their ability to make sense of the world. Some even speak of a "crisis of representation," in which old ways of thinking are increasingly inadequate to describe a world in transition (see Marcus and Fischer 1986).

These essays are part of a trend in anthropology that is global in vision, that links local cultural forms to broader political and economic processes. The essays confront contemporary human problems—such as racism, poverty, inequality—and draw upon anthropology's tradition of holism to make sense of cultural particularities. This world that is growing smaller is also growing more economically and politically polarized. Multinational textile factories and electronic assembly plants employ thousands of men, women, and children in Asia, Latin America, and the Caribbean who work for meager wages to produce clothing and luxury items for a largely Western consumer market. The oil shock of 1973–75, then the debt crisis of 1982 clearly revealed both the rapid rate of globalization and the increasing inequities between the First World and the

Third World, the North and South. The crisis showed that as governments and peoples were more directly drawn into the international economic system, they were incorporated unevenly and unequally. Lassalle shows how widely criticized youth leisure practices in Andalusia, Spain can only be understood within the broader context of the stagnant Andalusian economy. O'Dougherty points to the unusual consumerism among middle-class Brazilians as a not entirely predictable response to the world economic crisis.

Globalization is not only political and economic, but cultural. In South India, a rickshaw wallah blares a Michael Jackson cassette, while in Iran, a woman in a chodor sneaks a Marlboro cigarette. In a world where emblems of Western society seem ubiquitous, camera-clicking tourists and travelers disenchanted with Western ways set forth to remote corners of the globe, searching for more authentic peoples and timeless cultures. Yet McGuckin's article on Tibetan refugees suggests that the world these travelers encounter is already reconfigured by global politics and economics. What then is the meaning of tradition in this seemingly untraditional world? What is culture? What is community?

A common theme in many of these essays is the relationship between economic and social forms. The new international economy is producing a variety of cultural responses on a global scale. In Scotland, Hearn connects the rise of Scottish nationalism to the economic reverberations of the global oil crisis of the 70s and the retrenchment of the welfare state. In Cuba, Marcus argues that the deterioration of the socialist state threatens the social status of Afro-Cubans. In Taiwan, Lee argues that economic change is responsible for generational conflict within families over social roles and work responsibilities. And, as Menzies points out, there is no simple, one to one correspondence between economics and social forms. In Canada, Menzies examines the ways in which two men of essentially similar social origin are assigned different racial identities as "White" and "Indian," and how differently they therefore fit into a capitalist system of production that relies upon a racially segregated workforce for its perpetuation.

Several essays of the book point to the powerful effect of global forces on the lives of ordinary people as well as how they mediate such pressures. In Hart's article the economic devastation of World War II breaks deeply ingrained Mediterranean values of honor and shame in Naples, Italy. Warms also considers the cultural impact of the War on the life of an individual, Mory Samaké, one of many thousands of African youth recruited to serve in the French colonial army. Sawalha presents Palestinians forging a new identity in opposition to the forces that try to eliminate or assimilate them. Chin shows African-American girls in New Haven, Connecticut, transforming mass-produced symbols into ones with distinct, local cultural meaning.

NEW IDENTITIES IN A CHANGED WORLD

Rather than fearing the loss of culture, community, and self in today's world, many anthropologists celebrate the global consciousness that is currently developing. While we are disturbed by the terrible conflicts, fratricidal wars, and increased economic inequality that is currently ravaging the globe, we see tremendous possibilities in this new, smaller world. The increased international communication, travel, migration, production, and culture contacts provide both danger and opportunity. As anthropologists and citizens of the world we draw on our discipline's commitment to respect for cultural difference and an integrated and global view of humanity. Only with such a larger analysis and vision can we build a world where people are not just strangers across oceans, but neighbors in a global world.

REFERENCES

Bohannan, Paul and Mark Glazer
      1988   High Points in Anthropology. New York: Alfred A. Knopf.

Etienne, Mona, and Eleanor Leacock, eds.
      1980   Women and Colonization: Anthropological Perspectives. New York: Bergin and Garvey/Praeger.

Hymes, Dell, ed.
      1969   Reinventing Anthropology. New York: Pantheon.

Lewis, Oscar
      1966   La Vida: A Puerto Rican Family in the Culture of Poverty in San Juan and New York. New York: Random House.

Marcus, George and Michael Fischer
      1986   Anthropology as Cultural Critique: An experimental moment in the human sciences. Chicago: University of Chicago Press.

Mencher, Joan P.
      1974   The Caste System Upside Down or the Not-So-Mysterious East. Current Anthropology 15:469–494.

Mintz, Sidney
      1960   Worker in the Cane: A Puerto Rican Life History. New Haven, Yale University Press.

Nash, June and Helen Safa, eds.
      1976   Sex and Class in Latin America. New York: Praeger.

Redfield, Robert
      1960   The Little Community and Peasant Society and Culture. Chicago: University of Chicago Press.

Scott, James
      1976   The Moral Economy of the Peasant: Rebellion and Subsistence in Southeast Asia. New Haven: Yale University Press.

Smith, Carol
      1984   Local history in global context. Comparative Studies in Society and History 26:193–228.

Steward, Julian, ed.
   1956   The People of Puerto Rico: A study in social anthropology. Urbana:
          University of Illinois Press.

Vincent, Joan
   1990   Anthropology and Politics. Tucson: University of Arizona Press.

Wallace, Anthony
   1956   Revitalization movements. American Anthropologist 58:264–281.

Wessman, James
   1981   Anthropology and Marxism. Cambridge, Mass: Schenkman.

Wilmsen, E.
   1989   Land Filled With Flies: A Political Economy of the Kalahari.
          Chicago: University of Chicago Press.

Wolf, Eric R.
   1969   Peasant Wars of the Twentieth Century. New York: Harper Row.
   1982   Europe and the People Without History. Berkeley: University of
          California Press.

Worsley, P.
   1957   The Trumpet Shall Sound: A Study of "Cargo" Cults in Melanesia.
          London: MacGibbon and Kee.

PART
I

Race and Nationality

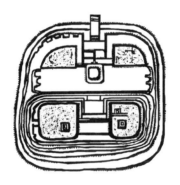

THROWING AWAY THE BONES

The Story of Mory Samaké, an African Veteran of the French Colonial Army

Richard L. Warms

Look, when you work for someone, he's got to recognize your efforts. They treat us like their dogs. They are white, we are black but we are all equal. If someone cuts my hand and someone cuts one of their hands, the blood is just the same. When we were there fighting the war, no one said "this one is white, this one is black." We didn't go to fight with ill will. We gave our blood and our bodies so that France could be liberated. But now, since they have their freedom, they have thrown us away, forgotten us. If you eat the meat, you throw away the bone. France has done just that to us.

Mory Samaké, Malian World War II veteran

INTRODUCTION

This is the story of Mory Samaké an African soldier who fought in Europe during World War II. He was a sergeant in the *Tirailleurs Sénégalais* or Senegalese Riflemen, one of the many African regiments that fought in Europe against the Nazis during World War II. These African soldiers risked their lives for countries that were not their own in a war fought far from home and found themselves forever changed by the experience. Their histories can give us insight into the process of European colonial expansion and the way that World War II changed the culture and politics of Africa, while leaving in place many colonial inequalities.

When most Americans think of World War II in Europe, they imagine American, English, and French troops (often led by a character resembling John Wayne) fighting Germans. It may come as a surprise to learn that almost a quarter million black African soldiers fought in Europe and North Africa between 1939 and 1945. It is particularly astonishing to learn that between 1940 and summer 1944, black Africans constituted the main rank and file of the Free French Army. Without their participation, critical Free French victories over the Nazis in the fall of 1944 would have been impossible. How did Mory Samaké, a young man from a village in the French Sudan (now Mali) in West Africa, come to be fighting in France?

While Europeans had been traveling to Africa in search of slaves and valuable trading goods since the 1400s, not until the nineteenth century did they establish colonies there. With the coming of the industrial revolution, Europeans needed tropical oils, gums, rubber, and other natural resources from Africa to fuel their tremendous industrial growth. French, British, and other Europeans established trading companies to buy these goods. The French built trading posts along the Senegal River (between modern day Senegal and Mauritania) and began to buy gum arabic, a tree resin used in cooking and in the manufacture of textiles, adhesives, and inks. French moves into Africa were not unopposed. Numerous African powers operated in the Senegal River basin so French trading posts needed military protection. At first troops were sent out from France to defend the posts but at that time Frenchmen considered service in Africa a virtual death sentence. Those who could be compelled to go were often "drunkards and marauders, disturbed and profoundly vicious men" (Schmaltz, an early colonial governor, cited in Echenberg 1991:8). Instead of relying on such troops, the French soon began to garrison their posts with men drawn from the local African population.

By the last third of the nineteenth century, the French and other European powers had substantial investments throughout Africa. Each power had staked out its own area of trade, but each feared competition from the others. The result was the so-called "scramble for Africa," a quarter century when European powers raced each other for control of African territory. In this contest, each nation made extensive use of African troops. The French officially formed the *Tirailleurs Sénégalais*, or Senegalese Riflemen, in 1857. Under French officers, African troops conquered the areas of West Africa that became French colonial possessions.

Finding men to serve in the *Tirailleurs* was very difficult. Africans rarely wanted to serve under people with whom they had no kinship in what they considered a rag-tag band of ruffians and mercenaries. The French solved this manpower problem by purchasing slaves to serve in the *Tirailleurs* and, when possible, incorporating the sons of nobles in areas they conquered. By the 1890s, the French had taken several steps such as increasing salaries and enlistment bonuses to make service in the

Tirailleurs more attractive, but even so, at the close of the era of colonial conquest in the first decade of the twentieth century, the *Tirailleurs Sénégalais* was largely composed of ex-slaves and other social elements considered undesirable.

Once colonial rule had been established, the role of military forces like the *Tirailleurs* changed. At first, they were used to suppress rebellions among colonized peoples and they formed a core of subjects whose loyalty was to French rule rather than any pre-existing state. Soon politicians and publicists in France began to look to Africa as a reservoir of military manpower. Propagandists such as Charles Mangin (1911) argued that Africans were natural soldiers—partially, so he claimed, because their nervous systems were less developed than those of Europeans—who could revitalize the French army and national spirit. Mangin and others proposed the conscription of a large standing African army to be used to achieve French imperialist aims. This notion passed its first real test in 1912 when West African troops were used to conquer Morocco. Using African troops thereafter became fundamental to French colonial policy. They were used extensively both in Europe and Africa in World War I (Page 1987). Each year after the war, mobile draft boards moved through French West Africa conscripting men for military service. The *Tirailleurs Sénégalais* changed from a small army of ex-slaves to a huge military force drawn from all levels of society.

Statesman, poet, and former soldier in the *Tirailleurs*, Léopold Senghor once called the *Tirailleurs* "the Empire's black watchdogs" (1991:71 orig 1945). They served France throughout her colonial possessions, in Morocco, Syria, Madagascar, Indochina (Vietnam), Algeria and many other places throughout the empire. Hundreds of thousands served in Europe in World Wars I and II. They were used not only to suppress colonial rebellions, but also against defiant French. During the French general strike of 1947, the *Tirailleurs* broke up protests outside the Nice post office and replaced striking dock workers at the port of Marseilles (Echenberg 1978). Their blood and their bodies were critical in holding the French colonial empire together.

In some ways, the international use of colonial troops proved to be an excellent policy for France. Colonial armies were less expensive to operate than those composed of French citizens and casualties among colonial troops had less political impact in France than losses of French troops. Beyond this, the notion of men from Africa (as well as colonial troops from other areas of the world) fighting for French power and French culture seemed itself to be proof of French imperial destiny and cultural strength.

Colonial officials, however, struggled with the policy. Conscripting men for the *Tirailleurs Sénégalais*—in effect, a blood tax—produced civil unrest and increased hostility to French rule. Further, service in the *Ti-*

railleurs Sénégalais created a large group of veterans with a cosmopolitan outlook. They could speak at least some French and many had acquired technical skills. Importantly, they knew that they and their comrades had suffered and sometimes died for the French. And they believed that France thereby owed them a profound debt. Veterans played a critical role in the national independence movements after World War II. Senghor, for example, became the first president of independent Senegal.

Upon returning to their countries after their tour of duty ended or when the *Tirailleurs* disbanded, once at home most veterans tried to enter the mainstream of African life. This was not easy. Men who served abroad were transformed by what they had seen. Their experiences were often incomprehensible to those who had neither traveled or served in an army. Their knowledge of French and of foreign ways often gave them an advantage in dealing with outsiders but—particularly if the returning veteran lacked a pension— the price of this was sometimes estrangement and marginalization within their own societies. While some veterans were handicapped by their experiences of violence, racism, and an alien cultural system, others became successful (Schleh 1968). The failures, like countless American veterans of Vietnam, suffered grave difficulties returning to society, often acquiring reputations for drunkenness and eccentric behavior (Echenberg 1980).

The story of Mory Samaké sheds light on the lives of the Africans who fought for France. Enlisting in the *Tirailleurs Sénégalais* in 1932 and serving first in Morocco and then in France and North Africa during World War II, he was a soldier during the heyday of French colonialism in Africa. He helped enforce French rule in Morocco and was part of the French army in Belgium that the Nazis crushed when France fell to the Germans in 1940. In 1944 he was a member of the victorious Free French forces that defeated the Nazis. His experiences of the army are typical of veterans of those years, particularly those who served at the beginning of World War II (Lawler 1988, 1992). He told his story to me in several interviews at his home in Mali, in January 1992 and December 1994.

SAMAKÉ'S STORY

Mory Samaké was born in 1911 in a village near Bougouni, a small town in the French Sudan (now Mali), and joined the *Tirailleurs Sénégalais* on November 26, 1932, at the age of 21. He enlisted for a four-year term. He told me that he joined because he had friends who were *Tirailleurs*. When they came back to his village on leave they were "well dressed, happy, and in good shape."

He was sent to Kati, the principal army camp in the French Sudan for basic training. Training included "learning how to use and care for their new weapons, physical training and conditioning, marching and general combat techniques" (Lawler 1988:102) as well as rudimentary instruction in French.

After six months of training, Samaké was sent to join the fifth *Régiment Tirailleurs Sénégalais* at Fez in Morocco. Samaké served in Morocco from 1933 until just before the start of World War II in 1939. Nationalist agitation was a common feature of urban life; civic unrest frequently erupted into violence and the *Tirailleurs* often broke up riots and enforced French control. This was particularly the case with the suppression of the nationalist *Comité d'Action Marocaine* in 1937 (Hoisington 1984). Mory Samaké has vivid memories of campaigns against these rebels:

> In Morocco, I was just a soldier. I had a machine-gun "Ouisse". It was really big, the "Ouisse." It's not the same as a machine-gun. The "Ouisse" is much heavier. There were times when I really abused the Moroccans. I had to because we were under the command of the French. When they say you have to do something, you do it.
>
> When you took a prisoner, if you wanted to, you killed him. If not, you could keep him captive. Me, I never kept prisoners, ah no. If he found me, he would have killed me so, if I got him, I killed him. It was only the officers who said that you shouldn't kill prisoners. They said that if you have a prisoner, you bring him to the rear and there were some who did that. Me, I never kept them. If he took me, he would have killed me. Why, if I got him, shouldn't I kill him? If someone is going to do evil to you, why, if you get him, should you let him live?

Samaké's attitudes toward prisoners of war are not particularly surprising. During the French conquest of Samaké's homeland, both French forces and the African forces who opposed them routinely executed prisoners (Balesi 1979:11–29). Samaké, who was born only slightly more than a decade after the end of this conquest, had grown up hearing stories of that war.

In Morocco, the brutality of warfare was counterbalanced by a vibrant and cosmopolitan social life. Samaké made many friends among other Sub-Saharan Africans, particularly men from Senegal and Guinea. Additionally, during this era, more than 150,000 French settlers lived in the colony and social contacts between them and African soldiers were frequent. Samaké remembers:

> When I was in Morocco, I was really well liked [by the French]. They gave me a Arab name up there. They called me Ali. They gave me that name even though I used to drink. I tell you, its

old age that has made me like I am today. Before, the whites liked me. Everyone liked me. Why? Because I am a man who grins, smiles, you know.

We had good times in Morocco too. We had big parties and danced with the French girls. Ah! I was young then. It was the French girls who gave me the name "Berber." I used to make everyone happy. When I went in to the bar, like that, to have a little drink, all the ladies said: "Berber, Berber." It was just like that.

I had a child with a Frenchwoman, the daughter of a master sergeant. I used to always hang out with her and I had a child with her. I left the child with her, and they went back to France.

In 1939, when war with Germany was imminent, France brought over 80,000 West African troops to defend the metropole (Lawler 1988). Samaké left Morocco for France, probably to the *Tirailleurs* camp at Fréjus, the traditional home of the African troops. Then, in early 1940, he was sent to fight in the disastrous campaign for Belgium. During this period he was promoted:

I was well liked by the whites because I worked really hard. I did really well in France. When someone doesn't do well, they don't promote him! You see, first I became a corporal, then a sergeant. They don't give you those if you don't obey the chief.

Samaké remembers the Germans as "much stronger than the Moroccans" and he remembers one battle particularly vividly:

There was a bridge between France and Belgium. The French had put half of their men on the Belgian side and the other half on the French side. Then they blew up the bridge themselves at 11:00 sharp. I was there, at that place. Lots of men died there. So many that we were all walking on their blood.

Since the early years of the century, propagandists had suggested that Africans were ferociously powerful and valiant soldiers and Samaké recalls that the French used the racial differences among their troops to encourage them to fight harder and believe in their own strength and superiority:

The French put the dead blacks in one place and the dead whites in another. They made it so that the blacks coming back from the front passed by the pile of dead whites and the white troops passed by the dead blacks. They did that so we wouldn't be afraid, so that fear didn't play with our heads.

The battles in Belgium were extraordinarily fierce. Lawler has estimated overall casualties for Africans of more than 25 percent in this phase of the war (1988:144). In the heated battles in which Samaké fought, the causality rate may well have been higher.

After the Nazi victory, France was partitioned into one area controlled directly by the Germans and a second region controlled by the puppet "Vichy" regime. Samaké's regiment retreated into Vichy France, eventually arriving in North Africa, which was also controlled by Vichy. The soldiers were involved in little but military exercises until Operation TORCH, the American-led invasion of French Africa in November 1942. After offering brief resistance, the *Tirailleurs Sénégalais* were placed under the command of De Gaulle and the Free French. Three divisions, including Mory Samaké's, were almost immediately dispatched to the battle for Tunisia. There they fought the Germans and Italians from February until May 1943, when over a quarter million German and Italian troops surrendered.

After the victory in Tunisia, Samaké fought with the Free French in Italy and in France. His last battle was at Toulon in August 1944, a bitter street-to-street contest culminating in a spectacular American bombing raid on the fort of Sainte-Marguerite, located on top of a cliff overlooking the harbor. Samaké remembers the ferocity of the battle, and particularly the role played by African-American troops:

> The Americans came and said that they would force the Germans out of Toulon. There were black Americans and they flew airplanes. They dropped many bombs on us and killed many civilians and soldiers. After, that war was finished.

Samaké came home from the war in 1945, but his trip was not without incident. Returning African troops were restive. France had created a powerful African army and now officials feared that, if united, these men might threaten France's hold on its colonial territories. For the French, it was imperative that Africans be returned to their separate homes rapidly and peacefully. They tried to encourage the soldiers to go home by promising them extra pay and bonuses, but the men were always told that they would be paid at the next stop . . . closer to home. In fact, the promised monies were never paid. In addition, the men complained about food, clothing, housing, and the sale of alcohol. Trouble, often sparked by racial slights, was frequent. The largest and best known episode of violence occurred on December 1, 1944, at Thiaroye, a military base in Senegal where thirty-five African soldiers were killed during a protest (Echenberg 1991:100). In this charged atmosphere, confrontations between African and French soldiers easily led to violence, which Samaké himself experienced:

> I was coming home for leave, in the train. When we got to Kayes (in Northwest Mali), there was a bugle call to say that the soldiers should get back on the train. I was a sergeant and in charge of the car. There were three soldiers under my command. These three soldiers were delayed getting back in the train.
>
> The head of the detachment, a captain came. He said "who is in charge of this car," I said: "It's me." I had a baton in my hand and when I said that, I waved the baton. The captain said that I was threatening him. Then he came over and tried to hit me. I wouldn't stand for that. Me! It's only God, my father, or my mother who can hit me! A man, even the devil himself, I'll hit him back! Oh yes, I was like that. I hit him. His finger was broken. That problem there, it put me in prison. It put me in prison for a year.

This incident shows that, by the end of his military service, Samaké was self-confident and unwilling to accept personal insult, even from a superior officer. He demanded respect from those he had served and was willing to fight them to get it. Because Samaké acknowledges that he breached military discipline, he bears no particular ill will for the year he spent in prison. He remains indignant, however, that after this incident the French stripped him of his sergeant's rank. Though his papers show that he left the service as a private, he denies that he was ever demoted and insists that the French owe him sergeant's pay:

> In the army, they tried me and sent me to prison, but they didn't say my rank was broken. When I got out of prison, I was still a sergeant. When I got to Thiaroye there was a captain. He said that I didn't deserve my rank. I said to him: "Why? I made a mistake and I paid for my mistake. Why do you refuse to give me what I deserve?"

After leaving prison, Samaké served briefly in Guinea and then, on November 26, 1946, he left the *Tirailleurs* and returned to his home. The length of his service entitled him to a small pension, and his having spent more than ninety days in combat entitled him to an additional small semi-annual sum after his sixtieth birthday.

The French, concerned that returning soldiers would foster unrest in the colonies, tried to mollify them by offering them jobs and other special concessions such as housing. In Bougouni, Maurice Meker, the French commandant tried to provide both jobs and land for housing to many veterans. While not all veterans I spoke with thought highly of the commandant, most believed that he had done more to support them than any other French official in Bougouni's colonial history. The Meker family retained an active interest in Bougouni for many years after he left the colony and many veterans remember him fondly. Yet the commandant did not have sufficient resources to meet the needs of the returning soldiers.

When Samaké returned from the army, Commandant Meker employed him as a chauffeur. However, Samaké, soon left to return to his natal village:

> When I was a chauffeur here, they paid me only 200 FCFA each month. I only stayed about six months and then I asked for permission to leave. I went back to my village to farm. I did this because I thought I'd be better off as a farmer than as a driver. 200 Francs a month! What's that?

Samaké returned to his natal village but like many other veterans with pensions, found life there difficult. For many veterans with pensions, village life led to disputes over control of money. Parents or older brothers of veterans often demanded that pension money be turned over to them. This is considered proper in the context of rural Malian society, but veterans often rebelled against it by journeying to the towns to distance themselves from their families and retain control over their pensions. Veterans with pensions often moved from their villages to larger towns. Living in town made it easier to collect one's pension. Since most towns had a *Maison des Anciens Combattants* (a meeting place for veterans), they also provided opportunities to socialize with old friends and others who had shared similar experiences. After spending six years in his village, Samaké moved to the town of Bougouni, and to the house he has lived in since.

With money from his military pension, Samaké established himself as a man of some means. After his return he married two additional wives. Among the three, he sired fifteen children. His possessions included a plow, a cart, and a mill to grind grain. While minimal by the standards of industrialized nations, these are still indicators of comparative wealth in Samaké's town.

Samaké believed that his success in the army and in the period immediately following his return was the result of the education he received while in the military:

> When I was in the army, I was a little bit smart . . . eh! I took classes like the European non-coms so I would know how to write a little. I wanted my children to go to school here.

Relatively few Malian children went to European-style schools in the 1950s, but Samaké made sure his children were educated in the French school system. He noted, however, that they did not benefit much from their education. Only one among them completed high school. He went on to become an agricultural extension agent, but

> he had problems with money. He stole 1,300,000 FCFA. When he had that "accident" he wasn't put in prison, but he did lose his job. I had to sell [all my possessions] so I could pay his debt and [he could] stay out of prison.

Now a relatively poor man, Samaké's family life began to collapse. One of his wives had died previously; now another left him. In 1992 he lived solely on his two pensions. He received about one hundred dollars a month from his regular pension and in addition, since he served more than ninety days in combat, an additional fifty dollars every six months. His remaining wife helped him with household chores. In 1992 he married another wife, a young girl. It was a marriage of convenience.

> But, look at that girl there [a woman in her early 20s], she's my wife. We haven't completely settled the marriage yet, but I've given the kola nuts. Her father is also a combat veteran. Since I knew she was sick, I went to her father and told him that I'd take care of her and marry her. The father agreed to it. But with that sickness there, I'm always looking for medicine for the girl. This sickness, it makes her turn her head [have seizures]; it makes her fall down. That's the way it is! If it wasn't like that, if she wasn't sick, she would never have agreed to marry me because I'm too old! She's young. I was born in 1911.

Samaké agreed to help pay for medicine for the woman in exchange for her taking care of him. The marriage, however, did not last long; in 1994, Samaké's young wife died of complications of her illness, probably epilepsy. In 1995, one of Samaké's sons and his family had returned to live with him.

Samaké looks back on his life in the military with pride mixed with regret and anger. He thinks that France has behaved shamefully with respect to African veterans. He believes that the French have rewarded him and other veterans insufficiently for their work and suffering on her behalf:

> The French have forgotten what we did for them. When I was in France, I was a sentinel. I didn't sleep. I made war. I put the rifle on my shoulder and shot where they told me to shoot. Now that we are out of the army, we should be eating well, we should be sleeping well.
>
> When someone helps you save your country, you should remember him. Look at my salary. I have 75,000 FCFA. What can I do with that? I've got to eat, and buy clothes. For that we

did with our youth and because of it, we have lost my children. They don't pay any extra for children. It's this out in our lives. You can't become a young man again, and I can't work any more. When we worked for the French, we thought that they would take care of us. They haven't done it. We went out and saw the world, but then just returned with nothing . . .

For me in the world now, it's all over. When you're really alive, it means you eat well, you dress well, you sleep well. Living like that, that's healthy. What I've got here and now isn't a life. Maybe in heaven everything is peaceful. But, when you're here, you have to have a little fun, you know.

All families have to think about how to find enough food, find a place to sleep, get clothes for their children, heal themselves when they are sick . . . it's very difficult. Look here. If I have a sick child today, he's going to die. If there is no medicine to make him well, he's going to die. Who's fault is all of this? It's all on account of France. If they paid us well, and if our wives or children fell ill, we'd go buy medicine to help them. But, what do we do if we don't have the money for that? We are all angry at heart. If things were right, our children should have nice clothes, like the children of the French veterans.

The issue of military pensions is of central concern to Samaké and most other veterans. The French promised lifetime pensions to those who had served fifteen years. It was, however, extremely slow to pay them. In 1950, five years after the close of the war, it is estimated that forty percent of veterans and their families were still waiting resolution of their pension claims (Echenberg 1991:160). By the mid-1950s, not only were these issues largely resolved but African veterans were making progress toward pay equity with French veterans. However, when African colonies opted for independence from France, the French government struck at military pensions. Article 71 of the law of 1959 was designed to punish Africans for promoting independence. It reduced the pensions of African veterans to one seventh that paid to French citizens and omitted cost-of-living indexing. There have been only a few raises in the pensions since 1959. The result is that since 1960, Africans have been paid only a small fraction of what Frenchmen with similar service receive. Samaké expresses his rage at this treatment eloquently:

Our French comrades who were in the war with us are treated 10 times better than we are. The French pay them well. Look at the "carte de combattant" that I have here. With this the French get paid 200,000 CFA each three months. Us here, we get paid 10,000 each six months. What kind of thing is that! For lack of

the right kind of skin! It's our lives that are ruined. We left to
fight the wars. We were young. We ran. The countries we took
in the war, who benefitted from that? It was France. Even if
they don't divide up what they won fairly, why don't they give
us at least a little so that we can live well also.

Sometimes they say they are going to give us a raise. Then
they add only 25 Francs to our pension. What's that? Among
us war veterans, no one is happy. We are all unhappy. If you
are young and you work without getting any benefit for yourself until you are too old to work anymore . . .

Despite his anger at the French, Samaké thinks of himself as their
willing servant. Soldiers were subject to a barrage of propaganda encouraging them to fight for the French nation and French culture. In 1940,
there was even a magazine called *La Gazette du Tirailleur* designed to
inspire and reassure them. These efforts probably had little influence
within West Africa, but they helped convince serving soldiers that their
cause was just. As Samaké tells it, he endured the hardships of war willingly. He looks back to the battlefield for confirmation of his endurance,
his strength, his fierceness and virility:

We did all of that. If you think too much about it during the
night, you can not sleep. There was snow there . . . We marched
in the snow. We are not accustomed to snow, but we put up
with everything. . . . During the war, we did nothing with ill
will. We were always willing to do what was asked.

Me, personally, me that you see here . . . I took Germans by
their hair and cut off their heads and drank their blood. You
can ask my comrades about that. I drank it, but what did I get?
I could have said "it's not my country I won't give my heart to
the fight," but I didn't.

During the war, there were some who were wounded and
who cried out and said come get me. I would come with my
machine gun and shoot at them. I did this so they wouldn't
make the others afraid. I was always game. Even in 1985, when
there was a war between Mali and Burkina, I wanted to be a
volunteer.

To be a man, you can't stay at home. You only get that on the
battlefield.

Not all veterans harbor the deep resentment of the French and the rage
Samaké has. Many of those who served in the early part of World War II
share his anger, but those who served later are not generally as disparag-
ing of the French. None of the veterans with whom I spoke were completely uncritical and none longed for the "good old days" of colonialism.

Nevertheless, some did praise the French and many believed they had benefited from their military experiences. Some gained skills that they were able to put to use in civilian life. After independence, others were able to move from the colonial military to either the civil service or the military of their own nation. One said:

> I got something good out of the army. It was the experience that I had there that permitted me to do well in trade. Even the French that I can understand, I learned that in the army. Even how to work well with others, I learned all that in the army [Kaka Diakite 1992].

Despite this, Mory Samaké and others who served the French have become in some respects men apart from their culture. Service in the *Tirailleurs* was a process of enculturation and acculturation. Conscripts learned a great deal about French culture and, in many cases, became skilled manipulators of French cultural symbols and values. The price of this, however, was a degree of alienation in their own culture. It was difficult for veterans to reintegrate into the village life they had left. The values they learned and the experiences they lived often proved incomprehensible to those who did not share them. Veterans reacted to this in various ways depending on their family connections and whether they had a pension. Some were well placed to take advantage of their situation. Others simply tried to forget as much as possible.

Veterans who served only three years or were, for various reasons, released without pensions were in very weak positions in Malian society. They had spent their time working for the French and were perceived as having received nothing in return. They generally went back to their villages and tried to resume the lives they had left. Often they had problems. They told stories that no one believed, and found little sympathy or understanding among former friends. One summed up his experience like this:

> When you come back, you have to follow the ideas of the people in the village. If not, if you try to tell them all about the army and what you have seen, they are never going to understand you. You can explain things and there are those who will just say you are lying. You just let them alone, at least that's the way I've gotten along. [Lassana Samaké 1995].

Some turned to drink and became increasingly estranged from their peers. One result is that, for many Malians, the idea of a veteran conjures up images of an eccentric old man prone to irrational and violent behavior. This image has been captured by African writers in stories such as "Sarzan" by the Senegalese author Birago Diop (1969) and *Le Lieutenant de Kouta* by Malian writer Massa Diabate (1983).

Those who served long enough to receive pensions or who came from prominent families did much better. Their relative wealth and social standing gave them a degree of power and authority within their own cultures. Their knowledge of French ways and the sufferings they had endured gave them legitimacy with French authorities. In the years between the end of World War II and the end of French colonial rule, such veterans became a moral and political force for African rights. Their support was critical to emerging African political parties. As independence was achieved, however, the position of veterans changed. Whereas before independence, African suffering for France could be used to leverage political and social concessions from the French government, afterwards veterans were seen as people who had aided colonial oppression. As a result, they faded from the political scene. The pride they felt in their service became tinged with embarrassment and a profound sense of grievance against the French.

CONCLUSION

Like many other veterans of his generation, Samaké is a failed hero, a man who fought for what he was taught was a noble cause only to have it revealed as shallow and corrupt; who placed faith in the paternalism of colonial rule to find that confidence betrayed. While Samaké may be particularly embittered, at some level his feelings are probably typical of those caught between their own societies and those of their colonial masters (see Nandy 1983, Memmi 1965, Fanon 1965, 1967). His life reveals the complexity of the material and psychological effects of colonialism. Samaké has learned French culture but has in no way become French. He has benefited materially from his association with the French, but remains a poor man in a poor country. The experiences that he understands as proving his strength and virility are the same as those that ultimately led to his sense of betrayal and rage. It is hard to say which of his words are more memorable: his ringing denunciation of the treatment of veterans by the French, "If you eat the meat, you throw away the bone," or his pronouncement that men are only made on the battlefield.

Samaké's story is also significant because it helps us to understand the nature of colonialism and its aftermath. As a soldier, Samaké was part of the system through which the French empire was created and maintained. The expansion of France altered cultures and individual destinies all over the world. It was a key part of the larger history of Western expansion that has created a world in which isolation is impossible and, for better or worse, cultures are inextricably intertwined, a world in which power and wealth are the prerogative of a relative few and poverty the lot of many.

Finally, Samaké's life is a reminder of the important role played by African troops on the world historical stage; of the sacrifices and hardships endured by subject peoples for their colonial rulers. This is a story that is unknown to most Americans, particularly those of the generations after World War II. Perhaps worse, it is a story that is virtually unknown to many young Africans as well. Veterans are often reluctant to speak of their experiences to those who did not share them. I often found that the children of veterans generally had little knowledge of their parents' experiences.

The men who served in the *Tirailleurs Sénégalais* are growing older. In a relatively few years, all will be gone. It is important that their stories, their sacrifices, and the memory of the injustices inflicted upon them does not vanish with them.

REFERENCES

Balesi, Charles J.
    1979   From Adversaries to Comrades-in-arms: West Africans and the French Military 1885–1918. Waltham (MA): Crossroads Press.

Diabate, Massa M.
    1983   *Le Lieutenant de Kouta*. Abidjan: Ceda.

Diop, Birago
    1969   *Les Conts d'Amadou Koumba*. Paris: Présence Africaine.

Echenberg, Myron
    1991   Colonial Conscripts: The *Tirailleurs Sénégalais* in French West Africa, 1857–1960. Portsmouth (NH): Heinemann.
    1980   *Les Migrations militaires en Afrique occidentale Francaise* 1900–1945. Canadian Journal of African Studies. 14(3):429–450.
    1978   Tragedy at Thiaroye: The Senegalese Soldiers' Uprising of 1944. *In* Peter Gutkind, Robin Cohen, and Jean Copans, eds. African Labor History: 109–128. Beverly Hills: Sage.

Fanon, Frantz
    1967   Black Skin, White Masks. New York: Grove.
    1965   The Wretched of the Earth. New York: Grove.

Hoisington, William A.
    1984   The Casablanca Connection: French colonial Policy, 1936–1943. Chapel Hill: University of North Carolina Press.

Lawler, Nancy E.
    1992   Soldiers of Misfortune: *Ivoirien Tirailleurs* of World War II. Athens (OH): Ohio University Press.
    1988   Soldiers of Misfortune: The *Tiraillleurs Senegalais* of the Cote d'Ivoire in World War Two. Ph.D. Dissertation, Department of History, Northwestern University.

Mangin, Charles
    1911   La Force Noire. Paris: Hachette.

Memmi, Albert
    1965   The Colonizer and the Colonized. Boston: Beacon Press.

Nandy, Ashis
    1983   The Intimate Enemy: Loss and Recovery of Self under Colonialism.
            Delhi: Oxford University Press.
Page, Melvin
    1987   Introduction: Black Men in a White Men's War. *In* Melvin Page, ed.
            Africa and the First World War: 1–27. New York: St. Martins.
Schleh, Eugene
    1968   The Post-War Careers of Ex-Servicemen in Ghana and Uganda.
            Journal of Modern African Studies 6(2):203–220.
Senghor, Léopold
    1991   (orig 1945) Prayer for Peace. *In* Léopold Sédar Senghor, The
            Collected Poetry: 69–72. Charlottesville (VA): University Press of
            Virginia.

IDENTITY,
THE SELF, AND THE OTHER

In a Poor Neighborhood in East Amman

Aseel Sawalha

> *"Although I have the Jordanian passport, and I lived in this same area (Wadi al-Rimam) since 1948, and my 8 sons and daughters were born here, I am not Jordanian and I will never become so. I and my sons and daughters are Palestinian refugees in Jordan. If I was given a Palace in Amman I won't take it, I will stay with other refugees."*

Abu Naser, fifty-seven-year-old Palestinian refugee

INTRODUCTION

In 1948, almost four hundred Arab villages were demolished by the Israelis. The Palestinians, as a consequence, sought refuge in surrounding Arab countries. Since then Palestinians have not been allowed to re-enter the land of their birth, forming a diaspora which today comprises approximately four million people scattered throughout the world (Morris 1986; Said 1983, 1986).

Here I will describe the different forms of identity among Palestinian refugees in a poor neighborhood in East Amman, Jordan. The interaction and performances of the refugees in daily life are to a large extent shaped by the way they conceive of their pasts, and by the way other people address them in various contexts. The various ways by which people identify themselves and are identified by others include their being members of a specific household or family; residents of a certain neighborhood in Amman; being of a specific village or town in Palestine of 1948; or simply as Palestinian refugees in Jordan. In what follows I will present the complex interaction between two places (exile and homeland) in relation to the past and the present and as they are manifested in everyday practices.

Both Palestinian people and many Arab writers refer to the cataclysmic period beginning in 1948 as *Al-Nakba*, (the Catastrophe, or the Disaster), a term that evokes loss, alienation, tragedy, and betrayal (Peteet 1991, Bisharat 1994). The *Nakba* year, 1948, has played a central role in the construction of Palestinian historical consciousness and identity. Palestinians in the refugee camps periodize their existence around the *Nakba* and consider it a cutting point in their history. They usually describe the period prior to 1948 as one of stability and happiness, while the "post-*Nakba*" stage is referred to as the starting point of a series of displacements, miseries, bad luck, and suffering.

WARDA'S LIFE

The story of Warda, a thirty-four-year-old mother of five children living in a one room apartment in a Palestinian refugee camp in Amman offers a representative history of displacement:[1]

> ... My father's family was living in a village on the Mediterranean coast of Palestine. They were farmers and they owned large farms of orange trees and olives. In 1948 they were forced out of their home village as all the Palestinians after the Israeli occupation of Palestine. My father's family settled in a refugee camp near Jerusalem. Ten years later, after they lost hope of going back to their home village, my father married my mother who is his relative from the same village of origin. I was born in the refugee camp in 1961. In 1967 we fled to Jordan after the second Arab-Israeli war and the occupation of the rest of Palestine by the Israelis. We stayed in this same refugee camp where there are families from our village. A few days after we came to Jordan my father went back to Palestine with the Palestinian resistance movement, and never came back. He was killed by the Israelis on the borders while he was crossing Jordan river. ...
>
> My mother took the responsibility of bringing up me and my sister and brother; my oldest brother was 9 years old. [Warda

---

1. In the following, the major incidents in Warda's life are arranged chronologically for the sake of analysis. This does not mean that this is the way she put them according to their priority in her own life.

pointed to her children saying that she and her brothers were at same age as her children.] We did not go to school when we first came to Jordan, because we . . . did not have any money; we lost everything, the house, the money and the father. A few years later my mother worked as a cleaning lady at one of the UNRWA schools. My brother and sister went to school but I did not; I had to stay home to do the housework and to take care of my younger brothers. I missed going to school, when I saw the boys and girls of my age, going and coming back from the school I was crying all the time. Because of this I will do anything to keep my children at school.

I got married when I was 18. My husband was a Palestinian refugee from a village close to my village in Palestine; he was working in Kuwait. I was sent to him to Kuwait with some of his relatives. I lived a relatively good life in Kuwait with my husband who was working as a driver. I thought that marriage will put an end to the days of poverty and misery, but during the Gulf war in 1991, we have to come back to Jordan without any money and without my husband. My husband died in a car accident during the war. We had some savings in a bank in Kuwait but because of the war we were unable to get any of it. I rented a truck to move my children and some furniture. At the beginning I stayed with my husband's family in this refugee camp, but a few months later the problems started after I spent all the money that I had in Kuwait. When the problems started between me and my in-laws I moved with my children to live with my brother and his wife and children, but their two-room house is not enough for me, my children and my mother. I rented this room and my mother moved with us, because the people around us will talk negatively about me as a young widow living on my own.

The experience of displacement and the loss of home have given the Palestinians a marked identity among other Arabs in the region. After they were forced out of their country, Palestinians started to identify themselves and be identified according to where they live in exile: the Palestinians of Jordan, the Palestinians of Lebanon, the Palestinians of Syria, and so on. In Jordan, since 1948, Palestinians of peasant origins who were forced to leave their villages have lived in refugee camps run by UNRWA (United Nations Relief and Works Agency) in Jordan and have tended to cluster in groups composed of refugees from neighboring villages in Palestine. Many families who were not able to gain access to UNRWA havens established squatter areas close to the camps of their relatives.

REPRESENTATIONS OF HOME
IN REFUGEE'S DAILY LIFE

This study is based on six months of field research in *Wadi al-Rimam*, a Palestinian squatter neighborhood in Amman.[2] The boundaries of the studied community are as ambiguous as the identities of its inhabitants. *Wadi al-Rimam* is a valley located between two mountains, *Jabal al-Taj* and *Jabal al-Nasir* in the center of the city of Amman. The houses in these areas are mostly owned or rented by Palestinian refugees who left in 1948. Close to *Wadi al-Rimam* is *Hayy al-Tafayleh* and *Hayy al-Mma'aniya*, whose residents are mostly from the towns of *Tafeela* and *Ma'an* in Southern Jordan who are not Palestinians. *Wadi al-Rimam* is surrounded on two sides by a wall made of cement, which separates it from the other two neighborhoods. The people of the area do not know who built this wall, but besides its symbolic significance this wall limits Palestinians of *Wadi al-Rimam* in their relations with residents of the neighboring areas.

Wadi al-Rimam is known by a number of names. Its inhabitants call it *Harat al-Mahasra* after the village of *Beit Mahseer*, since the majority of the first inhabitants of this valley were from this particular Palestinian village located west of Jerusalem. Being one of the first villages to be completely destroyed by the Israelis in the 1948 war, its people were among the first to be expelled from Palestine and head to Jordan. The boundaries of *Harat al-Mahasra* are not well defined. Sometimes the term is used to refer only to the upper part of the valley, and at other times to the whole valley. Inhabitants of other areas of East Amman call this area *Wadi al-Rimam*, while many of the people who live in wealthy West Amman do not even know of its existence. The term *Wadi al-Rimam* literally means "the valley of dead animals," referring to the pre-1948 period when people in the surrounding areas used to throw their garbage and dead animals in this valley. Palestinian refugees often boast that they "developed" and changed the area. They state that they usually build and improve the places where they settle, and offer the example of the Gulf States. One of the people of *Wadi al-Rimam* asserted "we (Palestinians) leave our green fingerprints wherever we go. We changed this place from a valley of the dead to a valley full of life, as you see."

Administratively, the area is registered as *Wadi al-Nasir* or valley of victory. Generally speaking, the houses look very poor from the outside, and are clustered very close to each other. The upper part of this area contains about 150 households included in an urban upgrading development project. These houses are separated by narrow paved alleys not

2. I chose the area for this specific research after participating in a survey on children and health in poor neighborhoods in Amman with Jocelyn DeJong.

exceeding the width of one meter. A number of houses in this part are built of concrete, and some have two stories. The land on which these houses are built was sold to the residents by the Urban Development Department. In contrast, the lower part of the valley comprises about one hundred households which are not included in the project and lack basic services such as water, electricity, and sewerage. The houses here are poorer and smaller, are built mostly of mud and corrugated metal, and the alleys separating the houses are not paved. Nor do the people in this part have legal ownership.

Both the upper and the lower parts of *Wadi al-Rimam* are crowded and many people, especially women and children, are in the alleys during the daytime. A number of houses operate as small shops usually run by older women. Often, women sit in front of these shops engaged in food processing like cleaning lentils and rice, or knitting and embroidering. The children play most of the time outside the houses because the houses are so small.

In addition to the majority of the inhabitants who come from *Beit Mahseer*, there are also people from a number of villages located near Jerusalem as well as from Lydda and Ramleh, two Palestinian cities which were occupied in 1948. Peteet notes that "the majority of Palestinian refugees living in camps—in Lebanon—(70–80%), were small landowning peasants or sharecroppers" (1991:20). When these Palestinian peasants first came to Jordan, they settled, wherever possible, in villages where they had family affiliations. Sayigh (1979) in a study about Palestinian refugees in Lebanon stated that the camps were arranged to re-create the pre-1948 Palestine villages. Streets, alleys, shops and markets which sprouted in the camps were named for the villages and towns from which the residents came. Similarly, in *Wadi al-Rimam* place names frequently refer to the village of origin or to the strong hope of return and the sacrifice and struggle connected to that hope. Examples include, *Al-Thawrah* (the revolution), *Al-Nasir* (the victory), *Al-Nidal* (the struggle), and *Al-`Awdah* (the return). Examples of other names include *Falasteen* (Palestine), *Al-Quds* (Jerusalem) and *Bab Al-Amoud* (a neighborhood in Jerusalem).

Upon their arrival in Jordan, Palestinian refugees formed committees upon request from UNRWA and the Jordanian government to organize receiving United Nation's aid. These committees consist of one or two persons from each village, including the *mukhtar* or the former headman of the village of origin (Plascov 1981) who received official recognition from the Jordanian government. At the beginning, these committees apparently did not have a political role, but were limited to carrying out relief policies and mediating between the refugees, the Jordanian state, and the relief agencies. Each *mukhtar* was given a government stamp to provide proof of identity for the people of his village of origin which is required to get official papers. The *mukhtar* also plays a crucial role in solving problems among the people of his village of origin. Later their activities expanded and their numbers increased. Now there are committees for almost each village and for most large families. Many of these committees and organizations are registered in Jordan as *rawabit* (organizations). Members of these organizations either meet in a rented place or some built their own space from designated contributions from members of the village of origin. All males from the village of origin who are over the age of eighteen pay a yearly membership fee. These committees are based upon the place of origin in Palestine regardless of the place of residence in diaspora. It must be noted that membership in these committees is restricted to men.

Currently, these committees help in collecting financial aid for families in crises, when the male provider of a family dies. Members of the *rawabit* also intervene in solving problems and conflicts at different levels as in the cases of fights with and accidents involving Jordanians or Palestinians from other villages. The *rawabit* also form a place for people from the same village to gather and exchange news, and provide a forum for younger people to meet the older generations. Since the houses of most of the Palestinian refugees are too small to perform ceremonies when the occasion arises, many weddings and funerals take place at the *rawabit*.

REFUGEES AS AN IDENTITY

The transformation in the meaning and the uses of the word "refugee" illustrates the way Palestinian refugees identify themselves in different situations. The people of *Wadi al-Rimam* are all of Palestinian origin and have Jordanian citizenship; at the same time they have UN refugee status, as do most Palestinian refugees in Jordan. The closest Palestinian camp to this area is the *Jabal al-Nasir*, an UNRWA refugee camp which is inhabited by people from the same villages as *Wadi al-Rimam*. People of both areas have access to UNRWA services at the *Jabal al-Nasir* camp, such as the UNRWA schools and health and training centers.

Since the 1950s there has been a constant movement in and out of *Wadi al-Rimam*. The first Palestinian inhabitants of the area bought small mud houses roofed with metal sheets from the bedouins who used to come seasonally to the area with their animals. Gradually, their relatives and neighbors from the villages of origin in Palestine started to move to this area after they too faced problems in finding places to stay. The price of land was cheap compared to the prices in other areas, and it was close to the city center where men used to look for work as daily laborers and women for domestic work. In 1967, after the occupation of the rest of Palestine by the Israelis, Palestinian *naziheen* (officially labeled as dis-

placed) from the West Bank and Gaza also came to this area.[3] The majority of the newcomers in 1967 were relatives of older residents of the area
either through kinship or marriage, or were from the same villages of
origin. At the time I conducted my research in 1992, a number of families
forced to leave Kuwait or other Gulf countries after the 1991 Gulf war
were looking to either buy or rent houses in the area. These people are
called 'a`ideen (returnees). Most of these families—Warda is repre-
sentative—either had kin in this area, or had grown up there before they
went to the Gulf.

In *Wadi al-Rimam*, the sons of the three groups of refugees (*laji`een* 1948,
naziheen 1967, and *'a`ideen* 1991) either stay in the same housing unit after
they marry in a separate room and share the kitchen and the bathroom,
or they try to rent a house in the area. Those with better economic conditions because of education or a regular job, move outside to other neighboring areas, mostly to *Jabal Al-Taj* or *Jabal Al-Nasir*. Immediately after
moving, people usually stay in touch with their relatives in the valley, but
gradually those who move away from the area reduce their participation
in the activities of the valley to the displeasure of their relatives.

THE IMAGE OF HOME IN REFUGEE'S DAILY LIFE

Memories of the former villages remain vivid in exile. When people feel
upset about their daily problems in Jordan like unemployment, discrimination, or poverty they usually blame it on their status as exiles, and their
immediate response is to remember *'ayyam al-`iz, 'ayyam li-blad* (the days
of happiness in the home-country). Rosemary Sayigh has written that
Palestinian refugees in Beirut, Lebanon remembered living in their village
as living in paradise (1979:10). Although people in *Wadi al-Rimam* romanticize their villages of origin, they still reflect the conflicts between people
back home in some of the relations of the refugees in exile. For example
one family refused to marry their daughter to a man from the same village
because of a land dispute between their families in the town of origin.

When I asked people in *Wadi al-Rimam* where they were from, most did
not refer to the place in which they presently live in Amman, especially
if they did not own the house they inhabited, or if their economic situation
was not good, or if non-Palestinians were present. The first response was
to give the name of the village of origin in Palestine; usually they followed
this with a comment that the village had been demolished by the Israelis;
sometimes they would also volunteer the Hebrew name of the Israeli

---

3. Palestinian refugees from 1948 are known as *laji'een* (refugees) whereas these of
1967 are known as *naziheen* (displaced). This is in conformity with UN regulations
which only recognize those who cross an international border as officially refugees.

settlement established after the destruction of the village. Many of them complained of the bad economic situation in Jordan, and compared life as refugees to what life was once like when they lived in their own villages. They talked painfully about the experience of leaving the village of origin "*al-qaryya al-asleyya*," and the hopes of returning home.

Few Palestinian refugees in Jordan have had the opportunity of visiting their birthplace after they were forced out. Those who have always tell stories about what remains of their villages, and everyone transmits and retells the story in his or her own way. There is a constant fixation on certain symbols that still exist of the village. For example, they would say "the whole village has been converted by the Israelis into a farm for raising cows, and all of the houses were demolished, but the wall of the cemetery is still there," or "the *ma`thaneh* (the minaret) of the big mosque is lying on the edge of the valley." Others mention that the house of so and so is still there, and the school is renovated and re-used as a kindergarten, or a flower garden has taken the place of the village, but the fields of oranges and the olive trees remain.

Many families retain the keys to their homes that were demolished by the Israelis as symbols of their determination to return. Other families still have the official papers which show their ownership of houses and land in their former villages. They keep these with their official papers like the family card, U.N. refugee card, and passports. Some have asked those who had the opportunity to visit the villages of origin to bring them back some of the soil of Palestine.

After forty-four years of living away from their home villages, the Palestinians may have become "more used" to it and may have developed some adaptation strategies or a new "Palestinian culture and tradition in exile" (Said 1986). But this is articulated with their memories of Palestine which they transmit to the new generation born outside Palestine. Mothers and grandmothers do most of this. Women relate narratives of life in Palestine, giving beautiful and romanticized descriptions of social life and relationships in home villages and compare it to the misery of their present daily life. The young people who have never been there repeat the same stories about their former villages; "misfortunes and poverty were explained to children by their parents as a consequence of the loss of homeland" (Peteet 1989:26). The children respond by blaming their parents for leaving their homes, and insist that they should have remained and defended their land instead of fleeing to these "bad places."

SELF REPRESENTATION PRE- AND POST *AL-NAKBA*

Palestinian identity has been politicized in the face of constant denial and dispossession in diaspora. Generally speaking, the refugees fall back on their past to overcome their demeaning present. Palestinian refugees in

Wadi al-Rimam use two kinds of symbols to show their Palestinian identity, one of them symbolizing their past before 1948, the other invented and reproduced in exile. The selection of these symbols—whether the people are aware of this or not—usually respond to other existing identities. On one hand is the enforcement of the Israeli state, with its continuous efforts to destroy the Palestinian identity, and on the other the different policies of the host countries—in this case Jordan—either to assimilate the Palestinians completely, or to marginalize them. Palestinian refugees find symbols and icons to continue distinguishing themselves from others.

SELF REPRESENTATION AS PEASANTS

Palestinian refugees in *Wadi al-Rimam* emphasize their peasant origin to demonstrate that they do not belong to their contemporary urban setting. Although "physically" living in a completely urban context, they articulate images and thoughts of being peasants from specific villages in Palestine in their everyday practices in a completely urban context. For example, they use the term *fallah* (peasant) to distinguish themselves from other people in Amman (Jordanians and non-peasant Palestinians). Despite their peasant origin, their current activities use none of their skills as peasants. The majority are working as daily wage laborers on an irregular bases, in construction, in car maintenance, etc. "The *fallah* has been made the symbolic representative of the cultural and historical continuity of the Palestinians. The peasant additionally signifies a prolonged attachment and deep love for the land of Palestine in the face of land expropriations and population transfers by the Israelis" (Swedenberg 1990:168).

The peasant identity is reinforced by the emphasis on speaking the Palestinian peasant dialect. Members of the community are quick to criticize those who mix their Palestinian peasant dialect with other words from Jordanian or urban Palestinian dialects. Women and children who spend most of their time in the valley speak the peasant's dialect more or less unalloyed. Boys and girls from the community who attend UNRWA schools until the ninth grade continue to speak the same peasant Palestinian dialect. These completely free schools are only for Palestinians and most of the teachers are also Palestinian refugees. When the students move to the secondary governmental schools with other students from different backgrounds, the boys start to mix their peasant dialect with the Jordanian dialect while the girls adapt terms from the urban Palestinian dialect. But both boys and girls speak only the peasant Palestinian dialect when they go back to their homes and their community in *Wadi al-Rimam*.

Another symbol Palestinians reproduce in their daily life is eating habits from the earlier peasant life. For example, olive oil and wild thyme are Palestinian food and powerful symbols of Palestine. The beauty of olive trees and the smell of thyme are now included in many of the songs the women sing while doing housework or in social gatherings. Both men and women tell stories of collecting the wild *zatar* from the fields in the earlier days. They also compare the vegetables and fruits they now buy from Amman with those their fields produced before 1948. Their products were "real" and authentic with a beautiful smell and taste, unlike today's market vegetables which taste like plastic. People in *Wadi al-Rimam* also emphasize their peasant's identity through dietary practices like eating olives and uncooked onions with all meals. They reminisce of the earlier days when they did not need to spend money on food, since they could eat from their own fields: we had "wheat for bread which we could eat with oil and olives and vegetables in all seasons. If we did not have money, we would not go hungry."

The women spend part of their time every day doing Palestinian embroidery. Younger girls are also encouraged to learn it. Women over the age of forty-five still regularly wear the Palestinian peasant dress *(thawb fallahi)*. If a woman from the community goes outside her house without wearing this Palestinian dress, other women will accuse her of trying to be *madaneyya* (urbanized), which is a negative indication that she wants to change her identity and, implicitly, gives up her right to go back to Palestine.

SELF PRESENTATION AS REFUGEES

At first, Palestinians considered it to be humiliating to be labeled as refugees. For the Palestinians, it meant a state of inferiority and need. But time has transformed this word, bringing it new meanings and making it more acceptable. Being a refugee has become an identity. A Palestinian from *Wadi al-Rimam* noted "now, we can't live without this word (refugee), it is a way of showing that we still have a homeland, and we are Palestinians living in temporary exile." In an interview conducted by Salman Rushdie, Edward Said stated "Palestinians are a people who move a lot, who are always carrying bags from one place to another. This gives us a further sense of identity as a people" (Rushdie 1991:174). An older man from *Wadi al-Rimam* described this refugee identity: "when we first came to Jordan we hated to be referred to as refugees. This was disgracing and humiliating; it meant that we are poor, waiting for aid from the relief agencies, and no one believed that we [once] had land and big beautiful houses. But now we are proud that we are refugees, and we will stay as refugees until we return to our homes. My refugee card and not my Jordanian passport proves my Palestinian *asil* (origin). Although the name of *Falasteen* (Palestine) has been changed, my village was demolished and given a Hebrew name, the day will come when all Palestinian refugees and all of their descendent will return home and build Palestine as we built all the Arab countries."

After 1948, UNRWA issued refugee cards for Palestinian refugees to receive aid and UN services. Now although many of these services do not exist any more, almost all refugees have kept their cards and they apply for refugee cards for their newborn children. Not only have needy Palestinians in camps demanded identity cards from UNRWA, but also some wealthier people have argued that refugee cards should be issued to all refugees regardless of their need for relief. The refugee card is a signifier of a temporary, unique status, and a tangible representation of the UN commitment to effect their return to Palestine. "The UNRWA identity cards were like the 'promissory note' on their right to return to Palestine" (Plascov 1981:49).

CONCLUSION

For a displaced community, narrating the past is often an oppositional process which takes place in the context of political contention and struggle. This process is further animated by the way the identity of the community is constructed by "others," in this case Arabs of the host countries and the Israelis. In the specific case of *Wadi al-Rimam*, one might say that the existence of thousands of refugees who share similar experiences and construct analogous pasts becomes an "authority" and "power" against all other forces threatening Palestinian identity by creating an obligation on this refugee community to keep and reproduce those practices and customs which have come to constitute the Palestinian "tradition."

REFERENCES

Bisharat, George
    1994   Displacement and Social Identity: Palestinian Refugees of the West Bank. *In* Population Displacement and Resettlement: Development and Conflict in the Middle East. Ed. by Seteney Shami. New York: Center for Migration Studies.

Khalidi, W.
    1992   All that Remains: The Palestinian Village Occupied and Depopulated by Israel in 1948. Washington D.C.: Institute of Palestine Studies.

Morris, M.
    1986   The Harvest of 1948 and the Creation of the Palestinian Refugee Problem. The Middle East Journal 40(40):671–685.

Peteet, Julie
    1991   Gender In Crisis: Women and the Palestinian Resistance Movement. New York: Columbia University Press.

Plascov, A.
      1981   The Palestinian Refugees in Jordan 1948–1957. London: Frank Press.
Rushdie, Salman
      1991   Imaginary Homelands: Essays and Criticism 1981–1991. London:
             Penguin Books.
Said, Edward
      1983   A Profile of the Palestinian People. Chicago: Palestine Human
             Rights Campaign.
      1986   After the Last Sky: Palestinian Lives. New York: Pantheon.
Sayigh, Rosemary
      1977   The Palestinian Identity Among Camp Residents. Journal of
             Palestine Studies 6(3):3–22.
      1979   Palestinians: From Peasants to Revolutionaries. London: Zed Press.
Swedenberg, Ted
      1990   The Palestinian Peasant As National Signifier. Anthropological
             Quarterly 63 (1).

RACISM AS A TRANSNATIONAL PROCESS

Afro-Cubans Between the Sword and the Wall[1]

Anthony Marcus

"This family was upper middle class before the revolution. They never lost their house to the revolution. They aren't that different from my own family. They understand what Americans are used to and they can provide it mostly. They understand us—they have relatives in Miami. The daughter even knows English. It's nicer than staying in some little apartment in old Havana, where the walls are falling down and the only foreign language they know is Russian."

Henry, an American journalist in Havana, 1995

INTRODUCTION

So spoke an American freelance journalist who was researching a story on Cuba as it changes from communism to capitalism. While in Havana he was paying $20 per night to stay at a *casa privada* run by a relatively

1. I received funding for research from CUNY Caribbean exchange. I wish to thank Mary Lennon for her invaluable contributions to my ethnography; Robert Marcus for convincing me to write the paper and then being there with his editor's pen when it was finished; Marc Edelman for helping me to clarify my thinking on Cuba; Tracy Morgan and Michael Weinstein for boundless support and thoughtful discussions; Molly Doane, Charles Menzies, Jonathan Hearn, Eliza Darling, and the 15 de Marzo group for useful editorial commentary; Philippe Bourgois, whose book *Ethnicity at Work* did much to shape my thinking about race in the Americas; and Martha Rodriguez who enables New York City and Cuba to share ideas and cultures.

comfortable white Cuban family, who live in an attractive well kept town house in the quiet and airy Havana neighborhood of Vedado. *Casas privadas* are private houses where families rent out rooms and provide meals to foreign visitors in exchange for dollars to purchase things that they no longer receive from the government. All over Cuba *casas privadas* compete for the foreigner's $20 per night—which is about 2–3 times the average monthly wage of a doctor or engineer working for the government.

In expressing his preference for staying with a family that was middle class before the revolution and still lives in its old town house in Vedado, this American journalist unconsciously became part of a much larger transnational process of racial inequality that threatens the gains made by Afro-Cubans in the Cuban revolution. This journalist, who regards himself as a very liberal and non-racist American, is open-minded enough to travel to Cuba, in violation of U.S. travel restrictions. However, it never occurred to him that racial divisions had anything to do with him staying with "a middle-class family" that has relatives in the United States rather than a less cultured and cosmopolitan family that lives in a crowded urban neighborhood like Old Havana. He was doing what any of us— other than an anthropologist—would do: using his $20 per night to stay at the most comfortable and familiar place he could find.

Instead of staying with an Afro-Cuban family in Old Havana, an historically Afro-Cuban neighborhood that is falling apart as the Cuban revolution crumbles, he was staying in a house with people who regularly receive money from their relatives in Miami to pay for paint, plaster, and other basic commodities that have lately become unavailable in Cuba. The daughter has learned some English instead of the Russian that was taught in the Cuban schools until recently, because of contact with cousins who live in the United States. While he stays with them, Henry will probably have his clothing cleaned by a relative of the family; he will use taxis called by the family; and he will occasionally use the daughter as an interpreter during interviews. But as the Miami Cubans continue to help out their families on the island with regular checks, the number of Henrys increases, and the Cuban government continues to struggle against brutal shortages in the state sector, the equality that the Cuban revolution has boasted of for 35 years will continue to erode and differentiation will occur.

These dollars from outside the island as they interact with life in Cuba cause big changes and re-create the very way Cubans see themselves and their neighbors. This paper explores the new dangers and new opportunities in the increasingly interconnected and interdependent economic and political system of the Americas. In particular it examines some of the ways in which the introduction of an internal market economy and the opening of Cuba to the economy and society of the capitalist world has differently affected the lives and perceptions of Afro-Cubans and their non-African identified compatriots.

RACISM TRANSNATIONALLY

As with the Jews before them who seemed to be hated by a multitude of peoples in a multitude of different countries in rather similar ways, peoples of the African diaspora have often heard the cross-cultural query, "if blacks are really the same as whites, why is it that they are always at the bottom of every society?" While there are some interesting examples of countries and regions where this is not the case such as Panama, where Afro-Panamanians have been considered to be middle class throughout much of the twentieth century, blacks provide an often sizable and socially very visible component of the poorest and most embattled sectors of society in much of the Americas.

Stereotyped in literature, popular culture, and mass media as a kind of perpetual urban problem, negative images of black people are present even in places where there are no significant African descended populations. In Asia, where there are virtually no black people, the prime minister of Japan provoked a scandal by making racist comments about black people and "Darky Toothpaste," a brand of toothpaste showing an offensively stereotypical African-American minstrel player with bright white teeth and a top hat, has been widely marketed. The drama of American race relations plays out on a world stage with those of African descent representing an international symbol of backwardness and social dysfunction.

While various forms of racism and tribalism have existed since ancient times, the anti-black racism of the present United States represents a more sharply defined and globally uniform racism than its older counterparts. In the pre-capitalist world, racism tended to be a more local set of prejudices based on a variety of characteristics that could be as particular as what kind of clothes people wore, what language they spoke, what god they prayed to, what kind of food they ate, or what specific country or region they came from. As capitalism brought the whole world together into one global system in the eighteenth and nineteenth centuries, whole sections of humanity were grouped into categories described as scientific but actually founded on biologically meaningless sets of superficial physical traits such as skin color, hair texture, or the dimensions of the head. Racism became even more globally uniform during World War II and through the entire postwar period, when the United States became the most powerful country in the world. Its economic structures, armies, products, television, radio, and media culture, military bases and its "American Dream" spread to the far corners of the globe. Not surprisingly, many of the U.S. understandings of race and racism accompanied these other aspects of American culture.

The process continues into the present with the increased globalization of the U.S. economy, the collapse of the Soviet Union as a counterweight to U.S. influence in Latin America and around the globe, and the widespread introduction of satellite broadcasts of U.S. cable television throughout the Americas. There is hardly a spot in the Americas where one can't watch Baywatch. With the full hemispheric economic integration that is planned for the year 2005, constantly improving communications technology, the increasing domination on a day-to-day basis of the United States and U.S. ideas, the transnationalization of racism, racial political economy, and racial ideologies in the Americas and beyond is very likely to increase.

While large sections of Latin America trace their ancestry back to Africa and Africans, many writers and social scientists have observed that most of the Spanish-speaking countries draw much less of a line between black and white than occurs in the United States. Seeing race more in terms of culture than biology, Latin Americans believe much less that "one drop of black blood" makes someone black. With many, sometimes hundreds of different categories, terms, and nicknames for describing a wide variety of peoples with a wide variety of combinations of colors, features, and social classes there is generally less of a sense that "racial difference" is a fundamental divide. The old saying in Spanish that "money whitens" suggests the ways in which race does influence social standing, but it is more "flexible" and "permeable" than in the United States.

This is not to say that racism against African descended people does not exist in Latin America. It is clear from looking at any set of economic statistics or doing interviews with a wide variety of different people that "blackness" is generally a social disadvantage in Latin America and whiteness an advantage. However, those who consider themselves to be Afro-Latin and are regarded as black are often part of specific communities that are only a small percentage of the people who have some African ancestry.

Cuba, a small island nation, ninety miles off the coast of Florida, has a history of race relations in many ways more like that of the United States than Latin America. The second to last country in the Americas to abolish slavery in 1886, Cuba has a long history of racial segregation, laws against intermarriage between black and white, separate cultural identifications for black and white, and a history of lynchings culminating in the "little war of 1912," an episode of mass lynching and torture of Afro-Cubans, in response to a struggle for civil rights.

Like much of the Caribbean, Cuba saw a retreat of European influence and a rise of U.S. domination in the last decades of the nineteenth century. The central prize that the U.S. fought over in the Spanish-American War,

Cuba is both the largest island in the Caribbean and the closest one to the United States (90 miles from Florida). It has for over a century been considered a crucial part of U.S. "hemispheric defense" and was briefly considered for statehood after the war with Spain. Cuba was occupied by the U.S. military in 1898–1901, 1906–1909, 1912, and again in 1917. From the American warships dispatched to the island, by Franklin Delano Roosevelt in 1933, in response to the political reformist regime led by Dr. Ramon Grau San Martin to the U.S. led invasion of the Bay of Pigs in 1961 there has been a long history of U.S. intervention into the internal affairs of Cuba. A U.S. military force remains to this day at Guantanamo Bay on the far eastern end of the island. Throughout much of the twentieth century, this direct U.S. control of Cuba was combined with a tremendous financial and institutional influence of U.S. corporations and organized crime leading pre-revolutionary Cuba to have many of the appearances of a U.S. colony.

This "intimate" relationship between Cuba and the United States during much of the twentieth century may have further added to the similarities between racial divisions in the U.S. and Cuba, doing much to create a separate group that identifies as black. Cuba, though, unlike the rest of the Caribbean and Latin America, had a radical rupture with the economic, political, and social system of the Americas. In 1959, when the July 26th movement seized power in Cuba and installed Fidel Castro as the leader of the government, Cuba began a social trajectory that linked it to a different world system than that of the capitalist countries of the Americas. On April 16, 1961, the night before the Bay of Pigs invasion, when Castro gave a speech at the funeral for victims of a U.S. bombing attack declaring that henceforth the Cuban revolution would be a socialist revolution, he embarked on a development path that brought Cuba closer to the workers' states of eastern Europe.

Even before this breach with the United States, Castro officially addressed the problem of racism in Cuban life. In one of his first speeches as leader of Cuba in March 1959 he shattered the long-standing taboo against even admitting to the existence of racism in Cuba. In this speech he asserted that "one of the battles which we must prioritize . . . is the battle to end racial discrimination." Cuba embarked on a radical course including literacy programs and affirmative action for all disadvantaged sectors without regard to color or background, with the goal of completely integrating all social groups into every aspect of the collective economy and the ending of segregation. While many scholars have assessed the success of these programs and many documented studies suggest that "pre-revolutionary" racial attitudes persist among many white Cubans (Serviat 1986, Carneado 1962, Moore 1988, Casal 1979), there is little doubt that for black Cubans these developments represented an unprecedented increase in relative social power.

The private school system which had formerly been the reserve of whites was eliminated and replaced with an integrated free public school system. Rents were dramatically lowered, with many houses simply deeded over to the inhabitants, (currently eleven years of residence con- stitutes automatic ownership of a house), making black Cubans the Afri- can descended population with by far the highest house ownership percentage in the world. With guarantees of adequate food, health care, housing, education, equal opportunity in employment, and a job for everyone, economically the revolution represented a major improvement in living conditions for all those at the bottom of the social opportunity structure, many of whom were Afro-Cubans. Post revolutionary Cuba has clearly been the country with the least inequality between blacks and whites in the Americas.

RACE AND RACISM IN REVOLUTIONARY CUBA

A significant percentage of the Cuban population identifies itself with Africa, "blackness," and the history of slavery in Cuba. One Afro-Cuban put it, "we are different. I knew people in my family who were born slaves. That is why we Cubans went to Africa (the Angola Campaign and the Ethiopian intervention) to help free our brothers who are still en- slaved. We have special feelings about Africans." Another black Cuban described her emotions about her daughter having married a white man "it was difficult at first, because we had to get used to him. At first I didn't want my daughter to marry a white. We black Cubans see whites as less attractive, the whites do not know our culture and there are many compromises that are necessary." Statements like these and the frequent references to the recent history of slavery as an historical experience re- veal a consciousness of being both Cuban and yet different from other Cubans.[2]

White Cubans are sharply aware of blackness and Africaness as a so- cial difference. They retain many stereotypical notions of black Cubans that are considered "pre-revolutionary." During an evening music and dance program on Cuban television the white Cubans with whom I was watching the show made numerous comments about how wonderful black Cubans were at dancing. Recognizing that these comments deviated from a social norm, they expressed defensiveness in the absence of any

---

2. While Afro-Cubans make frequent references to the collective memory of slav- ery, there was no mention of the race war of 1912. This war diminutively called "la guerrita del 12."(the little war of 12) saw the deaths of thousands of blacks and ordinary civilians through direct fighting and brutal torture. Cubans of mixed African/European descent, reputedly the majority of Cuba, seem to have little in the way of a separate racially-based cultural identity.

criticism or questioning on my part. As one woman said, "it isn't racist to say that blacks have something inside them that makes their dancing special. I can say the same thing about Cubans in general. They are better dancers than Americans. This is not racist. Look at them: there is nothing better." Clearly her comments about Afro-Cubans made her defensive in the presence of strangers from the United States.

Some white Cubans were much more explicit about their racialist beliefs. Claiming that communism had ruined Cuba and that the anti-Castro Cubans in the United States "still valued white people," these comments usually accompanied the English word nigger and invectives about Castro's rule. As one self-employed white Cuban told me, "the communist system makes blacks equal, but that is not natural and would be different under capitalism." Such attitudes were rare, and were invariably connected to identification with the United States or Cubans living there. This starkly confirmed the belief among most of my informants that whatever their personal feelings were about black Cubans, "to be a good and patriotic communist" was to reject the racism that they are taught is endemic to capitalism and imperialism. In a society in which the workforce is well integrated, salaries are roughly equal between black and white, and there is little residential or educational segregation, most Cubans appear to be very tolerant of differences or perceived differences.

Because of the great improvements in standards of living and opportunities, Afro-Cubans tend to be among the strongest defenders of Castro and the communist system. One older Afro-Cuban who told me "our memory of slavery is very recent," became nearly enraged when I asked him whether Cuba would ever be led by a black Cuban. "There already are black Cubans who lead this country", he said. "Look at any government office, look at the military, look at the National Assembly you will see all the colors of Cuba. There is not a country in the world that has done more for black people than Cuba. Our infant mortality rates are lower for blacks than the United States, literacy is higher, for blacks than anywhere in the world, our salaries are the same as white people's, nobody keeps us out of their imperialist suburbs, and I don't worry that my son will be beaten to death by a bunch of right-wing racist policemen. There isn't a father any place in the Americas who can say that, except Cubans. Castro is not white he is one of us."

While some Afro-Cubans noted that, indeed, more white Cubans than black ones sat at the very top of the Cuban government, the identification of Castro as "our leader and one of us" was very strong. Several black Cubans were quick to point out that "Castro was a good friend of Malcolm X." While Castro seems to still be very popular generally, Afro-Cubans were far more intensely loyal to "Fidel," the accomplishments of the Cuban revolution, and the communist system that has been in place for about 35 years than most other Cubans, particularly whites. As one Afro-Cuban woman said to me when she told the story of how the Havana town house that she had worked in as a servant before the revolution was given to her when the family that had lived there escaped to Florida: "They will have to kill me before those white shits in Florida take my house back. I would take a bullet for Fidel." Several informants made reference to the beating of Rodney King, insisting that such a thing would never happen in Cuba.

Cuba is clearly no racial paradise where prejudice, bigotry, and the legacy of hundreds of years of slavery and racial inequality have been eliminated once and for all. However, communist Cuba has greatly reduced the importance of race as a social division. Much of the whitest or most European descended 10% of the population abandoned Cuba after the revolution; the rates of intermarriage between white and black greatly increased; and Fidel Castro officially declared that "we are an African-Latin nation." As an Afro-Cuban taxi driver told me, "in the past, when the whites had all the power, we worried ourselves about their attitudes and ideas. Now I don't care about racial attitudes. I have an equal right to housing; an equal right to a job; and an equal right to medical care. Yes, there are white Cubans who still say racist things, but those are just words and that is their problem, not mine."

Virtually all Cubans agree that the Cuban revolution and the communist system has been very good for Afro-Cubans. The national claim, summed up nicely by an Afro-Cuban musician, that "Castro has done more for black people than any world leader in history," is one of the few things that most Cubans can agree on. This unprecedented leveling of political, economic, and social inequalities between black and white and the struggle to end racism in Cuba is so deeply tied in people's minds to Castro and communism that for many the coming collapse of communism in Cuba is seen as the automatic rebirth of racism, before it has even happened.

"THE SPECIAL PERIOD"

Cubans, who formerly enjoyed the highest standard of living in Latin America, based on heavily subsidized trade with the former communist countries, are currently facing a situation in which the basic necessities of life are no longer provided by the government. With the collapse of the Soviet Union and the end of the very favorable trade terms with the former countries of the Warsaw pact, Cuba has both been thrown abruptly into the world market and seen a massive effort on the part of the U.S. government to tighten the economic blockade. This has been accompanied by an increase in the extra-legal often violent activities of

CIA connected anti-Castro Cubans against the island. All this has increasingly isolated the Cuban workers' state from any "international community" and produced a debilitating spiral downwards of virtually all Cuban economic indicators.

It is estimated that with the fall of the Soviet Union Cuba has lost one to two billion dollars per year in trade leading to a decline of roughly 50% in its gross social product since 1989. This massive and nearly overnight collapse in the Cuban standard of living has led to the grinding shortages and severe rationing that Fidel Castro has dubbed "the special period." Milk, meat, and fresh vegetables are unavailable through state stores for all but young children, diabetics, and others with special medical conditions. Consumer products like toothpaste, shampoo, and normal bar soap[3] have also disappeared from the state sector. Blackouts are frequent. The tap water is becoming less clean in certain areas and often does not run for several hours per day. Public transportation is greatly reduced and there are no longer luxuries from eastern Europe in the stores. The isolation from the rest of the world has led panicked Cuban professionals, like computer technicians, doctors, and engineers who are unable to read the latest journal articles, learn the new machines, or attend international conferences to fear that by the time the special period is over, they will have been left behind by their various professions. Life has simply become much more difficult and uncertain for most Cubans. The general fatigue, malaise, and crankiness pervading Cuban society led many Cubans to seek escape to the United States in the summer of 1994.

In response to this crisis, the government has opened the economy to tourism and joint economic ventures with foreign capitalists in hopes of replacing the lost international investment and spurring private production through market incentives. In 1993 the Cuban government legalized the holding of U.S. dollars for the first time since the 1960s. This effectively legalized the black market and threw many of the luxuries and basic commodities no longer on the shelves of state stores onto the open market in dollar stores and informal markets across Cuba. With little work available and a massive retreat of the state sector, "self-employment" has also been encouraged. At present 210,000 people are legally licensed by the national government to be "self-employed." But with dollars legal again it is certain that the numbers of people who work in various semi-legal informal sector enterprises is far larger and petty capitalism has grown throughout the island.

---

3. In special period Cuba the variety of soap that is generally provided by the government is very caustic and abrasive due to the shortage of enough oil to produce adequate soap.

While the very barest necessities are still available to all the people through state stores, these bare necessities are hardly enough to survive on,[4] much less live a decent life. These privations are very difficult for Cubans who previously had the highest standard of living in Latin America. As one man put it "we Cubans don't have the normal Latin American expectations. We expect to live like people in the European countries." The problem is particularly difficult with regard to big-ticket consumer goods like kitchen appliances, air conditioners, televisions, and automobiles. No longer available through eastern European state sector industries at prices regulated by the government, these products are now for sale to individual Cubans only through the dollar market. This is virtually impossible without access to foreign money, when the average monthly salary in the state sector is about $4 per month, regardless of profession. Virtually all Cubans now must find a way to obtain dollars. As they are discovering, to be a capitalist you need something to sell.

The elimination of prostitution was an early point of pride for the revolution. Now, back with a vengeance, it is one of the major tourist draws in Havana for the many European and South American men who come to Cuba for vacations. People rent out extra bedrooms to tourists, use their cars as both licensed and unlicensed taxis, and provide a wide variety of services to tourists and Cubans who have the dollars to pay for them. Except for the lucky few who either have jobs that force them into regular contact with tourists or who run some kind of business that captures a regular flow of dollars, for most Cubans, the dollar economy is extremely chaotic, unplanned, and random.

This policy of encouraging the growth of an internal capitalist economy has reintroduced into Cuban society many inequalities unseen since the early 1960s. Miramar, a neighborhood of Havana where many of the more successful entrepreneurs are reputed to live, boasts nicely painted houses along well tended streets, with satellite dishes that sell U.S. cable television to residents of the community and dollar stores stocked with fax machines, Korean televisions, European washers and dryers, and a small supermarket with everything from European chocolate to powdered milk and German beer.

At the "Rapido," billed as genuine American-style fast food, red, white, and blue mini-skirt clad waitresses on roller skates are paid in dollars to serve customers in their Polish, East German, and Soviet built cars, while

---

4. An indicator of how low the Cuban rations actually are is that in 1993, the worst year of the special period, mass vitamin B deficiencies leading to temporary blindness were found in Cubans throughout the island. Unable to raise the rations of foods that provide vitamin B, the government instituted a program of regular distribution of B supplement tablets and injections throughout the island.

women dressed in stylish imported clothing pose and local Havana businessmen strip off fifty dollar bills from wads of American money to pay for hot dogs and beer for whole tables filled with people. At night the nightclubs and restaurants fill up not just with Argentine, Spanish, and German men on sexual safari, but also with local Havana entrepreneurs who, in the absence of a genuine capitalist financial sector, have little to do with their money but spend it on wine, women, song, and that most desired of Cuban commodities, powdered milk. There is a wild west quality to the dollar economy that belies its small size.

While these little big men of the Cuban cash economy carry around large sums of money and act like "pre-revolution" mobsters, they currently represent an extremely fragile petty capitalist class. The relatively small sums that they are dealing in and the few opportunities for investment leave them with little power beyond having a somewhat more comfortable life and the ability to make their neighbors jealous. For many Cubans who do not have easy access to hot dogs or any form of meat and who work in the state sector at low wages that pay for the basics and *"nada mas"* these "dollar men" are the source of envy. However for many black Cubans they represent the possibility of their worst nightmare invading the island: American style racism.

AFRO-CUBANS AND THE LONG SHADOW OF RODNEY KING

Black Cubans feel particularly vulnerable contemplating the change in the balance of forces away from the program of the Cuban revolution and toward attempts at integration with the capitalist world. Few Afro-Cubans have jobs in the tourist industry or relatives in the United States who send regular cash remittances, making it difficult to buy foreign-made products, act like big men at El Rapido, or go to clubs and tourist restaurants. Many Afro-Cubans talked of their fears of an "American solution." As an Afro-Cuban computer-technician told me, "If Cuba gets invaded by the Americans, we black Cubans will have no choice, we will have to fight to the death, every person. It is different for the others. They are faithful to their country and they know what a great leader Fidel is, but for us there is American racism. We know what happens to black people in the United States. We know what happened in Los Angeles with Rodney King and the police. We haven't had that here since before the revolution."

Cubans of every color and background express their consciousness of the role of the United States in the global spread of racism. One often hears that "really it was the Americans we fought in Angola and not Africans." The beating of Rodney King, the assassinations of Martin

Luther King and Malcolm X, and the U.S. government support for pro-apartheid forces in Southern Africa stand as proof for many black Cubans that whatever privations Fidel and the communist system have in store for them are better than "what is out there."

While Cubans are highly sensitive to race relations outside Cuba, due in part to Cuban government propaganda and the evening news which is often filled with reports of police brutality and other forms of discrimination against blacks in the United States, they also recognize a rising consciousness of racial discrimination in Cuba. As one black Cuban, who was actually doing quite well as a bartender in a tourist hotel put it, "the S.A. after all these businesses (S.A.— Sociedad Anonimo is Spanish for anonymous partnership, a rough equivalent of the English 'Corp,'), it means socios amigos (friends for partners), you have to have those kind of Amigos, like those whites in Miami." When I asked if there were better neighborhoods in Havana where the buildings were not in a state of permanent disrepair, I was sent to Miramar, where "there are white people who watch American television and live well." Many black Cubans noting white people's differential access to international capital and networks believe that the white Cubans in Miami and U.S. businesses in general will reproduce the U.S. racial system in Cuba. An Afro-Cuban teenager nicely summed up this feeling of being "iced out" of the developing capitalist market: "Whites in the United States prefer to make business with whites here."

Several different people pointed out the differences in how black and white Cuban defectors were treated when they arrived in the United States. A black Cuban woman who works in the informal sector taking in sewing jobs whose ex-husband left Cuba during the Mariel[5] exodus said, "when the white Cubans came to the United States, they were given welcome by the president and allowed to do whatever they wanted. When my husband went over there they were all locked up in prisons and camps and called criminals and lunatics—prejudice. That is why blacks in The United States like Fidel better than their own president." In economically stressed "special period" Cuba, the poor welcome given to the "*Marielitos*" has possibly permanent repercussions for the "on the

---

5. April of 1980 saw the first large-scale emigration of black Cubans to the United States. Released during Jimmy Carter's pre-election war drum beating against Cuba, the U.S. government was caught by surprise at thousands of nonwhite refugees on their shores. Instead of standing by these people that they had encouraged to leave, they sought to blame Castro and portrayed the *Marielitos* as a group of mentally ill criminals, and other dregs of Cuban society that Castro had gotten rid of at U.S. expense. For many black Cubans this was an ugly slap in the face to the fathers, uncles, brothers, and sons who had attempted to make the big journey that had previously been made by white Cubans.

ground" relationship between black Cubans and their non-black compatriots.

The simple fact that there were no sizable black Cuban immigrations to the United States until 1980 puts the entire Afro-Cuban community in the United States twenty years behind in the building of businesses, careers, and the accumulation of capital. This "late development" is further compounded by U.S. racism, the less affluent period in which they immigrated, the severe world economic downturn of 1982, and their stigmatization in U.S. public opinion. As a result, the *Marielitos* generally do not have enough money to send the kind of regular remittances back to the island that their white counterparts send. Furthermore, with each tightening of restrictions on the expatriating of U.S. money to Cuba, it becomes more difficult and expensive to help relatives on the island. This tends to reduce or even eliminate the remittances of the more recent and financially less secure *Marielitos*. Meanwhile, as white Cubans on the island circulate their remittances[6] and draw on foreign connections to obtain commodities for sale in the dollar economy, they show preferential hiring patterns in the rapidly growing dollar service economy.

A renewed racial differentiation threatens to consign black Cubans to the economic margins of the new Cuba. As only the most public face of this "new differentiation," an informal survey of the government-owned dollar stores in and around Western Havana showed that, with the exception of a parking lot attendant at El Rapido and a security guard at a dollar store, virtually none of the employees appeared to be Afro-Cuban. This confirmed what Afro-Cubans had told me about the heavily white character of the dollar economy. The legalization of dollars and the gradual liquidation of the state sector in favor of the private sector has therefore aided in the reproduction of U.S. racial inequalities in Cuba.

This Afro-Cuban identification of the external connection with increasing inequality and the feeling that there are only bad things waiting for them outside Cuba in the world of capitalism is the other side of the general belief among Cubans that the revolution benefitted Afro-Cubans the most of any group. It may partially explain why many black Cubans still put so much faith in Castro, in spite of the fact that it was he who introduced the market reforms. As almost everyone in Cuba says, "with the fall of the socialist camp Fidel has no choice."

---

6. It is currently estimated that roughly 40% of the foreign money coming to Cuba is in the form of remittances. Some estimates put it at nearly one half billion dollars per year. With the collapse of the state sector after the fall of the Soviet Union these remittances and the people who receive them become more and more important in Cuban society.

AFRO-CUBAN YOUTH:
BETWEEN COMMUNISM AND CAPITALISM

The U.S. press has recently featured reports of a generation gap in Cuba. It is commonly said that young people with no memory of the revolution and the way things were before the revolution are completely uninterested in communism and only want more consumer goods and to be plugged into international youth culture. This MTV-as-apple-of-knowledge argument seems very compelling on the surface. In fact, many young Cubans have little interest in communism, little patience with Castro and his "tasks of the revolution," and a tremendous desire to be connected to "what's happening out there" instead of being trapped on this slowly starving island with its rapidly unraveling political culture.

However, this lack of commitment to communism that many U.S. commentators have noticed among Cuban youth appears to be due more to their ignorance of the possibilities that their parents had in the 1960s, 1970s, and 1980s than their not knowing how bad it was before communism. Young people who are just beginning their adulthood have little ability to imagine themselves fitting into a system that offers nothing but the promise of extended crisis and waste of their youthful energy.

While there are certainly many young people of all backgrounds who have recently finished school and are beginning their work life in the state sector with much enthusiasm and a strong loyalty to the still two million person communist party, for many youth there are few appealing possibilities for employment at wages that only purchase the meager state supplies in the rapidly shrinking economy. The lack of opportunities in the special period to travel to eastern Europe, Africa, or other Latin American countries to be educated or participate in professional, military, or humanitarian activities is yet another loss of incentive to work within the system. There was a time in the not so distant past when good grades in school might get a student sent to a university in East Germany, a humanitarian project in Latin America, or a conference on the beach in Bulgaria. It is not so much the restrictions of the system that seem to make young people impatient with communism and yearn for the glitter of U.S. capitalism, but its loss of ability to provide economic incentives, rewards for achievement, or project the romantic image of a viable national project as it did in the past.

Despite their political education and apparent consciousness of U.S. racism, black Cuban youth are no exception to this "new alienation." They know about prejudice against blacks in the United States, but they see people with relatives in Miami and New Jersey getting satellite antennas, washing machines, and other luxuries that are no longer provided by the state. They see the government laying off thousands of people[7] and paying those who are employed starvation wages. Many of them would rather take their chances in a society that has the potential to reward their energies and efforts than in a society where misery, idleness, starvation, and increasing inequality await them. As one Afro-Cuban man of 18 years old told me, "I do not believe in God or the Devil or any of those religious things. This is the only life I have and I am dying here on this prison island. I would do anything to get to the United States." Another young black Cuban who had displayed a strong knowledge of the history of blacks in the United States and the U.S. repression of the Black Panther Party told me that his dream was to go to the United States and start a business, "because there is nothing to do here, but wait." He felt that in spite of the racism in the United States he would have more opportunity to succeed "where there are many opportunities for many people, than here where there are few opportunities and the government is thoroughly corrupt."

Many young Afro-Cuban women who have turned to prostitution feel that the government and the system has a lot less to offer them than the foreign tourists with their shiny cameras and easy ability to buy a chicken dinner or drink *mojitos* (the Cuban national mixed drink) in a $100 per night hotel. They see that black Cubans are not the ones who are managing the dollar enterprises and they would rather cast their lot with foreigners than wait for segregation and color stratification to slowly return to the island and strangle them. As a young professional woman who made extra money in the evenings "getting to know foreign men" told me, "I am mixed and my friend is a black and many foreigners think we are unusual and will give us more."

For many young people in Cuba between 15 and 25 who see no viable future, have increasingly distant memories of life before the special period, and know little else but privations and defeats, the stories of money, success, glamour and glitter in the land of capitalism beyond their shores fires their imaginations.

---

7. In 1995 the Cuban government announced the end of full employment and the right to a job. While this legal change does not represent a major change in the current lives of Cubans who are still provided with food, housing, education, and health care by the government, it has some major repercussions for the future. It could be seen as a major step in laying the basis for a full-blown capitalist economy, with a competitive labor market and a reserve army of labor. When one looks at the proportion of African descended peoples in the Americas who are consigned to this fate by capitalist economies it is not unreasonable to imagine this same fate for black Cubans in a capitalist Cuban society. One of the fundamental tenets of Marxism-Leninism as it is both theorized and has been practiced is the notion that everyone, regardless of abilities, has both the right to work and the obligation to work. In this quiet way Cuba has retreated from one of the most basic aspects of its system.

AFRO-CUBANS
BETWEEN THE SWORD AND THE WALL

Afro-Cubans look at the disintegration of the Cuban revolution and feel themselves to be "between the sword and the wall." In this case the sword is the sword of U.S. racism and the system of racial inequality that they had hoped they had left behind in 1959. The wall is the weakness of the isolated Cuban economy and the fragmentation of the collective state system into which they have invested massive amounts of labor and political support. While a few Afro-Cubans articulated a kind of pan-African nationalism, most of my informants were much more worried about day-to-day problems such as getting powdered milk or new clothing that is not provided by the state stores and finding a way to pay for it. They saw that while there is still a rough equality for the majority of people in the state sector, in the increasingly important private sector inequality rapidly grows. They attribute this to "corruption" rampant within the government and the power white cubans have to mobilize "pre-revolutionary" resources and networks. In the words of a black Cuban woman who teaches judo in the state sector, "the best businessmen here are whites. The whites have the rich families in Miami, the whites have the business knowledge, the whites have the connections in the United States that this corrupt government wants. Of course the whites run all the businesses here, they do it because they can do it and the government needs them to do it." Thus old divisions are causing new inequalities.

While the policies of Fidel Castro are directly leading to this "new inequality" in which not everybody starts with an equal opportunity to become a capitalist, it seems likely that Castro can still count on black Cubans to provide a central pillar of support for his policies, his government, and his bloated military apparatus. These changes have the contradictory effect of both alienating many black Cubans, as citizens with less recourse to the private economy, from some of the most important trends in contemporary Cuban society and yet driving them deeper into defending the government that is promoting these changes that do not seem to be in their interests. This contradictory position seems to be pretty well understood as a "tactical retreat" by those black Cubans who do remember pre-revolutionary racism or grew up after the revolution. As one black Cuban woman of about 30, who was working part-time as a prostitute for the tourists told me, "my grandparents didn't even know how to read or write and look at me, I am a chemist and I know Russian. These are things the revolution has given us that cannot be put into numbers or statistics. If Fidel has to follow the rules of the market for a time, ok, he has no choice."

However, most young black Cubans, like virtually all Cuban youth, have little patience with the whole business of adjustments, tactics, and the protection of a revolution that has given them little and pours their youth down a hopeless geo-political sinkhole. They have heard stories of incredible riches and high wages. They have heard the music, seen the movies, and watched the television shows of the millionaires of the U.S. African diaspora. Many Cuban teenagers follow U.S. professional sports and have seen the glamour, wealth, and opportunities that are enjoyed by U.S. black athletes whose only athletic competition in this hemisphere are Cubans. For many Cubans it is a point of pride that "U.S. heavy weight boxers made millions of dollars throughout the 1970s and 1980s and none of them could beat Teofilo Stevenson," the great Cuban Olympic boxer, who was reputed to be the best fighter in the world throughout much of the 70s and 80s. Cubans watch U.S. baseball on TV, listen to sports on U.S. radio, and become very excited about the Pan-American games, in which all Latin American countries participate, but where every event amounts to a competition between Cuba and the U.S. for the gold and silver medals.

During the 1995 Pan-American games Cubans were quick to point out that "their boys and girls" were beating future millionaires. Although Cuba won more total metals than nearly all of the other Latin American countries put together, they were sorely disappointed that the United States had taken more metals in contrast to the previous Pan-American games in which Cuba had beaten the U.S. Between the identification of U.S. sports being dominated by African Americans and the popularity of African-American music, many Afro-Cuban youth, regardless of their ideological leanings view U.S. African Americans as dynamic producers of culture and excellence in sports. They see them as a group that in spite of racial prejudice has accumulated more wealth and has a higher standard of living than any other African peoples in the Americas. For a young person who sees no future in Cuba and has been lied to over and over again by a corrupt government and a megalomaniacal leader, the "American dream" is something to live for and a way to "get on with your life." They want to go to the United States and get a jump on the world of capitalism, which everybody including Fidel seems to suggest in one way or another will come to Cuba anyhow.

CONCLUSION:
RACISM AS A TRANSNATIONAL PROCESS

The function of racism to divide black and white workers, both to reduce their bargaining power over wages and as a means of political control is still very much the foundation on which local systems of racism are based.

However, the contemporary capitalist world system is based on an unequal distribution of wealth and resources and an international division of labor in which "blackness" or "non-whiteness" is a transnational category that divides society on more than a local basis. The diffusion of these transnational divisions brutally reproduces inequalities and the justifications for them around the globe. These inequalities have many different sources: the reinforcement of ancient prejudices; the political, economic, and cultural links between Third-World ruling classes and North Atlantic economies and societies; the still very nonblack character of U.S. business; the world predominance of U.S. media; preferential access to doing business with a U.S. military base or firm; and the historic legacy of inequalities produced by the African slave system of the Americas.

However, the U.S. "black question" is becoming both the metaphor for articulating difference and the organizational principle for implementing that difference as it is diffused throughout the world. This dominant political, economic, and cultural role has increased with the spread of satellite technologies and the collapse of the Soviet counterweight to U.S. domination, homogenizing culture and ideology. This "new world order" in which "blackness" represents an international division in the world working class that is becoming more transnational has the potential to become increasingly universal as more isolated and peripheral or previously closed sections of the world are integrated into "the new world order."

Regardless of how much inequality has developed in contemporary Cuba, Afro-Cubans articulate a very clear message. They are apprehensive about the coming changes and fear racial injustice tied to the notion of an international category of race or "blackness." Just as the anti-Latino law in California entitled "Proposition 187" has become a famous symbol of U.S. prejudice and bigotry throughout *mestizo* Latin America, there are whole countries and regions of the world particularly here in the Americas over which hang the long shadow of Rodney King blocking the sun.

REFERENCES

The Black Scholar
  1985   Roundtable on the History of Racial Prejudice in Cuba. January: 36.
Bourgois, Philippe
  1989   Ethnicity at Work: Divided Labor on a Central American Banana Plantation. Baltimore: Johns Hopkins University Press.
Brenner, Philip, ed.
  1989   The Cuba Reader: The Making of a Revolutionary Society. NY: Grove Press.
Carneado, Jose Felipe
  1962   *La discriminación racial en Cuba no volverá jamás.* Cuba Socialista. La Habana: Minrex.

Casal, Lourdes
    1979   Race Relations in Contemporary Cuba. *In* Anani Dzidzienyo and
    Lourdes Casal. The Position of Blacks in Brazil and Cuban Society.
    London: Minority Rights Group.

Fagen, Richard
    1969   The Transformation of Political Culture in Cuba. Stanford, Ca.:
    Stanford University Press.

Fernandez, Nadine T.
    1996   The Color of Love: Young Interracial Couples in Cuba. Latin
    American Perspectives 23 (Winter).

Fuente, Alejandro de la
    1995   Race and Inequality in Cuba 1899–1981. Journal of Contemporary
    History 30.

Glazer, Jon
    1992   Working for the Tourist Dollar. The Nation 254 (June 15): 820.

Habel, Janette
    1991   Cuba the Revolution in Peril. London: Verso.

Mintz, Sidney W.
    1992   The Birth of African-American Culture: An Anthropological
    Perspective. Boston: Beacon Press.

Moore, Carlos
    1988   Castro, the Blacks and Africa. Los Angeles: Center for
    Afro-American Studies, University of California.

Serviat, Pedro
    1986   *El problema negro en Cuba y su solucion definitiva*. La Habana: Editora
    Politica.

Taber, Michael, ed.
    1983   Fidel Castro Speeches: Our Power Is That of the Working People.
    New York: Pathfinder Press.

Zeitlin, Maurice
    1967   Revolutionary Politics and the Cuban Working Class. Princeton:
    Princeton University Press.

THE COLONY AT THE CORE

*Scottish Nationalism
and the Rhetoric of Colonialism*

Jonathan S. Hearn

INTRODUCTION

In the fall of 1993, during the early months of my fieldwork on the nationalist movement in Scotland, a series of news stories appeared in the press about a controversial new campaigning group called Scottish Watch. An opening passage from a Scottish Watch flyer entitled *The Struggle for Scotland* gives a sense of the group's concerns, and rhetorical style:

> Scotland is being cleared, cleansed, and colonized by a greedy Thatcherite generation of English exploiters, who, having already looted their own land to ruin, are now loose in ours. Whether by accident or design the English are pushing our people to the margins of society and even out of Scotland altogether. While the English seize every opportunity to make money at our expense the Scots are becoming a nation of dupes on the dole. Only a people duped into despair would allow a country rich in land and raw materials to slip into the grasping control of English exploitation. Scots should never forget that despair and fear are tactics used by the English Tory establishment to deprive us of that will to resist the deliberate colonial exploitation of our country. They are the tried and tested weapons of a ruling class that has laid waste to country after country in a centuries old experience of imperialist coloniza-

tion. Scottish Watch is an organization devoted to uncovering the activities of the new economic exploiters of the Scottish people. We will just as ruthlessly expose the methods of those who seek to usurp the Scots from their lands and livelihoods. We will educate, agitate and organize, we will defend the right to work and the right to have a home for Scots in Scotland. We will prevent our people from becoming refugees in their own land. Join us now in the struggle for Scotland.

This manifesto shows the widespread, though inaccurate perception in Scotland that well-off English people are moving into Scotland in ever increasing numbers, displacing Scots from housing—especially in rural communities, better paying managerial jobs, and places at universities. Still, Scottish Watch and its strident anti-English rhetoric met with a mixed reception, many Scots being highly uncomfortable with its quasi-racist overtones. Detractors balanced supporters at a series of public meetings it held around Scotland in 1993–94; newspaper editorials were generally hostile; and the Scottish National Party (SNP), which campaigns for Scottish national independence, took pains to dissociate itself from Scottish Watch and proscribed its members from joining. A fringe of the nationalist movement, however, remains sympathetic to Scottish Watch and a few other small and somewhat shadowy groups similar to it.

Scottish Watch's core argument is that Scotland has continuously been colonized by England. Few outside of Scotland will find this persuasive: as part of the British Empire, Scotland has been in the position of the colonizer as well. As this essay stresses, Scots realize the problems and ambiguities of the notion of Scotland as a colony. Nonetheless, with the growth of the nationalist movement since the 1970s, it has emerged as a powerful and pervasive analogy for Scotland's political situation. Why does this colonial analogy, despite obvious logical difficulties, carry such force? During my fieldwork I pursued, with people involved in the na-tionalist movement what it means to call Scotland a colony. Replies inevi-tably made many references to Scotland's long and complex historical relationship with England. After providing some historical background, I will return to their responses, considering how and why they vary. More generally, I will illustrate how political rhetoric is grounded in cultural experiences, and how such analogies work as rhetoric because they have many, rather than single meanings.

THE BASICS

Scotland and England are both historical nations within the larger politi-cal state of the United Kingdom (UK), which also includes Wales and Northern Ireland. The term Britain generally refers to the island territory that England, Scotland, and Wales share, and thus technically does not include the territory of Northern Ireland, part of the separate island of Ireland. Nonetheless, "Britain" is often used to refer to the entire political system of the United Kingdom. Scotland occupies roughly the northern third of the British Isles, including several much smaller outlying islands to the west (the Hebrides) and north (Orkney and Shetland).

England, by far the largest and most populated part of the United Kingdom,[1] has dominated the history, politics, and very conception of "Britain." English people rarely make a clear distinction between being English and being British (cf. Crick 1991), whereas for the Scots and the Welsh, Britishness is more clearly a separate, alternate identity. The United Kingdom's constitutional history also blurs England and Britain. Unlike the United States for instance, which was created at a particular historical moment, the United Kingdom, having no written constitution nor any single moment of creation, is a gradual and piecemeal history of England's conquest and incorporation of neighboring kingdoms.

SCOTTISH HISTORY

Numerous conflicts over the centuries kept Scotland and England separate kingdoms until 1603 when the Scottish king James VI inherited the English throne and the United Kingdom was born. James moved his court to London, the heart of the larger and more powerful country. Ironically, Scotland found itself governed by a distant royal line that, though originating in Scotland, increasingly viewed political matters from an English perspective. Meanwhile, the Scottish Reformation of the previous century (1560) had created a new Presbyterian Protestant Church, which became a major political force that often competed with the king for power and authority in Scotland. This power struggle led to a century of conflict which took its toll on Scotland. In 1707 the Scottish aristocracy agreed to a Treaty of Union with England, combining the Scottish and English parliaments into one body.

The Union of 1707 preserved the dominant institutions of Scottish society: the national Presbyterian Church, its educational system, and the separate legal system. The Union also gave Scotland access to England's imperial overseas trade, and after an initial period of adjustment, the Scottish economy began to grow. Scotland was now a "Junior Partner" in the developing British Empire, importing tobacco from the American colonies and developing its weaving industries.

---

1. In 1981 the UK total population was 55.7 million. 46.2 million (83%) lived in England, and 5.1 million (9.2%) lived in Scotland. The rest lived in Wales and Northern Ireland (Kellas 1989:10).

But not all Scotland prospered. Centuries earlier Scotland had developed an internal division between the "highlands" in the north and west, and the "lowlands" in the south and east. The highland economy, based on subsistence agriculture and cattle raising was weak. Its people spoke Gaelic, a Celtic language, were at least nominally Catholic, and were organized politically into clans, extended kin groups that could be mobilized by their clan chiefs (also part of the Scottish nobility) for military action. The more prosperous lowland economy stressed urban manufacture and trade, larger-scale agriculture, and the developing trade with the New World. Lowlanders spoke Scots, closely related to English, were staunchly Presbyterian, and viewed the highlanders as backward and dangerous. The highlands, increasingly marginalized, erupted in a series of uprisings (in 1715, 1719, and 1745) that vainly sought to reinstate a Catholic royal line and preserve a more traditional political order. But the lowland Scots and the English crushed these rebellions, treating the highlands as an internal colony to be pacified. In the period known as the "highland clearances" (c. 1790–1830) clan chiefs who had become anglicized landowning nobles forcibly removed large numbers of highland tenants, relocating some to newly created coastal fishing villages, and compelling others to immigrate either abroad or to the industrializing lowlands of Scotland.

In the nineteenth century the economy and empire continued to grow. New large-scale manufactures and industry developed, especially cotton textiles, which thrived until the American Civil War cut off a major supply of cotton. In the later part of the century, heavier industries, such as coal and steel mining, and especially shipbuilding, thrived. Meanwhile, the British empire offered an escape from the limited opportunities in Scotland. Upwardly mobile middle-class Scots found careers as colonial administrators, doctors, and missionaries, while the working classes found employment in the British army and navy. The Scottish middle classes demonstrated nationalistic pride, building monuments to such figures as the novelist Walter Scott and the medieval hero William Wallace, a nationalism entirely compatible with British pride in the Empire (Morris and Morton 1993). The establishment of a secretary of state to administer Scottish affairs in 1886 recognized the country's important place in the British political and economic system.

By the early years of this century, however, the weakening Empire cost Scotland foreign markets for its goods. World War One marked a turning point: the Scottish economy went into a long, slow decline, as capital once generated and reinvested in Scotland was increasingly invested elsewhere (Harvie 1981). The massive growth in heavy industry had created an organized industrial working class that played a major role in the formation of the British Labour Party. Socialism, and in some areas communism (especially in mining communities), became well established in Scotland,

though often fused with a kind of Calvinist Protestant ethic, the legacy of
the powerful role of the Presbyterian Church in Scottish society (Smout
1987:231–275). As the British economy declined, the Labour Party advo-
cated a stronger role for government in managing the economy and protecting citizens from the unpredictable forces of the market. After World
War Two a new and highly activist Labour Government considerably
expanded the welfare state, including pensions, unemployment protection, national health care. They also nationalized many of the key industries and fostered new industries to create employment throughout the
United Kingdom. During these years the Scottish secretaries of state and
the Scottish Office promoted regional interests within this new, much
more centralized and planned economy, making the country a distinctive
unit of economic management within the larger UK system.

Nonetheless, despite centuries of incorporation into a larger system
and a tendency of many outsiders to view Scots as a regional variation on
the English, Scotland remains set apart by a unique heritage of language,
religion, and culture embedded in a set of concrete institutions. These
include the Church, the schools and universities, the legal system, the
political parties, all of which have separate organizations at the Scottish
level, trade unions, local government, newspapers and television networks, football teams, not to mention all sorts of organizations representing various special interests within Scotland, whether the elderly,
tenants rights, Gaelic speakers, or the business community. All these
groups and organizations articulate their political demands in a Scottish
context before they are channeled to the British Parliament at Westminster
and the Prime Minister's cabinet through the Scottish Office and secretary
of state. Thus, Scotland is both a discrete cultural unit as well as a structural component of how politics works in the United Kingdom (Paterson
1994).

Since the 1970s Britain has been a leader in the global political shift
away from a belief in the effectiveness of the welfare state and centrally
planned national economies. The Labour Governments of the 1970s had
already begun to move in this direction, but the election of the Conservative Prime Minister Margaret Thatcher in 1979 initiated an aggressive
move to the right. Deregulation and privatization has stimulated trade
and business in the heartland of the Conservative (or "Tory") Party, the
southeast of England in and around London. But much of the north of
England, as well as Wales and Scotland, have not enjoyed the same economic revival, instead experiencing higher per capita unemployment, and
lower per capita incomes. This has been called the "north-south divide"
(Taylor 1991), a general polarization of support for the right-wing Conservative Party in the south, with its advocacy of smaller government and a
greater role for the free market, versus support for the Labour Party in the
north, with its advocacy of a stronger role for government and more

emphasis on redistribution of wealth. As I will explain in the next section, Scottish nationalism in part reflects this "north-south divide."

THE NATIONALIST MOVEMENT

Nineteenth-century Scottish nationalism, usually complementary to a larger British nationalism, began to change around the turn of the century. The combination of economic decline and creeping centralization created anxieties in Scotland about its weakening world role and increasing subordination within the British system. In this context the Scottish National Party (SNP) was formed in 1934, to campaign for Scottish independence. For many years, the SNP had little political effect. Though many expressed sympathy for the cause, political realism channeled electoral support toward the Labour Party, and more generally toward the entire agenda of centralized state planning, which was seen as the only way of sustaining Scotland's economy. For years hard-core Scottish nationalists were an eccentric band on the fringe of "real" politics. But in the 1960s, this began to change. Economic prospects brightened after the hard and bleak decade or so following World War Two, as the benefits and greater security of the expanded welfare state became more established. With increased confidence in Scotland's economic and political prospects, SNP membership began to grow. Then, in the 1970s, newly discovered oil reserves off the Scottish coast in the North Sea, combined with the global oil crisis, made an independent Scotland look much more possible, and a sudden surge in support sent eleven SNP ministers to the United Kingdom parliament in 1974. But this peak was short-lived and in 1979 the Tories, who are resolutely pro-union and against any change in Scotland's constitutional status, came to power.

There are two basic possibilities for constitutional change in Scotland. The less likely alternative is for Scotland to become an independent nation-state. Were this to happen, Scotland would probably become a member of the European Union (EU), a supranational organization designed to coordinate and integrate the economies of its member states. The EU, a major political and economic force in Europe today, puts serious limits on the self-determination of its members. If Scotland were to follow this path, its "independence" would be constrained by EU membership. The more likely possibility is that Scotland will gain its own parliament with limited powers over domestic affairs. This would make it more like a state in the United States, with an elected body running things at the Scottish level, but still a part of the United Kingdom. Some nationalists who advocate independence see a Scottish parliament as a trick to deflate the independence movement. Others view it as a necessary first step toward full independence. Still others think that a parliament alone is sufficient for Scotland's needs. Based on poll data and voting behavior over the last twenty years, we can estimate that around a quarter of the population favor full independence, half favor a parliament within the UK, and the remaining quarter the status quo of union. These preferences are primarily associated with the SNP, the Labour Party, and the Conservative Party, respectively. Thus a theoretical distinction can be made between the "hard" nationalism of the SNP and independence, and the "soft" nationalism of Labour and a parliament. But in practice, individuals shift back and forth between these positions and make tactical decisions about who to support and how to vote. Further, similar political views and cultural pride inform both positions.

In 1979 Scotland held a popular referendum on establishing its own parliament. At that time the Labour Party was deeply divided on the issue, and the Conservatives strongly opposed. Together Labour and Conservative opposition defeated the referendum. Since then, the Labour Party has strongly favored a parliament, largely due to the efforts of the Scottish Constitutional Convention, a broadly based cross-party organization established in 1989 to foster unity around the pro-parliament cause. The north-south divide, and a profound antipathy between Prime Minister Thatcher and most Scots has strengthened Scottish nationalism, both "hard" and "soft," which has developed deeper and more diverse roots in Scottish political culture in recent years. At present the SNP has four ministers in the United Kingdom parliament (out of seventy-two Scottish seats), and two ministers in the European Parliament (out of eight Scottish seats).

What do nationalists, in this broad "hard and soft" sense, want? The answer can be summarized in several categories. A written constitution, with a Bill of Rights, should entrench basic political rights (many Scots think that the present political system is archaic, concentrating too much power in the hands of the Prime Minister and Cabinet). Parliament is viewed as inevitably biased toward the needs of the southeast of England with fiscal policies addressing the needs of the London-based core of the economy, so that measures taken to stimulate investment or reduce unemployment are reversed before they have had a chance to take effect in Scotland. The country's economic future lies in expanding trade within the European Union, and many Scots believe that they could position themselves better within this economic environment as a small independent nation than as a submerged part of the UK economy. An activist, redistributive state is needed with a commitment to social and economic welfare. Scots still tend to believe in the welfare state built up in the middle of this century; there is a broad consensus that the free market should be kept within limits, and that the state has an appropriate role to play in the provision of such basics as housing, health care, and employment.

Cultural recognition is more difficult to pin down, and some place more emphasis on it than others. Scots are used to existing in the cultural shadow of England, having their history, language, and culture measured against the English standard. For centuries Scots have been told that historical progress was a matter of following England's example. Getting ahead has meant suppressing the Scots language and adopting middle-class English speech. Scottish culture has tended to be stereotyped, portrayed as quaint and romantic, the stuff of kilts, clans, and bagpipes, and somehow suspended in a distant past, no longer truly relevant. These attitudes have been created as much by the Scots, especially the middle class, as by the English. But a legacy of resentment remains, and many Scots believe that greater control over their own politics would foster a more confident and self-assured cultural identity (Beveridge and Turnbull 1989). Though I analyze them here into separate parts, all these concerns blend into the larger, complex phenomenon of nationalism. Different people emphasize different views, but no one agenda should be mistaken for the whole (Edwards 1989, and Marr 1992).

TALKING COLONIALISM

Having sketched the big picture, let me return to the question of Scotland as a colony, and why this problematic analogy is so compelling. During my fieldwork I interviewed both "hard" and "soft" nationalists. Interviewees were chosen for their participation in key organizations: the SNP; pro-parliament pressure groups within the Labour Party; as well as numerous pro-parliament, cross-party campaigning groups with names such as Campaign for a Scottish Parliament, Democracy for Scotland, Common Cause, and Scotland United. I also included opinion creators such as artists, writers, journalists, and educators. I asked these people what they thought of the idea that Scotland is a colony. This section presents some representative responses, beginning with those that generally affirmed the colonial analogy, and working toward those more skeptical.

Stuart McHardy (b. 1947) was raised in a communist household, has a degree in history from Edinburgh University, and has been involved in Democracy for Scotland. He has been both a journalist and a teacher, and currently works for the Scots Language Resource Center, which seeks to preserve and promote the many varieties of Scots. When I asked him about the applicability of colonialism to Scotland, he responded:

> I see Scotland in many ways as being the model for colonialism. Because the English when they invaded Ireland, particularly under Cromwell, it was absolutely brutal, and it was almost universally brutal. The colonization of Scotland was

done in a much more subtle way, and the way that Scotland was colonized was that the lairds [major landowners], and the middle classes, the merchant classes, whatever you want to call them, were brought increasingly into the ambit of power. And it's something . . . this is the basic pattern for divide and rule, that the British Empire used so well across the world. And in many cases . . . Scotsmen were the best at it. We were very, very good at being colonial administrators, forgetting that the same thing had been done to us. But it's clearly seen in the fact that to this day, major landowners claim to be Scottish, and there's, you know, nothing Scottish about them. They're educated in England, they're generally raised in England, they spend most of their time abroad, they only come here for several weeks of the year, yet they claim to be Scottish.

McHardy emphasizes the co-optation of the upper and middle classes and their abandonment of Scottish culture as the defining feature of colonialism.

John MacLean (b. 1962) is a rank and file SNP member, and active in Scotland United, an organization established in 1992 to foster cooperation between Labour and the SNP in organizing a new popular referendum on the constitutional question. Though his parents, a policeman and a nurse, are Tories, his politics are socialist, which is typical of many of the younger, active SNP members. The first in his family to go to university, he took a degree in politics at Glasgow and is a civil servant. Here is his take on the idea of Scotland as a colony:

I think . . . yeah, we are a colony I think . . . in terms of the equation perhaps if we were a more obvious colony . . . We don't fit the model of the colonies . . . the African and Asian colonies, but on the basis of having an economy that's dominated by, basically an imperial power, we are a colony. It's not an analogy I would use to try to convince people to vote SNP, though that's what people do . . . because unlike a lot of colonies, we've been retaining a separate legal and educational system, where there haven't been any real efforts to sort of swamp those, by the English . . . so on that basis I wouldn't . . . I think economic colonization, far more than any cultural . . . there's certainly control of the economy from outside of Scotland, and the stripping of resources. . . .

In contrast to McHardy, MacLean emphasizes that Scotland doesn't fit the ideal model of colonization. He places more emphasis on external control of the economy, arguing that a degree of institutional autonomy has helped preserve cultural differences in Scotland.

Kevin Pringle (b. 1967), employed as a Research Officer at the SNP Headquarters, has a degree in politics and has a working-class background comparable to John MacLean's, though his parents were Labour voters. He argued that the colonial analogy was "partially" true, stressing Scotland's lack of control over its own economy, but offered the usual qualifications: that Ireland was more truly colonized, and that Scotland was a "fellow traveler" with England in the British Empire. He also pointed to one of the present reasons for relevance of this analogy: "The whole way we are governed is of a colonial nature. To the extent that, in a kind of jokey boast, about five or six years ago the then Secretary of State for Scotland Malcolm Rifkind [a Tory], said that he enjoyed the powers not dissimilar from those of a colonial governor . . . so he actually likened his role in Scotland . . . as a colonial governor . . . so both sides of the argument you can find that kind of language being used from time to time. And certainly over the past fourteen years, when you take the view that Scotland's never ever endorsed the Tory Party, over the past fourteen and a half years, and yet we've had these policies, these unwanted policies, forced upon us. You can argue that is a colonial way of being governed."

This is an argument I encountered frequently during my fieldwork. It differs in an important way from the first two responses, in that it refers to the current structure of government, not to an historical legacy. This ability of the colonial analogy to encompass and link long-term history with immediate problems of political structure helps account for its appeal.

Isobel Lindsay (b. 1943) is a Lecturer in Sociology at the University of Strathclyde. Long the leading member of the SNP, in recent years she has been the Convener of the cross-party organization Campaign for a Scottish Parliament (CSP), and has recently joined the Labour Party, whose current pro-parliament position has been significantly influenced by the work of the CSP. She is from an industrial working-class family from central Scotland: her father worked for an engineering company before her parents bought a small news agents shop. He supported the Communist Party, while her mother was a typical Labour voter. Despite having reservations about the colonial analogy, she attempted to shed light on its salience by focusing on the everyday experiences of Scots: "I think, in relation to the experience of many ordinary Scots, it has some resonance . . . because the kind of English that the Scots tended to have dealings with in Scotland came here in, shall we say, a managerial capacity, or a professional capacity. Because of our relatively adverse employment situation historically, this was not the place that working-class English came to get work. The work prospects were worse than you'd have down south. . . . You might come across the very occasional working-class person who had come here because of marriage, but that wasn't very common, and . . . Scotland in many ways was a very homogeneous place, and in some sense still is. But you did come across a few English, but it was usually in authority positions."

This passage adds another dimension to the overall picture: the way the prestige and power associated with Englishness mapped on to Scottish daily life when she was growing up. Her argument reflects a general tendency in Scotland to equate Scottishness with being working class, and Englishness with being middle-upper class. Upwardly mobile Scots usually were more anglicized and often moved south in pursuing professional and managerial careers, just as similar English people might move north. The geographic mobility of professional middle classes tends to disassociate them from a national/regional context.

Willie Storrar (b. 1953) is a leading figure behind the campaigning group Common Cause. Appealing to many Scottish intellectuals, it fosters public discussion of the constitutional issues and pressures the political parties to cooperate in working toward a parliament. Storrar comes from a lower-middle-class shopkeeping family, his parents being classic Conservatives of the World War Two–Winston Churchill era. He is a Church of Scotland minister, and the author of *Scottish Identity: A Christian Vision* (1990). He offered a very detailed historical analysis in response to my question:

> Overall I would say that Scotland is not a straight example of colonialism. One undoubtedly finds after 1707 and before, indeed from the union of 1603, the anglicizing of the elites, and their looking increasingly to London, metropolitan, and English upper class models . . . for power, status, for culture . . . normative, linguistic, educational patterns. . . . If you want to call that colonialism, it is a very particular kind of self-colonialization. I think if you look at the Scottish highlands, you see a very brutal form of colonial politics, that that Gaelic, Celtic, Jacobite culture was brutally repressed. But it was repressed not only by England and Hanoverians, but by the lowland Presbyterian Scots. So it's a much more complex phenomenon, I mean there's some patterns of colonialism in terms of what happened to the highlands in the early eighteenth century and subsequently in Gaelic culture and society, and there's some evidence of a kind of colonialism in what happened to the anglicized upper classes. . . . But overall I don't think we explain or understand Scotland's situation and politics of nationhood on a straight colonial model.

Though he too mentions elite co-optation, Storrar is reluctant to treat this as a true example of colonialism. But he does point to another major ingredient—the colonization of the highlands, which does fit the model much more closely, and is historically bound up with the anglicization of Scottish elites. Highland culture is often treated as emblematic of Scotland as a whole, and today many lowland Scots, especially in the West, have highland ancestry, partly as a result of the "clearances" of the later eighteenth and early nineteenth centuries. Thus a substantial part of Scotland did experience something closely related to colonialism, and that part of Scotland is often taken to symbolize the whole. Here is another way in which the colonial analogy takes root.

CONCLUSION

For all their different perspectives on this question, the people I have quoted would agree on many points. Some are more comfortable, and some less, with the image of Scotland as a colony, and the comparison with classic examples of colonialism. Their opinions form a continuum, not a controversy. Though these informants, because of their relatively high level of involvement in the movement, are probably more reflective and articulate on this question than the average Scot, my experience is that the range of certainty versus ambivalence, and the kinds of evidence these speakers cite, are representative of attitudes in the population as a whole.

One important division in how Scots approach this analogy is the relative emphasis on culture versus economics. Not surprisingly, people I interviewed who were involved in cultural production—the arts, literature, and language—were more likely to emphasize cultural colonialism, while those primarily involved in party politics, especially younger party activists, were more concerned with economic colonialism. But there are peculiar wrinkles. The Communist Party (CP) in Scotland has long been a behind-the-scenes force in support of home rule, and is also very concerned with Scottish popular folk culture and history, linking these to the Scottish working class. One elderly couple with a long involvement with the Scottish CP described to me camping weekends when comrades would sit around the fire reciting the poetry of Robert Burns by heart, or singing old Jacobite songs. So while one might expect people practically involved in the philosophy of Marxism to privilege economics over culture, in Scotland this does not appear to be the case.

Ideas have histories, and this one is no exception. In the 1970s, and early 80s, academics wrote a number of books that developed this colonial analogy (for example, Dickson et al. 1980; Hechter 1975). McCrone (1992:62–87) has shown that this mode of analysis applies only to the highlands. In most of Scotland economic trends including industrial and occupational structures are much more parallel to than divergent from the UK as a whole. The basic story here is not the economic conquest of Scotland by England, but rather that of a laissez-faire system where capi-

tal had a lot of freedom. This led to the rapid and often turbulent industrialization of Scotland in the nineteenth century, followed by the massive
flight of indigenous capital in this century, as the empire shrunk and
Scotland was no longer able to fulfill its industrial role within that system.
Ultimately capital, more than England, is the key agent in Scotland's
marginalization. Despite the inaccuracy of the economic version of the
colonial model, the ideas of these books and others have disseminated
through Scottish culture during the period of Tory government, broadly
influencing political and nationalist discourse. This partly explains why
the economic colonial model has attracted younger, left-oriented party
activists. They have, in a sense, grown up with it.

I conclude with a more general point. As an idea associated with a
political movement, should we consider the colonial analogy to be "ideology," or "culture"? These concepts tend to shade into one another, and
if we define ideology as a relatively explicit political analysis and agenda,
and culture as a more loosely cohering set of assumptions and beliefs, I
think we can place this colonial idea in a kind of middle ground, and this
is precisely its significance. The clearest examples of ideology are associated with tightly bound groups with common social and political goals,
while culture tends to create a diffuse sense of communality among people who often have quite different interests and perspectives on reality.
The colonial model brings together a diverse set of historical facts, political and economic conditions, and lived experiences, giving them a certain
politicized reading. As a hypothesis, I would suggest that broad social
movements such as Scottish nationalism will tend to generate and foster
such ambiguous, in-between concepts precisely because they provide a
conceptual path for people to move from cultural assumptions toward
more explicit ideological convictions, thus facilitating political mobilization. Like any path, individuals may ultimately depart from it, having
reached a new political position from which they can view the idea more
critically. But the general need to ground specific forms of practical political action in a broader cultural context remains, and so the peculiar concept of Scotland as a colony endures, because of, rather than in spite of,
its ambiguities.

REFERENCES

Beveridge, Craig and Ronald Turnbull
    1989   The Eclipse of Scottish Culture. Edinburgh: Polygon.

Crick, Bernard
    1991   The English and the British. In B. Crick, ed. National Identities: The
             Constitution of the United Kingdom. pp. 90–104. Oxford: Blackwell.

Dickson, Tony, ed.
　　1980　Scottish Capitalism: Class, State, and Nation from Before the Union to the Present. London: Lawrence and Wishart.

Edwards, Owen Dudley, ed.
　　1989　A Claim of Right for Scotland. Edinburgh: Polygon.

Harvie, Christopher
　　1981　No Gods and Precious Few Heroes: Scotland Since 1914. London: Edward Arnold.

Hechter, Michael
　　1975　Internal Colonialism: The Celtic Fringe in British National Development, 1536–1966. Berkeley: University of California Press.

Kellas, James
　　1989　The Scottish Political System. Fourth edition. Cambridge: Cambridge University Press.

Marr, Andrew
　　1992　The Battle for Scotland. London: Penguin.

McCrone, David
　　1992　Understanding Scotland: The Sociology of a Stateless Nation. London and New York: Routledge.

Morris, R. J. and Graeme Morton
　　1993　The Re-making of Scotland: a Nation within a Nation, 1850–1920. In Scotland, 1850–1979: Society, Politics and the Union. M. Lynch, ed. pp. 13–18. London: Historical Association Committee for Scotland and The Historical Association.

Paterson, Lindsay
　　1994　The Autonomy of Modern Scotland. Edinburgh: Edinburgh University Press.

Smout, T. C.
　　1987　A Century of the Scottish People, 1830–1950. London: Fontana.

Storrar, William
　　1990　Scottish Identity: A Christian Vision. Edinburgh: Handsel.

Taylor, Peter J.
　　1991　The Changing Political Geography. In The Changing Geography of the United Kingdom. R. J. Johnston and V. Gardiner, eds. pp. 316–42. London: Routledge.

Wallerstein, Immanuel
　　1974　The Modern World System: Capitalist Agriculture and the Origins of the European World Economy in the 16th Century. London: Academic Press.

PART II

Gender, Sexuality, and Kinship

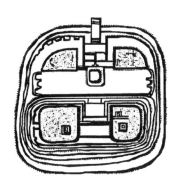

A TALE OF TWO SISTERS

Gender in Taiwan's Small-Scale Industry[1]

Anru Lee

SISTERS TELLING STORIES: A TAIWANESE MANUFACTURING FAMILY[2]

When I was in high school, I disliked weekends so much. Whenever it was Saturday, my classmates all became so excited because they were going to have a day and half off. They always planned to have fun after school. I didn't get excited. My life was so different from theirs. I just went straight home and worked in the factory. I knew I would not have time off. I was doubly busy on weekends.

Wang Mei-Hwa once told me this when I was sitting in her computer appliance shop and sipping the tea she made for me. Her sister Mei-Ling listened; she did not say anything but nodded her head so vividly to show us that she could not have agreed more.

Wang Mei-Hwa was 32 in 1995, and Mei-Ling, 30. The two sisters used to work in their father's weaving factory, side by side with the employees

1. The research reported in this article was supported in part by a grant from the Wenn-Gren Foundation for Anthropological Research (No. 5784). This research has also received support from the Institute of Ethnology, Academia Sinica, in Taipei, Taiwan.
2. All Chinese names and words are romanized in the Wade-Giles system.

on the shop floor, producing fabric to make garments for the U.S. market. Their eldest sister, said to have the best "mathematics mind" in the family, was the accountant; she also cooked for the workers as well as tended the looms when they were short on labor. The son in the family, Mei-Hwa and Mei-Ling's elder brother, was the mechanic. They all worked under the supervision of their father, the owner and manager of the factory. However, this seemed to be a long time ago. Since Mei-Hwa married in 1990, she helps her husband in his computer shop. In her free time she also works as a salesperson in Taiwan's booming insurance industry making her own money from commission. Wang Mei-Hwa and her husband are their own bosses. They make up their working schedule. No more working on weekends!

FROM AGRICULTURE TO INDUSTRY

I met Wang Mei-Hwa and Wang Mei-Ling in the very first week after I came to Hai-kou, a small town in central Taiwan, to study the local textile industry. A friend, introducing Mei-Hwa to me, said that she knew everything about textiles because her family owned a factory. However, instead of telling me everything, Mei-Hwa first took me to her parents' house/ factory compound for a trip, and later arranged for me to live there to learn more. Mei-Hwa's parents' house, located in the middle of farmland, is a large three-story, gray cement building; downstairs is the weaving mill and the top two floors are the family's living space. A brook runs through the back of the house. Behind the brook is the Wang family's asparagus field.

Asparagus used to be the family's major source of income. Thirty years ago, in the late 1960s, when Mei-Hwa's grandfather was still alive and in charge of the family, asparagus was an important cash crop in the local economy and a major item in Taiwan's agricultural exports to Japan and the West. In the heyday of asparagus cultivation, the Wang family hired some hands to help them with the daily harvest. Mei-Hwa's father, along with his brothers and sisters, acted like modern factory line leaders in the asparagus field; each of them was assigned an area to work with four or five hired hands. The Wang family was quite well-known for its asparagus business. Once I was told by an old neighbor that Mei-Hwa's aunts used to be called the "Asparagus Princesses" in the region before they married.

However, the good days of asparagus seemed to be gone with Mei-Hwa's grandfather when he died in 1975. After his death, following the local tradition, the three sons, Mei-Hwa's father and his two younger brothers, divided the family's land and property and went their own way. They continued to grow asparagus for a while, but the profit quickly declined.[3] The youngest brother gave up asparagus first; he started a small workshop making small, assembled parts for faucets. The second brother soon followed: he began a weaving mill. Mei-Hwa's father, the eldest brother, continued asparagus cultivation the longest, but the profit in industrial production finally led him to purchase 24 looms and he began weaving in 1978. A few years later he acquired more machines to seize the opportunities provided by the rapidly expanded local textile industry. At its peak the Wang family owned 68 looms and hired 15 workers.

FAMILY MEMBERS WORKING TOGETHER

The Wang family had always hired workers to produce textiles but the family children always comprised an essential part of the workforce. Mei-Hwa and Mei-Ling's brother, who first worked as a mechanic then gradually took over the supervisory role from the father on the shop floor, as the only son in the family would undoubtedly inherit the family business in the future, and the family took for granted that he would be given the opportunity to learn to operate the factory. Mei-Hwa and Mei-Ling, the two younger daughters, were still going to school in the evening when their father started the mill. Regularly they worked for four hours in the morning and took a nap in the afternoon before they went to school. However, they would have to work for longer hours if any workers took the day off.

Family labor plays a crucial role in Taiwan's small-scale industry. Many recently converted industrialists like Mei-Hwa's father rely heavily on family members to assure a smooth flow of production and a profit and industrialists can always count on them to work overtime whenever it is needed. Most importantly, they are cheap. In many family mills, they are not paid but given a "monthly stipend" with a value much less than the wages they might otherwise make in the labor market.

LOCAL INDUSTRIALIZATION IN THE GLOBAL CONTEXT

Family members working together under the supervision of their male patriarchs is nothing new in the Han Chinese culture. Past literature has recorded numerous cases of Chinese families acting as a corporate unit in

---

3. Taiwan's Asparagus crop dramatically lost its overseas market after the European Economic Community canceled Taiwan's quota and gave it to China in 1979.

various socio-historical circumstances.[4] However, the engagement of family labor has become even more crucial for Taiwanese families in the current industrial setting. This has to be understood in relation to Taiwan's structural position in the global economy.

Taiwan was a colony of Japan before 1945 and therefore served as a base of the Japanese empire during its war in Asia and the Pacific. As a result, Taiwan was under heavy bombardment by the U.S. Airforce at the end of World War II, and its infrastructure was badly damaged. After the Second World War ended, Taiwan's economy was further devastated by the Chinese civil war on the Mainland; its resources were taken by the Nationalist Party (KMT) to support its military action against the Communist Party as well as to stabilize the fiscal/monetary crises caused by the war. Only after the KMT was defeated and forced to retreat to the Taiwan Island in 1949, was Taiwan given the chance to rebuild its economy.

Taiwan's postwar economy is closely connected with the United States and Japan. From the very beginning, the economy gradually regained its momentum with the assistance of the U.S. Using raw materials supplied by the U.S., particularly cotton, the government launched an import-substitution policy to foster the development of light industries. This economic policy served three purposes. First, it required only minimum levels of technology and capital to initiate but quickly produced urgently needed consumer goods for the domestic market. Second, by promoting import-substitution industrialization (ISI), the Taiwanese government prevented further draining of precious (and extremely limited) foreign exchange reserve. Third, ISI enabled Taiwan to accumulate capital as well as to acquire technical knowledge which facilitated later economic development.

The period of ISI did not last long. The domestic market was becoming saturated in the late 1950s, and the government introduced new economic policies to encourage export expansion. In the meantime, more and more people in the rural areas had become familiar with industrial work. Although most of the older generation remained in agriculture, an increasing number of the young entered manufacturing industries. In Hai-kou, girls became weavers and young male apprentices learned to repair the looms and do the maintenance in the local textile industry. Labor participation in the industrial sector grew as export-oriented industrialization (EOI) boomed and many former farmers/landowners like Mei-Hwa and Mei-Ling's father began to invest their money in textile manufacturing in the 1970s. According to local observers, there were almost 600 textile

---

4. For example, Skinner, 1957; Cohen, 1976, 1992; Harrell, 1985; Niehoff, 1987; Oxfeld, 1993; Ka, 1993; Li and Ka, 1994; Hsiung, 1996.

factories in Hai-kou in the peak days of the industry. Even though most of these factories were small with a labor force under 30 workers, they hired the majority of the working population in town.

Export-oriented industrialization proved a successful economic strategy for Taiwan. Since the 1970s Taiwan has experienced a remarkably high growth rate. The income distribution is relatively equal and the gap between the rich and the poor is low in comparison to most of the developing countries. Within three decades Taiwan has transformed itself from an agriculture-based to an industrial society (and it is gradually becoming service-centered in the 1990s, with booming insurance, banking, and retail industries).

The success story of Taiwan, along with the stories of the other three East Asian newly industrializing countries (NICs: Hong Kong, South Korea, and Singapore) has received wide attention in the developmental literature. It has also inspired many other countries to replicate the experience. Even so, one should not romanticize Taiwan's achievement. In fact, Taiwan's export expansion runs parallel to economic restructuring in advanced capitalist countries and a relocation of manufacturing production from these countries to less industrialized regions in the world. In the case of the textile industry, Taiwan was first benefited from the Japanese who sold synthetic fiber to the island in the late 1950s and later brought in orders for garments made of such material for the U.S. market (Lin C.-C. 1994). Textile manufacturers in Taiwan thereby learned the technology to produce fabric from synthetic fiber. The industry was further advanced when U.S. retailers sought cheap apparel to sell in their domestic market in the 1960s (Cheng and Gereffi 1994, Gereffi and Pan 1994). The relation between the garment and textile industry is an effect of backward linkage, that is, when a down-stream industry is growing, it will stimulate its upper-stream industries to grow as well. As Taiwan's garment industry expanded, the demand for yarn and fabric increased as well, which in turn animated the domestic spinning and weaving industries.

SUBCONTRACTING AND DECENTRALIZED PRODUCTION SYSTEMS

Taiwan's link with both Japanese and U.S. retailers denotes a pattern of "marketing-dependent development" in the global system (Skoggard 1996). That is to say, direct foreign investment in industrial production—for example, large multinational factories in export processing zones—plays only a minor role in Taiwan's EOI. Instead, Taiwan has based its "economic miracle" on small-scale, decentralized, family-centered subcontracting firms, which rely on foreign retailers, brand-named marketers, and trading companies to supply them with orders.

Foreign buyers are primarily looking for cheap commodities. However, as the competition in their domestic markets as well as the international market intensifies, they also ask for increasingly shorter turn-around time for products. Manufacturers in Taiwan have proved themselves to be highly effective in meeting those demands. They are efficient and flexible, maintaining quality at a given price, while ensuring reliable, on-time delivery.

Nonetheless, the division of labor between the Taiwan manufacturers and foreign buyers is not an equal one. While Taiwanese firms manage the decentralized manufacturing stages, foreign capital generally controls the more profitable export and marketing networks (Gereffi and Pan 1994:134). Moreover, the manufacturers constantly have to reduce their production cost and adjust their production organization to comply with stringent trading terms. In order to accomplish this, they need to have the cooperation of a workforce willing to work cheaply around the production cycle, i.e. to work overtime for days or even weeks when meeting deadlines and to take unpaid time off when the market is slow. Who will more ideally fulfill these conditions than manufacturers' own families?

FROM SUNRISE TO SUNSET: THE CURRENT PREDICAMENT OF TEXTILE MANUFACTURERS

Textiles used to be the leading industry in Taiwan's export economy, but for several reasons it has rapidly declined since the late 1980s and has now become a "sunset industry." The first hard blow came from the U.S. government, which in order to reduce its own foreign trade deficit pressured Taiwan to appreciate its currency (Schive 1992). The exchange rate of the New Taiwan dollar vis-a-vis the U.S. dollar plunged from forty in 1985 to twenty-six in 1990, which severely impeded Taiwan's export capability just when it was facing increased competition from other industrializing countries in Southeast Asia and China.

Labor shortages further shattered the prospects of textile manufacturing. Cheap labor was always a key to success for Taiwan's labor-intensive industries such as textiles. However, textile manufacturers have confronted an insufficient labor supply since the early 1980s, a result both of a declining birthrate after the 1960s and recent changes in the economy. Young people entering the wage labor market for the first time now prefer to work in the booming service sector instead of manufacturing industries. Also, more and more young women in rural areas continue their education to senior high school or even beyond to prepare for white-collar jobs. Their families no longer push them to take on factory work right after elementary or junior high school, as their counterparts in prior generations were expected to do.

The wages in the textile industry have rapidly risen as a result of the labor shortage. Textile manufacturers in Taiwan have responded to the appreciation of the New Taiwan dollar, labor shortages, competition from other industrializing countries, and international protectionism with two major strategies: relocating and downsizing.

RELOCATING AND DOWNSIZING:
STRATEGIES FOR SURVIVAL

By the late 1980s many textile producers, in search of cheap labor and inexpensive raw materials, had closed down their plants in Taiwan and relocated production to China and Southeast Asia. (Klein 1992, Chang & Chang 1992, Bonacich et al 1994). In Hai-kou, according to local observers, more than half of the looms were removed from the production line in the past five years or so. Those who remain in business in Hai-kou have rearranged the labor division on the shop floor, or they have upgraded their machinery to reduce the number of workers needed. Only a few wealthy industrialists in town could afford to purchase new machines. Many of the small factory owners just sold part of their looms and downsized production to the extent that family members alone would make up a sufficient workforce. Responding to the labor shortage, in the early 1990s, the Taiwan government finally legalized the employment of foreign workers for some industries including textiles. Yet, the manufacturers have complained that the quotas are too low and the hiring procedures are too cumbersome to meet their pressing needs.

CONFORMITY AND CONFLICT IN THE FAMILY

For those families who can neither find native workers nor get the government's approval to hire foreign labor, once again and even more crucial than ever before, they have relied on family labor to make up for the missing workforce. However, the husband and wife—or the father and mother—bear the burden this time. Young people having attained (or attaining) higher education, are more interested in the booming financial/commercial world than in working for their parents in the declining manufacturing sector. Parents who are running a factory may desperately need their children's labor now, but to their misfortune, they can no longer count on their children.

Parents are losing control over their children's lives. The transformation of the economy plays a major role here. Young girls in particular are benefiting from the newly granted educational opportunities and sometimes the wide range of jobs in the wage labor market. They have more alternatives now. Yet, conflict and struggle between the generations seem also aggravated as a result. If one looks closely into the dynamics in a patriarchal corporate family like the Wang's, one discovers that the elder and male authority in such a family is always on the verge of being challenged. In the Wang family, for example, even though the children had been working together under their father, the daughters were not submissive. On the contrary, each of them has striven for a life of her own outside the family factory, albeit still under the constraint of her particular social circumstance.

MEI-HWA:
THE DAUGHTER WHO'S MARRIED OUT

Mei-Hwa always speaks in a light-hearted tone when she tells me about those "old days." Despite the fact that she had worked so hard and was often forced to juggle her time among school, factory, and her job in the insurance company after her graduation from junior college in 1987—and later, dating her boyfriend in secrecy—she rarely shows hard feelings towards her parents. She usually laughs at the silly things she did before. The one story she loves to tell is how she "stole" half an hour daily on the way home from the insurance company in order to meet her boyfriend.

> I had to sign in at 8:00 in the morning, and went to the rou-
> tine meeting that followed after. The meeting usually ended
> around 10:30, and I would immediately leave the company and
> rush home to tend looms. I worked at home till 4:30 in the
> afternoon, and hurried back to the company at five, signed out,
> and hurried out again to meet my boyfriend. We met around
> 5:15, and had a bowl of shaved ice or a glass of juice together.
> I had to say good-bye to him at 5:45, that left me fifteen min-
> utes to rush home so I would not be late for my 6:00 shift, and
> nobody would be suspicious about my movement. And we did
> it all over again the next day!

After she came back from the insurance company at 6:00 in the evening, Mei-Hwa continued to work on the shop floor usually till midnight. "I was always working, working, and working. There was no time left for me to think of anything else," she told me.

Mei-Hwa not only lived an extremely busy life, she also lived a life with a "double" identity: she was an insurance salesperson in the professional world and a weaver in her family. Pursuing her own career did not release her from her duty in the family business. She was expected to fulfill her family role first before she could do other things. Despite the fact that she had been deliberately arranging her daily schedule to fit the family's demands, her job eventually caused tension in the family. Her brother, the supervisor on the shop floor, frequently complained to their father that Mei-Hwa was irresponsible because she did not do her share of work until it was too late, i.e. in the late afternoon after she came back from the insurance company. He wanted their father to force Mei-Hwa to quit. But Mei-Hwa insisted in keeping her job, and according to her sister Mei-Ling, the more the father and the brother pushed, the more determined Mei-Hwa became. Consequently, the brother and sister were in disagreement all the time.

As time went by, the family's objection seemingly waned and they gradually accepted Mei-Hwa's divergent attention as part of the reality they had to live with, although they were never happy about it. On Mei-Hwa's part, by taking a job outside the family in the first place and later resisting the pressure from the elder, she was negotiating for more space of her own, although the family duty was still an important guideline for her decisions and actions. The recognition that she had her own ideas about life did not come easily, however, and the tension continually simmered beneath the compromise made by the family. The conflict of interests was only solved by Mei-Hwa's marriage.

Mei-Hwa now looks back with amusement. After all, she is a daughter who is "married out." She is no longer obliged to work for her natal family. Instead, as a married woman, her fate is linked with her husband (or rather, her husband's family), as is her labor. Nevertheless, Mei-Hwa is fortunate because her parents-in-law neither run a factory nor own a company; her labor is thus not bound by her husband's family. Furthermore, her parents-in-law have already retired from farming, therefore, they are able to take care of Mei-Hwa's children, which sets her free to explore new possibilities for herself and her husband.

MEI-LING:
THE DAUGHTER WHO'S LEFT BEHIND

Mei-Ling, the youngest sister in the Wang family, has a different story to tell.

As a woman who is over 30 but still remains single, she is under tremendous pressure not only from her family but also from relatives and neighbors who all urge her to get married. Mei-Ling always becomes very demoralized when we touch this topic in our conversation. "You know how gossipy those old women are in the village? They often tease my mom by asking her how much longer she is going to keep me home. They say I must be a treasured daughter so that she is reluctant to marry me out even though I have passed the age already. My mother said to me that if I do not get married soon, she will have no face to live in the village anymore." Mei-Ling's parents are clearly bearing the stigma of having a middle-aged unmarried daughter.

Mei-Ling's parents have been trying very hard to arrange for her to meet prospective mates, but Mei-Ling was either unimpressed by the arrangement or too upset to go. " I have told them [the parents] many times that I am not going to get married unless I graduate from college, but they just do not listen"; she became really upset when she said this to me: "It is all their fault that I am still in school now and have not got married yet. I always wanted to study, and I have expressed myself very clearly to them ever since Mei-Hwa graduated from college. And they kept saying yes to me, but never really supported my decision in action. But even if they had been willing to let me go, with a constant problem of labor shortage, what could they have done otherwise? They had no choice but to keep me working in the factory."

Mei-Ling explained to me why she insisted on schooling first and marriage second. She said, "Eventually I will be married out. If I do not get my education now, I will not have any chance at all after I get married. My own parents do not even support me on such matter, who else in the world do you think will support me? My husband's family? Ha, you imagine it!"

Neither Mei-Hwa nor Mei-Ling continued their college education right after high school. Both of them had waited for a few years. Mei-Hwa waited three years and finally went back to school in 1984; she was 21 and Mei-Ling was 19. Mei-Ling had expressed her wish to go to school with her sister, but the parents disagreed. They could not afford to lose two workers at the same time; they could allow only one daughter to study, and therefore lose one worker, each time. Nevertheless, Mei-Ling was discouraged again even after her sister had graduated from college. Mei-Hwa was about to get married, and the family would lose her labor permanently upon such occasion. Mei-Ling's labor had become even more indispensable than before. Once again, the family could not afford to let her go.

FAMILY WELL-BEING VS. INDIVIDUAL INTEREST— BUT WHOSE FAMILY IS IT ANYWAY?

After Mei-Hwa married, Mei-Ling became the only daughter who worked for her parents. Meanwhile, the Wang factory had been affected by the current crisis and was suffering from a lack of labor. Mei-Ling's father decided that he was too old to endure the pressure anymore. He retired in 1991 and passed the business to his son, the only heir of the family. Mei-Ling's brother made the decision to downsize the factory. He sold all of the old machines and bought six more advanced ones. In his plan, which was supported by his parents, he only needed one worker on each shift for this minimized production scale. He was going to perform the mechanic's task. Having Mei-Ling work on one shift, he simply needed to find two more weavers. Mei-Ling's labor was obviously seen as part of the factory assets which were naturally transferred from the father to the son in his inheritance. As long as she was not married, she belonged to the family, and so did her labor.

Mei-Ling eventually went back to school in 1991, after many years of waiting. While she was going to school in the evening, she continued to work in her brother's factory on the day shift. In fact, she was her brother's only weaver because he could not find another. Although he had to turn off the machines at night to accommodate Mei-Ling's schedule, he had tried to keep Mei-Ling at work except for the time he had to let her go to school.

Mei-Ling's relationship with her brother and her parents began to turn sour when she insisted on having Sundays off in addition to her school time. There was a long struggle before the brother and the parents finally yielded to her will.

> My mother was particularly upset. She was offended by my request. She felt that I was letting down the family by taking Sundays off. Without me there, my brother would either have to tend the looms himself or shut down the production completely. It would cut back his profit either way. How could I do this to my brother, particularly in such a difficult time? She had refused to talk to me for a very long time.
>
> But they [the parents] only care about their son! This is their son's factory, not mine. I will not be able to live under my brother's roof for all of my life, even if I want to. I will have to find something for myself.

Mei-Ling is aware of the possibility that she may have to stay single, although she does not reject the idea of getting married. But until she marries, she wants to have a career of her own. She believes that to pursue more education will help her in finding a job she really likes.

CONCLUSION: GENDER IN TAIWAN'S FAMILY-CENTERED SMALL-SCALE INDUSTRY

When Taiwan began its export-oriented industrialization in the 1960s, many farmers set up factories on their own land and mobilized their family members to perform the production tasks. Although family members working together and acting as a corporate unit was not new in the Han Chinese culture, the newly emerged economic opportunities gave the cooperation a new meaning. Family labor proved crucial in the success of Taiwan's small-scale industry. It provided a cheap, steady, flexible, and efficient workforce which enabled Taiwanese manufacturers to produce goods at a low price while ensuring reliable, on-time delivery.

Under the current predicament within which Taiwan's labor-intensive industries and the producers are troubled by the problem of labor shortage, family labor becomes even more important than ever before. However, when family labor is desperately in need, the elder in the family can no longer count on their children for help. The economic changes in the past three decades have created new opportunities for the younger generations. Young people — and young women in particular — nowadays have attained higher education, and they are more inclined to acquire jobs in the booming service sector rather than in the declining manufacturing industries.

Conflict between generations has been exacerbated in recent times when young women have alternatives other than working in factories. Even in a patriarchal corporate family like the Wang's, the senior and male authority has always been on the verge of challenge. Although the daughters had worked for their father and helped to accumulate the family wealth which would one day be inherited by their brother, they were not docile. Each of them has striven for a life of her own, despite the fact that they are still under the constraint of their social circumstances.

REFERENCES

Bonacich, Edna, Lucie Cheng, Norma Chinchilla, Hamilton, and Paul Ong, eds.
    1994   Global Production: The Apparel Industry in the Pacific Rim. Philadelphia: Temple University Press.

Chang, Raymond J. M. and Pei-Chen Chang
    1992   Taiwan's Emerging Economic Relations with the PRC. In Denis Fred Simon and Michael Y. M. Kau, eds. Taiwan: Beyond the Economic Miracle. Armonk (NY): M.E. Sharpe, pp. 275–98.

Cheng, Lucie and Gary Gereffi
    1994   U.S. Retailers and Asian Garment Production. In Edna Bonacich et al., eds. Global Production: The Apparel Industry in the Pacific Rim. Philadelphia: Temple University Press, pp. 63–79.

Cohen, Myron
    1976   House United, House Divided: The Chinese Family in Taiwan. New York: Columbia University Press.
    1992   Family Management and Family Division in Contemporary Rural China. China Quarterly, 130:357–77.

Gereffi, Gary and Mei-Lin Pan
    1994   The Globalization of Taiwan's Garment Industry. In Edna Bonacich et al., eds. Global Production: The Apparel Industry in the Pacific Rim. Philadelphia: Temple University Press, pp. 126–146.

Harrell, Stevan
    1985   Why Do the Chinese Work So Hard? Reflections on An Entrepreneurial Ethic. Modern China 11(2):203–26.

Hsiung, Ping-Chun
    1996   Living Rooms as Factories: Class, Gender and Satellite Factory
            System. Philadelphia: Temple University Press.
Klein, Donald W.
    1992   The Political Economy of Taiwan's International Commercial Links.
            In Denis Fred Simon and Michael Y. M. Kau, eds. Taiwan: Beyond
            the Economic Miracle. Armonk (NY): M.E. Sharpe, pp. 257–74.
Niehoff, Justin D.
    1987   The Villager as Industrialist: Ideologies of Household
            Manufacturing in Rural Taiwan. Modern China 13(3):278–309.
Oxfeld, Ellen
    1993   Blood, Sweat, and Mahjong. Ithaca: Cornell University Press.
Schive, Chi
    1992   Taiwan's Emerging Position in the International Division of Labor.
            In Denis Fred Simon and Michael Y. M. Kau, eds. Taiwan: Beyond
            the Economic Miracle. Armonk (NY): M.E. Sharpe, pp. 101–122.
Skoggard, Ian
    1996   The Indigenous Dynamics in Taiwan's Postwar Development.
            Armonk (NY): M.E. Sharpe.
Stites, Richard
    1982   Small-Scale Industry in Yingge, Taiwan. Modern China 8 (2):
            247–279.

PRIVATE LITTLE WARS

*Prostitution and Economic Collapse in Naples
During World War II*

Maria Ramona Hart

THE WORST OF TIMES

*Hunger governed all. . . . What we are witnessing in fact was the
moral collapse of a people. They had no pride any more, or dignity. The
animal struggle for existence governed everything. Food. That was the
only thing that mattered. Food for the children. Food for yourself. Food
at the cost of any debasement and depravity. And after food, a little
warmth and shelter* (cited in Ellwood 1985:49, emphasis added).

These words, by Alan Moorehead, a journalist writing in *Eclipse* magazine, describe the desperate plight of the city of Naples during the Allied
occupation in 1945. They describe conditions that were in no way new.
As early as September 1943, *The New York Times* reported that "the food
situation in Naples is acute. No supplies are moving into the metropolis
from the farms where there are abundant harvests of grapes, apples,
peaches, nuts and vegetables. Disease has broken out to increase the fear
and misery. . . ." Contemporary observers tell of children searching for
dandelions in the hills around Naples and mothers prying limpets from
rocks in the bay in search of anything that might be construed as edible.

During the years 1941–1945, while the Second World War raged
throughout the European, African, and Pacific theaters of operations, industry, business, and commerce on the Italian peninsula ground to a halt.
In these years, wholesale prices for consumer goods increased almost
twentyfold and the cost of living rose commensurately (Statistical Ab-
stract 1953:144), while farm and industrial wages rose only listlessly
(1953:148) and caloric consumption plummeted.

The city of Naples was particularly hard-hit by the economic devastation. With Allied blockades and German bombing in the Bay of Naples,
its commercial shipping industry slowed and its agricultural production
was paralyzed, reducing both imports and exports. Shortages of grain,
meat, sugar, milk, salt, potable water, soap, clothing, and cooking oil
indicate the extent of the emergency.

The scarcity of food and absence of high protein staples in the regular
markets forced Neapolitans to the black market where prices were four
times what they were elsewhere. This created a desperate need for cash
among the already impoverished population. With most Neapolitans'
very survival in question, the social norms and values by which the population lived in peacetime were submerged under the swelling misery. By
1944, approximately one in three Neapolitan women had turned to prostitution (April 1944, British Bureau of Psychological Warfare). As astound-
ing as this percentage is, it masks the even more overwhelming tally of
mothers, fathers, and brothers who solicited for their daughters and sisters;
it is perhaps this which makes wartime prostitution such a singular case.

Traditional Mediterranean societies consider honor as more important
even than life. Up until the early years of the twentieth century, illegiti-
mate children were "sacrificed for honor," or given up to foundling
homes (Kertzer 1993). "Omerta," the code of silence held by Mafia entrepreneurs punished loss of honor with death (Blok 1974). Women's reputations hinged in part upon the cleanliness of their houses and the
contents of their tables because these were thought to be indicators of
their sexual conduct (Goddard 1987). And yet, for the duration of the
Second World War, prostitution, the conclusive renunciation of honor,
became part of a *family* strategy for *survival*, and women and girls who
had once been safeguarded in some cases even from contact with the
opposite sex were encouraged and often forced to take up the most dis-
honorable profession of all. Not only did women offer themselves to
passing German and then Allied troops without question, they were often
sold by their relatives in an attempt to salvage the last remnants of the
family unit and to guarantee the survival of its members. During the war
years these women broke the ingrained Mediterranean polarities of honor
and shame, behaving literally as whores in the name of kinship and filial
obligation. Only through this ultimate sacrifice could they assure that
their families would eat.

THE COMFORTS OF HOME:
WAR, PROSTITUTION, AND THE STATE

Civilian populations overrun by a conquering army always suffer tremendous dislocations and transformations in their lives and expectations.
Honest and upstanding citizens turn to theft, and faithful wives and

young sexually inexperienced girls to prostitution. In wartime, the survival instinct often forces people to do things they could never have imagined in peacetime.

This is as true for a conquering army as it is for the people conquered. The generals and staff whose job it is to administer an occupied territory must keep the soldiers fed, sheltered, and happy and at the same time see that the host population remains relatively safe and under control. Ensuring that the civilian population does not become a breeding ground for guerrilla warfare and terrorism and that their own armies do not become mutinous is a delicate balancing act.

Far from the normal rules and regulations of daily life, soldiers are young men who have been uprooted from their homes, families, and towns and ordered to kill, an act that during peacetime is the ultimate violation of basic social norms. They descend on the conquered population with the same needs that they have in their everyday lives: to eat, sleep, socialize, and express their sexuality. The commanders of an occupation army need to solve the problem of how this large group of young men will express their sexuality just as they must secure enough of the local food to keep them from starving or enough shelter to keep them out of the rain. Like food and shelter, sexual expression usually comes at the expense of the local population.

During World War Two different governments had a wide variety of policies for enabling the sexual expression of their troops. While on the surface many of these policies looked very different, they all had in common the way in which to varying degrees they reduced the local women to sexual objects and instruments of the military machine. As Enloe (1993) notes, in Honolulu, Hawaii, during World War II, the United States tacitly encouraged widespread prostitution by allowing the brothels to open at 9:00 a.m. and remain open all day and most of the night. With the largest contingent of troops in the Pacific theater quartered in Hawaii between 1941–44, the brothels became an institution of "militarized masculinity" that was protected by the American Army.

For the Japanese, the presence of Korean "comfort women" on Japanese lines required the complicity of the Japanese government and was tantamount to "legalized military rape" on a scale not before seen. Sold into sexual servitude and shipped all over the Japanese "empire," "comfort women" were sexual captives. The military considered them so important that they often preceded munitions and weaponry to the front lines and were designated "war supplies" (Hicks 1994:16). Japanese troops thought it unlucky to go into battle without first visiting a prostitute, and so many of the designated "comfort women" were obliged to service up to twenty men per day. The so-called "Joy Division" performed the same function for the German army, and even the French Resistance relied upon the existence of brothels, which were at times "safe houses," secured from Vichy command (Roberts 1992). In each case, military governments exploited local women.

Solving the problem of sexual expression for the soldiers created another problem: sexually transmitted diseases. The longer that troops stayed, the greater the incidence of sexually transmitted disease. By the end of the war, such diseases had assumed truly monumental proportions (Kennett 1987:203), causing both male and female patients to occupy precious beds, use up medical supplies, and divert the attention of already overworked staff. A letter to the editor of *Stars and Stripes* in May 1945 written by the quartermaster in charge of "R and R" complained about the problem of enforcing the suspension of rest passes for enlisted men afflicted with venereal disease.

Such diseases became a focal point of wartime propaganda. Both the Germans and Allies accused each other of using venereal disease as a sort of biological weapon. A circular sent to Allied troops in 1944 claimed that the Axis powers were encouraging prostitution to undermine the effectiveness of Allied troops (Lewis 1993:96). In another incident, the Allied occupiers themselves devised a "plan" to use syphilitic but asymptomatic prostitutes, "recruited" and deliberately left untreated for their illness, to spread venereal disease among the German troops (Lewis 1993). However, the German army command was extremely meticulous about the sexual needs of its forces, setting up special brothels reserved for the use of its troops. These brothels featured extensive public health advisories and notices. One poster on many of the walls of German army brothels read, "Use a condom. Danger of venereal disease. Memorize your partner's registration number! Disinfect after intercourse!" (quoted in Hicks 1994:32).

Military involvement in prostitution, however tacit, is common, especially during periods of war. What is most injurious to the local population, however, is its bias against indigenous women. For the city of Naples, subjected to an occupation by first German and then Allied troops, the extent of abuses generated out of these policies was unusually great.

ARMIES OF THE NIGHT:
SEX AND SURVIVAL IN OCCUPIED NAPLES

On September 26, 1943, *The New York Times* reported that "the drama of Naples held the center of the Mediterranean stage" as the two German armies commanded by Field Marshal Albert Kesselring attempted to reduce Naples to "mud and ashes," leaving ruin in their wake. But the terror of German occupation and indiscriminate bombing would soon be replaced with ambivalence over the Allied occupiers.

A month after "liberation," the Allied liberators began to take on overtones of the oppressor and the Allied occupation army came to be regarded with mistrust, suspicion, and, at times, fear, as alcoholism escalated and drunkenness became, as an American army spokesperson put it, "the greatest ambassador of ill will" (Kennett 1987:207). Although the army attempted to instill a sense of responsibility in its recruits, urging them to be careful of violating local customs, the Italian government was increasingly anxious about the conduct of the American troops (Kennett 1987:122). The government in turn worried about the possibility of large numbers of war brides entering the United States (Kennett 1987:122).

One of the ways of preventing war brides was the tacit encouragement of prostitution. Prostitutes, in theory at least, do not expect marriage. Allied policies in Naples actively promoted the wholesale entrance into prostitution of Neapolitan women, as starvation compelled men to sell their sisters and daughters, and women to sell themselves for food. In some ways, the Allied occupation was even worse than the German. Under German occupation, the Third Reich imposed a grueling nutritional regimen upon the Neapolitans, rationing each citizen only 1378 calories, and then crushing the food riots which ensued as a result (Kennett 1987:203). Yet, the Allied occupation provided only a blatantly insufficient 615 calories daily (Ellwood 1985:127) with additional calories only provided to those who worked for Allied forces in some capacity.

The commodification or sale of women involved persons of all ages. Perhaps most seriously, the prostitution of minors reached momentous proportions as families offered girls as young as seven and eight to passersby. Minors were treated for venereal disease in increasing numbers. In one two-week period in August 1944, some 4,000 cases of venereal disease in one Neapolitan hospital alone were of minors (Lambiase and Battista 1993:138). Such statistics suggest a precursor to the present situation in many Asian countries where the fear of AIDS and other sexually transmitted diseases inflates the value of ever younger women, pulling young, virginal girls into the sex trade. In wartime Naples, although some children turned to prostitution because they were sought after for their youth or because they had been orphaned by the war, most did so to help out their starving families (West 1957).

Prostitution reached staggering proportions in Naples during the war in part because of sharpened conditions of supply and demand, and in part because the Allied presence was a fixture on the local landscape for a period of over two years. During this time, Naples was the station through which much of the advancing Allied army passed on their way to the front lines, as well as a rest camp. Although prostitution is an expected companion to military occupation, American G.I.s, viewing prostitutes as "fallen" women who had taken up the profession as a matter of choice, affinity, or desire, were at times confused by the purely economic nature of prostitution in Naples in 1944. Norman Lewis, then a British officer stationed in Naples, relates a standard encounter between prostitutes and the men, as soldiers jostled one another with typical ribaldry:

> A row of ladies sat at intervals of about a yard with their backs to the wall. These women were dressed in their street clothes, and had the ordinary well-washed respectable shopping and gossiping faces of working-class housewives. By the side of each woman stood a small pile of tins[1], and it soon became clear that it was possible to make love to any one of them in this very public place by adding another tin to the pile. The women kept absolutely still, they said nothing, and their faces were as empty of expression as graven images. They might have been selling fish, except that this place lacked the excitement of a fish market. There was no soliciting, no suggestion, no enticement, not even the discreetest and most accidental display of flesh (1993:26).

Once a hapless soldier, encouraged by his buddies, negotiated with one of the women, the tone of the encounter changed:

> One soldier, a little tipsy, and egged on constantly by his friends, finally put down his tin of rations at a woman's side, unbuttoned and lowered himself on her. A perfunctory jogging of the haunches began and abruptly came to an end. A moment later, he was on his feet and buttoning up again. It had been something to get over as soon as possible. He might have been submitting to field punishment rather than the act of love (Lewis 1993:26).

An entire generation of American servicemen and women was shaped by their formative years in wartime Europe, and perhaps had their vision of Europe skewed by the extraordinary pitch of desperation which they encountered among the population. A former United States Army Military Police (MP) officer stationed in Naples, responsible for incarcerating

---

1. K-rations, the daily ration of dehydrated food received by the Allied troops. U.S. army troops received packets containing a small can of food, three cigarettes, Nescafe dried coffee, a sugar packet and an "emergency" chocolate bar, which was so highly concentrated that with the addition of water, the chocolate bar alone was a quick energy supply. K-rations were received daily, whether or not the soldier ate in the mess hall at camp; their purpose was to fortify troops in battle or on maneuvers. Informants who were stationed in the city of Naples itself tell of trading their rations, and most especially the cigarettes and chocolate bar, for everything, from items in the black market to prostitutes.

prostitutes among other duties, related that after emerging from church services one Sunday morning he was accosted by an attractive young woman who promptly offered herself to him. When he refused, her mother, who had accompanied her to church, then also proceeded to proposition him, and was insulted when he declined. Family involvement was typical: mothers commonly prostituted their children (Lewis 1993:109), brothers prostituted their sisters (1994:56), and fathers prostituted their daughters (1993:42) with the emotional detachment typical of any other economic interchange. In Lewis' account, *Naples '44*, several instances stand out clearly; in one, two siblings of aristocratic lineage in desperate need of cash approached Allied personnel to assure the sister's entrance into an army brothel, an officially nonexisting entity. In a second instance, a man trying to sell his daughter's services had almost certainly received the aid of the local priest in formulating this request; the letter presented to Lewis was written in impeccable Italian, which itself nearly guaranteed that this illiterate father could not have written it. The letter stated that the girl had no mother, had not eaten for days, and proposed that "perhaps we could come to some mutually satisfactory understanding in due course" (1993:43).

Since American G.I.s were better provisioned overall and higher paid than other occupation armies, receiving pay packets four times that of the British infantry, for example, American soldiers were most often solicited for purposes of prostitution. Among American troops, African Americans came to be among the most desired men for sexual encounters largely because of their segregation to the low status Allied quartermaster corps, which was responsible for supplying the army with food, supplies, and requisitions. Although many Neapolitan women became involved with African-American soldiers and some bore children by them, actual emigration to the United States after the war was a rare occurrence because of strong anti-miscegenation sentiments among both Italians and Americans.

These interracial sexual encounters in themselves were indicative of vastly changed social mores; among Europeans, Italians were no more open-minded about race mixing than were Americans. Just prior to the Second World War, Mussolini fought a disastrous war in Ethiopia and many Italians sent to fight remained behind, intermarrying with the locals. Their mixed-race progeny were not accepted on the Italian peninsula and were in effect forced to remain in North Africa, as Mussolini's fascist decrees sought to improve the Italian "stock" and to seek "births, more births" (de Grazia 1992). And yet during the occupation of Naples, many social prohibitions against race mixing broke down. One Italian-American World War II veteran explained this based upon his apparent disbelief that Italian girls could be interested in African-American G.I.s for any other than economic reasons by saying, "they were the quartermaster troops, the suppliers; Italian girls went out with them because they had the food."

The control of food by the army generally was the key to many of the sexual contacts between Neapolitans and their "liberators." American troops were astounded that in the days after liberation the cost of a prostitute was only twenty-five cents (Kennett 1987:203). Although inflation proceeded apace and rendered the cost six times higher within the space of a few weeks, military officials would soon deplore the high number of women lured into this trade.

Veterans of the Italian campaign tell of young boys selling their sisters with the well-worn phrase, "hey, do you want to have a good time?" Although these veterans still have little understanding of the urgency inherent in most of these transactions, not all of the prostitutes' clientele were indifferent to their plight. An army private, Samuel J. David, expressed his understanding of the Neapolitan woman's dilemma in the Mediterranean edition of *Stars and Stripes*, and in the process admonished his fellow G.I.s to think about the cost of their actions, with the following verse:

> You do not really think it was her wish
> To sell her only heritage so cheap?
> Do you believe she yielded for a dish
> Of beans before the pangs of life cut deep?
> Do you believe she easy sleeps who keeps
> Her bed at all the crossroads of the town?
> Can you conceive that in her something weeps
> Each time you pour some rum and put her down?
> Or does her laughter not betray to you
> Its empty ring and deeply sunken hate
> Of all the things that she was forced to do,
> And for the world that dealt her such a fate?
> Well, Buddy, do what you feel you must,
> But don't berate the soul you tramp in dust.
> (September 11, 1944, Naples).

THEORIZING PROSTITUTION:
DOES PROSTITUTION CREATE PROSTITUTES?

Many questions need to be asked about the nature of prostitution as an economic activity in the Neapolitan context during the war. Prostitution is most often a marginal economic activity, and prostitutes usually among the most highly marginalized members of society. Yet, during the war in Naples, prostitutes bore little disgrace.

How did this disreputable trade become almost acceptable, allowing 42,000 out of 150,000 women (April, 1944, British Bureau of Psychological Warfare) to help support their families with the proceeds? Perhaps answers are best sought by comparison with such present-day situations as Thailand, the Dominican Republic, and other economically depressed Third-World regions where a woman's primary obligation is to feed her children and herself. The means by which she does this are secondary, and women who are prostitutes in order to be the family "breadwinners" are accorded respect because they are often the sole support of their households thus averting the far greater disgrace of family disintegration. It is possible also that prostitution in Naples during the war did not comply with the accepted definition of prostitution, the sale of sexual services for money, because the lira was so devalued that it was almost valueless, and the Amlire, the U.S. imposed wartime currency, was not used for payment nearly as often as food, clothing, army blankets, or other commodities.

This is a critical point. Barnett (1976:63) asks if a trade of sex for food *is* prostitution, mirroring as it does the unequal exchange found in marriage. The only difference between marriage and prostitution, says Barnett, is that prostitution is usually illegal, although this was not the case in Italy prior to 1958. Engels stated long ago that the difference between prostitution and marriage may be that in the institution of marriage, a woman "does not let out her body on piece-work as a wage worker, but sells it once and for all into slavery" (1970:134). Although prostitution is the ultimate imbalance of power, where powerless women sell to more powerful men, the line between full-fledged prostitution, gifts to a sexual partner, and actual marriage are often blurred under conditions of economic necessity. As G.I.s and British infantry personnel alike regularly shared tins of food, cigarettes, and army requisitions with the local women's families, and given that prostitutes were often paid with k-rations and army supplies rather than money, the question needs to be asked as to just what constitutes the difference.

During the war in Naples, prostitution escalated to such a scale that females were "breadwinners" in one in three families, overturning, at least temporarily, the idea of female submissiveness. Women of all classes in society, from the aristocracy through the working class, resorted to prostitution for the first time in recent memory in Italy. Women rather than men supported their families economically and in addition continued to attend to the physical and emotional needs of their families as they always had done. In the process they—again temporarily—redrew the sexual division of labor and realigned the class structure. Under these unique conditions, all women, regardless of their class origins, earned the same amount while performing some semblance of "equal work."

In a recent article, Matthaei (1995) states that sex work often seems threatening precisely because it empowers women at the same time that it degrades them, and allows them to both break with traditional family structures and to support themselves in times of economic necessity. Along the same lines, White (1986:273) has argued that prostitution in Nairobi during World War II was not "an interlude in the survival strategies of poor women," but rather was a response to poor economic conditions that changed both women's labor process and their lives. In Nairobi, prostitutes commonly provided domestic services such as cooking, cleaning, and bathing to male clients for an additional fee. White argues that such integrated services made prostitutes into owners of their own enterprise rather than wage workers. Yet, the situation in Naples during the same period was vastly different, as women remained entrapped in traditional patriarchal power structures, within their families' control, yet were sexually exploited by the military rank and file.

PRIVATE LITTLE WARS: REBUILDING A LIFE

War is in a sense the ultimate economic crisis because it both uproots people and eliminates the preconditions for survival. The food, clothing, and shelter upon which life depends are taken away at the same time that human life itself is destroyed. Although prostitution during peacetime may itself be a reaction to economic crisis, in most industrialized countries it is one option among many. In wartime, however, there may simply be no choice except the sale of the one commodity which cannot be separated from the human person: the body itself. Although not all cultures place as much emphasis upon female chastity as Mediterranean Europe does, this process is never without conflict since all societies possess notions of honor that are not easily overturned. Censored from many of the newspapers of the day (*La Voce* and *Risorgimento*), and proclaimed nonexistent by Mussolini himself, prostitution was nevertheless a critical means of survival for much of the civilian population while the war and the emergency lasted.

The war's end in Naples transformed the majority of "prostitutes" back into "housewives" as the preconditions for their entrance into the sex trade disappeared. Although an argument can be made that with the cessation of hostilities, patriarchal notions of honor and shame reasserted themselves, driving women back into the domestic sphere and restoring normative values upset by the war, it is also possible that women forced to such extremes were psychologically and emotionally scarred by the experience, and wished to bury all memory of their wartime travails. Perhaps the most lasting testament to the emotional duress and human tragedy endured by women prostitutes is that after the war, the majority disappeared into society, becoming "invisible," and never speaking of this era again except in the most confidential manner.

Because the "causes" of prostitution had been wholly economic, women's dependence upon prostitution as a livelihood lasted only as long as barriers to other types of work remained. Once industry, which in 1945 was merely one quarter of what it had been in 1938, resumed, in part with funding from the Marshall Plan, both men and women went to work in more conventional occupations. It is a truism of most patriarchically organized economic systems that women often can earn more from prostitution than from the limited "female-typed" jobs available to them. However, at the conclusion of hostilities in 1945, women turned from prostitution in vast numbers and a collective amnesia set in as most of the city's prostitutes faded from sight. By 1952 most were self-described "housewives" (*casalinghe*), hidden among the folds of the undifferentiated social fabric of the Neapolitan working class, and upholding a wall of silence about their wartime ordeal.

Shortly after the war ended, legislation was implemented to ensure that such widespread flouting of "public morals" never occurred again. The Merlin Law (a law, proposed by the progressive Socialist Senator, Lina Merlin in 1955 and passed in 1958) finally addressed the exploitative nature of the sex trade, but ultimately represented a misreading of the nation's wartime experience. Anti-prostitution legislation was in some senses unnecessary or even superfluous, because the war years had been an anomaly that no one, least of all Neapolitans, wished to repeat. Yet in another sense, the law was perhaps a belated reminder of the anguish of war and the impermanence of peace, as legislation attempted to do what the nation itself could not, restore honor to a generation whose innocence, if not whose memory, was forever lost.

REFERENCES

Barnett, Harold C.
    1976   The Political Economy of Rape and Prostitution. Review of Radical
           Political Economy 8 (1) Spring.

Blok, Anton
    1974   The Mafia of a Sicilian Village, 1860–1960: A study of violent
           peasant entrepreneurs. Oxford: Basil Blackwell.

David, Samuel J., Pvt.
    1944   Fair Enough. The Stars and Stripes. The Mediterranean, Italy
           Edition. (Naples) Monday, September 11, 1944.

De Grazia, Victoria
    1992   How Fascism Ruled Women: Italy 1922–1945. Berkeley: University
           of California Press.

Ellwood, David W.
    1985   Italy, 1943–1945. New York: Holmes and Meier.

Engels, Friedrich
    1972   The Origin of The Family, Private Property and The State. New
            York: International Publishers.

Enloe, Cynthia
    1993   The Morning After: Sexual Politics at the End of the Cold War.
            Berkeley: University of California Press.

Goddard, Victoria
    1987   Honor and Shame: The Control of Women's Sexuality and Group
            Identity in Naples. *In* The Cultural Construction of Sexuality. Pat
            Caplan, ed. London and New York: Tavistock Publications.

Hargrove, Hondon B.
    1985   Buffalo Soldiers in Italy: Black Americans in World War II.
            Jefferson, N.C.: McFarland.

Hicks, George
    1994   The Comfort Women: Japan's Brutal Regime of Enforced
            Prostitution in the Second World War. New York: W.W. Norton.

Kennett, Lee
    1987   G.I. The American Soldier in World War II. New York: Charles
            Scribner and Sons.

Kertzer, David I.
    1993   Sacrificed for Honor: Italian Infant Abandonment and the Politics of
            Reproductive Control. Boston: Beacon Press.

Lambiase, Sergio and Enzo Battista
    1993   Napoli 1940–1945. Longanesi & C. Milano.

Lewis, Norman
    1993   Naples '44. New York: Pantheon Books.

Matthaei, Julie.
    1995   The Sexual Division of Labor, Sexuality, and Lesbian/Gay
            Liberation: Towards a Marxist-Feminist Analysis of Sexuality in
            U.S. Capitalism. Review of Radical Political Economy 27(2) June.

Roberts, Nickie
    1992   Whores in History: Prostitution in Western society. London: Harper
            Collins.

West, Morris
    1957   Children of the Shadows: The True Story of the Street Urchins of
            Naples. Garden City, NY: Doubleday.

White, Luise
    1986   Prostitution, Identity and Class Consciousness in Nairobi During
            WW II. Signs 2(21).

SERIOUS FUN IN SHANGRI-LA

Tourism, Gender, and Interethnic Relations in a
Tibetan Refugee Settlement

Eric McGuckin

Holidays are serious business. Tourism is fast becoming one of the world's most important economic activities, employing over 200 million people globally. Some 528 million people traveled abroad in 1994 (Sloan, 1995). Anthropologists now encounter travelers in even the most remote fieldsites. Tourism's enormous economic and cultural impact is finally being studied by a growing number of social scientists. Their work is easily overlooked as a flood of travel writing recounting personal adventures in the remaining exotic hinterlands of the planet overflows the shelves of bookstores everywhere.

Once regarded as a painless path to Third-World development, tourism is now widely recognized as a risky business, vulnerable to "political instability" that scares off visitors, unpredictable fashions or recession in the wealthy societies of the North, and seasonal booms and busts. Expensive infrastructure development—hotels, airports, sewage systems—is often under foreign control. Profits then flow out of the country and into the hands of multinational corporations, while environmental costs burden the local community, and little benefit ripples outward into the rural areas surrounding tourist enclaves. As farmlands are transformed into pool decks, overdevelopment and pollution often follow. Existing social and economic inequalities are frequently exacerbated as prices for land and commodities skyrocket. Until recently, social scientists were almost uniformly critical of the impacts of tourism, particularly the transformation of traditional culture into spectacles for the consumption of outsiders. In *The Golden Hordes*, Turner and Ash (1975) lamented the growth of a "leisure periphery" in the Third World. Tourism, they claimed, is the enemy of authenticity.

Since their book was published, tourism has continued to grow, but in a new direction. Hordes of mass tourists, disgorged from their air-conditioned buses, cameras clicking, have been joined by legions of intrepid travelers—eco-tourists, ethnic tourists, adventure tourists—in search of unspoiled locales. Traveling on low budgets, much of their money is spent in small, locally-owned enterprises. Many of these new travelers are young and disenchanted with the consumer culture of the West. Their quest for "authentic" people and handmade goods now subsidizes many endangered cultural and artistic traditions. Nature tourism has led to the creation of a number of ecological preserves, such as the Annapurna Conservation Area in Nepal favored by mountain trekkers. In the context of Third-World debt and First-World industrial dominance, tourism and handicraft production are among the few viable options that remain for many rural communities and particularly for landless refugees. But "alternative travelers," who are often at pains to differentiate themselves from ordinary, destructive tourists, inevitably bring change to the "timeless" peoples they visit. Tourism pulls indigenous communities farther into international flows of money, goods, and culture over which they exert little control. Alternative travelers often form the first wave of the very commercialism they are attempting to escape. The Annapurna region now bristles with signs in English advertising lodges serving pizza and Coca-cola, and toilet paper lines the trails.

The impacts of tourism are complex, effecting local economies, culture, and even interpersonal relationships. This chapter describes some of the positive and negative impacts of tourism in Dharamsala, India. Dharamsala is home to the Dalai Lama and a Tibetan refugee community largely supporting itself through tourism and cultural entrepreneurship, a host Indian population with whom relations are increasingly tense, and a growing number of Western visitors. While this chapter focuses particularly on gender and interethnic relations in Dharamsala, it will illustrate several general points: opportunities and problems brought by tourism and international relationships are unevenly distributed along gender, ethnic, and class lines; travelers' myths about "traditional" societies are often appropriated by indigenous peoples for political and economic self-promotion, while in fact their cultural expressions and arts begin to mirror the expectations and desires of outsiders; and while travel is sometimes hyped as promoting cross-cultural cooperation and understanding, the sincere attempts by foreign visitors to form personal relationships with and improve the lives of their hosts often conflict with local interests and bring unintended consequences, different for men and women, that linger long after the travelers have safely returned home.

TIBET OPENS TO THE WORLD

Tibet, on the "roof of the world" behind the Himalayas, remained relatively aloof from global imperial struggles until the twentieth century. Although nominally under Chinese authority for centuries, Tibet enjoyed a practical independence, maintaining an imperfectly unified political-religious state dominated by competing Tibetan Buddhist sects. The Dalai Lama, believed to be an incarnation of Avalokitesvara, the Buddha of Compassion, was the head of the most powerful monastic sect in Tibet.

The army of the newly founded People's Republic of China "liberated" Tibet in 1951, when the present Dalai Lama was sixteen years old. At first their reforms appeared beneficial to many Tibetans, especially the poor. Soon, however, the occupying force became more restrictive. Heavy taxation, forced collectivization and labor, and the adoption of agrarian practices ill-suited to the Tibetan environment led to the deterioration of most people's living standards. Buddhism, inseparable from Tibetan culture and identity, was suppressed. For a time even the Tibetan language was forbidden in schools. Tibet is now an internal colony of China, exploited for its minerals and timber, its people becoming a minority in their own land.

After a failed rebellion in 1959, the Dalai Lama fled to India. Thousands of Tibetans, both members of the elite and ordinary farmers, artisans, and traders, followed him into exile. Over the years, thousands more have fled the Chinese occupation, and today over 100,000 Tibetans live in settlements in India and Nepal. With the help of host country governments, international aid agencies, and investments of the treasure smuggled out with the Dalai Lama, the Tibetans have established a thriving welfare state-in-exile that provides employment, education, and medical care for many of the refugees. The production and sale of Tibetan handicrafts to tourists helps support refugee institutions and preserve Tibetan religion and culture.

McLeod Ganj, once a deteriorating British hill-station above Dharamsala in the foothills of the Indian Himalayas, is now host to the Dalai Lama, the Central Tibetan Administration, and a Tibetan community of some 5,000. Tibetans in Dharamsala engage in both co-operative and private enterprises including hotel and restaurant services, petty trade, and cultural industries such as handicraft production and religious teaching. McLeod Ganj is now on the international tourist map as a mini-

Kathmandu, attracting growing numbers of spiritual seekers, anthropologists, volunteers, and tourists.

Before the Chinese occupation, Tibetan elites attempted to keep foreign influences out of Tibet, and few Westerners were allowed to set foot in the capital city of Lhasa. Today, the exile administration aims to maintain a distinct Tibetan identity, hoping to keep Tibetans in compact settlements and discourage interethnic marriages, assimilation, and citizenship in host nations. However, Tibetan autonomy is limited because the refugees—lacking a state, arms, or land—are dependent on the hospitality of India and Nepal and on international aid and foreign consumers. While the refugees and their supporters advertise an urgent need for the preservation of traditional Tibetan culture, some crafts have been radically altered for the tourist and export trade. Many enterprises are initiated by foreign sympathizers and entrepreneurs, and a few "Tibetan" souvenirs are actually made by non-Tibetans. A growing interest in Buddhism in the West has led several Tibetan monastic sects to establish businesses and teaching centers, helping these institutions regain some of their past strength. In Dharamsala, however, some monks now seem to spend as much time serving pizza as praying.

SHANGRI-LA IDEAL; SHANGRI-LA REAL

In Dharamsala, an old nun and a wizened monk earned their daily bread by striking poses for tourists. The monk was particularly picturesque, his wrinkled and smiling face adorned with a huge walrus mustache. He would station himself in front of groups of foreigners, always spinning a much-used prayer wheel. Few could resist taking his photograph—plucky Tibetan faith preserved incarnate—upon which he would retrieve from under his ancient robes solicitations for money in German and English. Charming the first time, he and his female counterpart rapidly became nuisances. The old monk never seemed to remember who he had just hit up, and would appear before the same travelers day after day, staring directly at them, grinning broadly, twirling away with his prayer wheel. He did manage to hold the focus of quite a number of the documentary film makers constantly passing through Dharamsala, stationing themselves importantly with their equipment in the middle of whatever event appeared most traditional, spoiling the snapshots of mere tourists. My young Tibetan friends were embarrassed by the behavior of these two. They called the nun "Thukpa Ani" (literally Noodle Nun) since she lived in large part off meals solicited from Westerners in restaurants, where she could be seen in her robes, sipping a newly available Pepsi, in a haze of cigarette smoke and Rock and Roll.

Westerners come to Dharamsala in part for the "scene." They have heard it is full of other interesting people and offers a restful mountain retreat from the hassles, heat, and dust of the Indian plains. But many travelers are also drawn to the spiritual mystique that surrounds the Tibetans. Knowing that much political support and tourist business are at stake, the Tibetans have become extremely image-conscious, and manipulate the Shangri-la myth to their advantage. Hotels or restaurants with the name "Shangri-la"—the invention of a Western novelist—can be found in nearly every Tibetan settlement catering to travelers. Behaviors that disturb the mirage, such as Thukpa Ani's, are discouraged.

In *The Myth of Shangri-La* (1989), Peter Bishop writes that as the European and American landscapes were "disenchanted" by science and development, faraway Tibet, like other places not fully explored and categorized by Westerners, was imagined as a magical, sacred space where Abominable Snowmen and Himalayan gurus lived in a spiritual land outside history. The timelessness, internal harmony, and innocence of disappearing cultures are regular themes of coffee-table books, charitable solicitations, and travel advertisements. The alleged isolation of such societies grants them a special interest to Western travelers precisely because they have not yet been "contaminated" by the West. This imagining relies on excluding accounts of the internal violence and hierarchy that actually existed within many such societies, as well as overlooking the impact of the world economic and political system on even the most isolated peoples. For many Westerners alienated from consumer society, an idealized, egalitarian, and otherworldly Tibet has become a key symbol of spirituality and tradition struggling against the onslaught of modernity, meaninglessness, and materialism. But the image of traditional Tibet as an isolated, harmonious, and unified nation contrasts with the actual historical record. Tibetan history reveals foreign alliances, social inequalities, and bloody power struggles between aristocratic, religious, and regional factions. In exile, regional rivalries persist and sometimes threaten refugee unity, and tourism brings commercialism and competition.

The Tibetan refugee administration is concerned to counter propaganda from the People's Republic about the evils of the old society. It attempts to present idealized portraits of traditional Tibet both to foster nationalism within the refugee community and to elicit support from foreigners. Many travelers, for their part, are eager to project their utopian fantasies upon the Tibetans. Public discussions of commercialism, sexism, and conflict within Tibetan society undermine the harmonious image both groups desire.

Like the idea of the noble savage, however, the myth of Shangri-la largely reflects Western desires and places impossible expectations upon the refugees. Western visitors are often bitterly disillusioned when they discover that even the Tibetans are only human, and refugee values and interests do not always coincide with those of their benefactors.

WESTERNERS AND THE IMAGE OF TIBETAN WOMEN

Dependent on foreign generosity and political interest, Tibetan political activists must make appeals to Western concerns. Through contact with Western scholars and activists, for example, Tibetans have become more sophisticated about the destructive environmental impacts of the Chinese occupation, and the cause of Tibetan independence is now sometimes rhetorically linked to environmental issues.

Equality of the sexes is crucial for many Westerners' vision of a perfect society, of a contemporary Shangri-la. The Tibetan Women's Association makes appeals to the women of the world to help the women and children of Tibet. Stories of Tibetan women's resistance to Chinese repression and torture are inspirational for many travelers. Numbers of Western travelers, more women than men, stay or return to Dharamsala for prolonged periods to work as volunteers in Tibetan institutions. However, travelers' perceptions and ideas about gender relations conflict with local values and realities. While the status of Tibetan women is quite high relative to other Asian societies, gender inequality persists in the refugee community, and tourism has brought unequal opportunities to men and women.

While most Tibetans probably think of women as members of households and nunneries, many Westerners see women as a separate social category with unique problems and rights. Following Western academic fashion, where once anthropologists analyzed the "adaptation" of Tibetans to a new environment, many young students now arrive in Dharamsala hoping to conduct research on Tibetan women. In 1992–93, when research for this article was conducted, studying some aspect of gender—marriage forms, Buddhist nuns, or simply "women"—was probably the most popular topic among at least eleven anthropologists simultaneously conducting research in Dharamsala. The presence of so many Western visitors and researchers has made Tibetans feel they are under a microscope, their every behavior scrutinized. Tibetans sometimes resent foreign influences on gender relations and criticism of inequality. It is difficult to generalize about the "status of Tibetan women" because little empirical research on gender relations has yet been completed, and because much regional variation exists. Accounts of travelers, British officials, missionaries, and anthropologists do, however, report a high degree of female autonomy in pre-occupation Tibet. Charles Bell, a British official and Tibetologist who traveled widely in Tibet at the turn of the century, claimed that "when a traveler enters Tibet from the neighboring nations in China or India, few things impress him more vigorously or more deeply that the position of the Tibetan women" (Bell 1968 [1928]:147). Tibetan women engaged in trade, inherited property, and initiated divorce. There were no traditions of foot binding, veiling, or female seclusion, and little sexual segregation outside of religious institutions.

Today, the Tibetan community in Dharamsala appears comparatively egalitarian to travelers having recently journeyed through India or other parts of Asia. Reflecting new Western ideas of democracy, the exile Tibetan constitution declares that men and women are equal. Women can vote and hold office, and some have risen to positions of influence. Refugee women constitute about 45 percent of the working force and are important in the sale and promotion of Tibetan goods. Many travelers to Dharamsala contrast the position of Tibetan women with the oppression they see experienced by local Indian women. As one female traveler from Australia observed, Tibetan women enjoy "a lot of respect. They're allowed to show themselves. They have courage and strength."

It cannot be expected that short-term visitors—now or in the past—will perceive subtle forms of women's disadvantage. The impressions of travelers are formed in hotels, restaurants, and in the marketplace. Many travelers engage with local individuals only in brief exchanges of goods, services, and money. Ideas about a host society are necessarily constructed through superficial appearances. Travelers, historians, and scholars of Tibetan Buddhism have generally limited their substantial conversations, by choice or necessity, to male representatives of the aristocracy and monasteries. Portrayals of women's status in Tibetan society and religion have therefore been idealized. Although Tibetan society portrays women as largely self-sufficient and autonomously engaged in economic life, at the higher regional, state, and monastic levels power has always been in the hands of men. In exile, although women are influential at the household level, men retain dominance in most community-wide political and economic decision making.

WOMEN IN TIBETAN CULTURAL INDUSTRIES

Tibetan religion, probably the cultural sphere that most identifies Tibetans and appeals to foreigners, is almost completely represented to the outside world by men. While some deities in Tibetan Buddhism are female, and there were several significant female religious figures in pre-occupation Tibet, the most important reincarnations, who wield significant political as well as spiritual power, were and are male. Women are seen as less spiritually capable, and female practitioners still pray to be released in the next life from their "lower birth" (the literal meaning of the Tibetan word for woman) and to be reborn as men. Although foreign women are quite active in Buddhist studies in Dharamsala, Tibetan monks receive far more attention and donations than do nuns, even from females. This is due in part to the greater wealth and political influence of the monasteries, but also to the monk's higher levels of education, bilingualism, and public relations savvy. They far more frequently play the role of teacher or guru to Western seekers. Monasteries operate craft shops, restaurants, and guest houses in Dharamsala, and organize tours of monastic artisans and performers abroad. The nunneries have few such enterprises, instead relying on Western volunteers and the Tibetan administration for support. A push to improve the status of nuns by some Western Buddhists is often dismissed by mostly male Tibetan intellectuals as a foreign intrusion irrelevant to the nuns' true interests. Most tourists have no idea where the nunneries are located, and few tourists have any contact with Tibetan nuns.

Like Tibetan religious culture, artistic production is largely directed and represented by men. Tibetan women are generally engaged in handicraft production as employees rather than managers, more likely to be photographed as picturesque weavers in carpet factories than interviewed as master artisans. Men almost completely monopolize the higher status arts such as painting, metal work, and woodcarving. However, the goal of artistic preservation, and the need to provide employment to the refugees, has somewhat loosened traditional gender restrictions. A few Tibetan women are now apprenticed as religious painters, formerly a male monopoly.

In general, however, women work in the lower status, less spiritually significant crafts such as tailoring and carpet weaving, in which there is more of an emphasis on rapid, standardized production. Because Tibetan women retain domestic responsibilities, they often accept part-time work and lower wages than men. This allows the refugee enterprises to employ numbers of less-affluent women, providing them with a safe, if small income to supplement that of their husbands and family. Sometimes left alone with children, women are often more concerned with security than men, and take less economic risks.

The largest Tibetan craft industry in exile is carpet production. The handicraft co-operative run by the Tibetan administration in Dharamsala employs approximately one hundred weavers, all women. Whereas weavers once generally chose their own designs, often copying old carpets, most now follow sketches on graph paper drawn by male designers, sometimes to the specification of Western tourists or importers. The manager of the co-operative is male, as is the elderly carpet designer, a former religious painter. Carpet clippers, who finish the carpets by leveling their surfaces and contouring designs, are all men. Their job, it is said, requires strength, and they earn substantially more than the female weavers.

"Nyima" is a middle-aged woman who weaves in the co-operative. I interviewed her on one rainy afternoon in 1993 in her two small rooms supplied by the co-operative. Her friend "Yangchen" was my translator. In one corner of the living and sleeping room was a small table set up as an altar, upon which sat a line of metal bowls half filled with water for offering, and two butter lamps. Nearby was a framed photo of the Dalai Lama with former President Bush. A very large poster of the London Bridge in its new incarnation as a tourist attraction in the Arizona desert hung on one wall. I noticed Nyima had no carpets in the room. Many weavers cannot afford the carpets they produce. I asked if the weavers get a special price on carpets.

Yangchen snorted: "This is a dream!"

"We are like coolies," Nyima laughed.

Nyima had been weaving for nineteen years. She weaves twenty-six days a month from around eight in the morning to seven at night, with an hour break for lunch, earning some 600 rupees a month (about U.S. $20). Although she admitted the wages are low, Nyima stays with the co-operative for the secure income and the cheap rooms it provides. She also enjoys the sociable atmosphere in the factory. "Fingers going, mouth going, joking, singing," she said. "We play around. When we get paid I get sick when I see how little it is, then I forget after a few days." The work is hard on her hands. At one point, she put out her hand to show me her swollen knuckles. "My hands look like ginger!"

Tourists often come and watch the weavers. They stand at the open doors of the factory watching the women sitting cross-legged in rows on the floor in front of their wooden looms. Many of the weavers wear Tibetan clothes, their long, braided hair tied with colorful cloth ribbons. In some societies the appearance of women has taken on a new significance. Ethnic dress can simultaneously assert the preservation of group identity in a transnational world and announce that women retain traditional domestic roles. Men are generally integrated into wage labor markets wearing Western pants and shirts. Many tourists in Dharamsala take pictures of the weavers at work. Some of the women turn to smile at the tourists' cameras. Others are embarrassed, laugh, and turn their faces into a neighbor's shoulder. Some simply ignore the intrusion and continue weaving. Nyima said she likes it when Westerners take pictures. "Some look in the window but are too shy to come in, so I wave them in." Because Nyima cannot speak English, she cannot ask them to send her copies.

Nyima told me that the co-operative used to employ both male and female weavers, but now very few Tibetan men weave. She gave two very different reasons for this. "Women are better weavers," she explained. "Men have clumsy hands; women have small, skilled hands. Carpet weaving is women's work; if I see a man weaving it doesn't look right." However Nyima also recognized that this idea had something to do with different gender expectations and options. "Before many men wove," she said, "but the income was small and the work hard, so the men left. But women like the cheap rooms the co-operative provides. If they leave they have no house." Her own husband used to work in the Co-op, but now has a stall selling "Free Tibet" T-shirts, shoes, flip-flops, and the like. "Hong Kong things, Taiwan things," Nyima explained. "This has a little better income; also less hard work!"

Tibetans are often considered natural traders. The streets of Dharamsala are lined with small shops offering Tibetan crafts, clothes with Tibetan motifs, jewelry, and knock-offs of Western goods such as jeans and watches. In pre-occupation Tibet, wealthy families and the monasteries maintained trading monopolies, and large-scale commerce was largely under the control of men. However, women in Tibet engaged in petty trade and often ran their own shops. In exile, women are often the preferred sales representatives. Tibetan girls often work behind the counter of crafts shops while their brothers hang out with their friends or Western tourists. While I was talking to Nyima, her husband arrived and broke into the conversation, expounding on the capabilities of women. "Selling is good, and caring for the children and caring for the home," he said. "Business—they can sell more. Girls can sell sweaters better." Nyima's friend Yangchen added: "If two women and two men have stalls, the Indians go to the women. Women can talk more frankly and Indians like women better."

Despite inequalities, the growth of tourism and the market in ethnic handicrafts offer new opportunities for indigenous and refugee women. Women who once married quite young and remained subservient to their families can earn a new autonomy. In Dharamsala, with no land to work or keep within corporate households, many Tibetan women supplement family incomes or support themselves independently through handicraft production and trade. With subsidized living quarters from the crafts co-operatives, divorced, single, and widowed women can sometimes maintain their own households. "Love marriages," rather than arranged marriages, are becoming more common. Today, few India-born Tibetan women choose to enter nunneries, a former alternative to family life. Women are generally considered more financially prudent than men, and some Tibetans now say it is no special economic advantage to have male children.

THE STRATIFIED MARKETPLACE

Despite the many real benefits that tourism can bring to indigenous women and their communities, the industry can exacerbate gender, ethnic, and class conflicts. The ability to take advantage of new markets and international relationships is highly unequal. Some entrepreneurs exploit uneven international exchange rates as well as social differences within communities for their own profit. Traditional arts may be cheapened and degraded as craft industries, dependent on foreign consumers, employ the poorest segments of the community at low wages.

Merchants with international connections, often made through encounters with travelers, can sometimes sell ethnic handicrafts in Europe or the United States for many times their cost of production. Their profits depend on keeping sale prices well above the cost of local labor and materials. The Tibetan carpet industry in Nepal provides a good example. Tibetan carpets have become Nepal's largest earner of foreign currency, generating significant fortunes for a few families. However, the only thing "Tibetan" about many of these carpets is the ownership of the means of their production. Carpets are often so altered for foreign tastes that they retain no Tibetan motifs at all. The carpet industry in Nepal relies on the labor of some 300,000 non-Tibetan Nepalis, many of them driven into the carpet factories by rural poverty. About half these workers are underpaid children.

In contrast to Nepal, Tibetan settlements in India need to employ poor and less educated members of a much larger and expanding refugee population. The handicraft market in Dharamsala is dominated by craft schools and co-operatives run by exile institutions. Tibetans are also limited by Indian law in the amount of land they may obtain, and private industries cannot expand indefinitely. Most successful private entrepreneurs in Dharamsala remain petty traders, rising into a growing Tibetan middle class, rather than forming a new economic elite.

This Tibetan middle class, however, is doing better than much of the surrounding Indian population. The Tibetan administration has attempted to limit direct competition between the refugees and host communities, and new economic opportunities have opened to Indians with the means to take advantage of them. An ethnic division of labor has developed, in which Tibetans operate most of the Tibetan craft industries, stalls selling Western clothes and trinkets, and small restaurants and hotels. The Indians, who hold all the agricultural land, operate most of the food shops and monopolize the taxi union and most of the phone and travel services. Land prices are rising quickly in surrounding Indian villages, and some Indians are selling their land, giving up farming, and buying taxis or opening cafes. Should the Tibetans return to Tibet, these investments could prove disastrous.

The Indian community generally resents the Tibetans who refuse to assimilate and receive much more attention and support from Western travelers. In April 1994, these tensions exploded when a young man of the Gaddi community, the traditionally agrarian and pastoral people of the area, was stabbed to death by a young Tibetan after a fight over a taxi. In response, local Indians carrying clubs and iron rods ransacked and looted the Tibetan administration's complex and many Tibetan shops and homes. Egged on by members of the Hindu chauvinist Bharatriya Janata Party (BJP), local Indians marched through Dharamsala demanding the expulsion of the Tibetans. They also sought an inquiry into land deals that Tibetans had allegedly obtained through bribes, linking them to skyrocketing land and commodity prices. Although the Tibetans are sometimes in competition with small local merchants—much of the BJP's constituency—other Indian business interests dependent on tourism would be devastated should the Dalai Lama relocate, in addition to the considerable political embarrassment this would create. After threatening to move, the Dalai Lama was persuaded to stay, and the presence of the Tibetans continues to benefit many Indians, while angering others.

Depending on one's perspective, entrepreneurs either offer desperately needed income or exploit the weakest members of both the Indian and Tibetan communities. Taking advantage of rural poverty, some Tibetans pay Indian women low rates to knit sweaters and other woolen goods for resale to travelers, and Indian children are often employed by Tibetans as domestic help and restaurant workers. Cheap labor rebounds to the advantage of Western travelers, who find goods and services in Dharamsala a bargain.

Refugees newly arrived from Tibet are also at a disadvantage, particularly if they have few local ties or do not speak English, and single mothers are generally poor, with no husband to complement their incomes. These refugees often become dependent on the Tibetan administration or on better connected private entrepreneurs. The weaver Nyima, for example, supplements her income by weaving nights and holidays for a woman whose son sells carpets in the United States. Many refugees seek "sponsors" among travelers and foreign residents who regularly send money for education, living expenses, or even starting businesses. While raising the quality of life for many Tibetans, such sponsorships foster a dependence on the often temporary generosity of Western patrons. The case of "Songmo" and "Nancy" will illustrate the interweaving of class and ethnic divisions, unequal international relationships and exchange rates, and dependency.

Nancy, an American volunteer, planned to organize a women's co-op to produce and sell fine handicrafts. Her main purpose, she said, was to meet the needs of her friend "Songmo," a new arrival from Tibet, and her infant son. Her husband was an artisan whose income did not meet their needs. Songmo had no kin in India and her small family was about to lose the room provided by the Tibetan administration. "She fell through the cracks in the Tibetan safety net," Nancy explained.

Songmo's former job in a Tibetan restaurant had paid a pittance for a long, hard working day. Songmo also tried knitting socks for a Swiss couple who supported themselves and their Buddhist studies in Dharamsala by buying crafts in India and selling them for a much higher price in

Europe. They bought Indian shawls for eighty rupees, using Tibetan women to bargain with the Indians. The couple then sold the shawls in Switzerland for the equivalent of 1200 rupees. They bought socks Songmo knitted for thirty rupees and sold them for ten times that sum. Although the Swiss paid Songmo a better wage than they paid Indian women, Songmo quit when she discovered how little of the eventual profit she received.

Nancy wanted to form a co-operative of newly arrived refugee women to knit higher quality goods than those usually produced in Dharamsala. The co-operative would share profits fairly and be run by the producers. Nancy had already found some prospective buyers in Delhi. Although she had some initial problems locating sources of fine wool, the women themselves were the biggest obstacle. They were reluctant to give up whatever small security their current jobs might provide, and afraid of the opinions of others. The leveling mechanisms common to many peasant societies still persist to a degree in Dharamsala. The women "wanted it all to be secret," Nancy told me. They were "afraid that people would be jealous and even try to sabotage it." Songmo never really wanted a co-operative; she wanted her own private business. Songmo imagined hiring poor Tibetans and Indian women who would work for low wages, while Nancy found clients in the West. Having learned that the cost of labor and goods are ethnically and nationally unequal, she wanted to take advantage of the differentials herself. Not only was Indian labor cheaper, should the venture fail she would not be accountable to her peers in the Tibetan community. Nancy was troubled by this. "To sell in the West," she said, "you need sympathy [for the Tibetan cause] and I already had potential backers for a *Tibetan* women's co-op. It would be dishonest if we employed Indian women."

The idea fizzled out, although Nancy later took carpets Songmo made to sell to Western friends. Songmo "feels she'd be exploited dealing with shopkeepers here," Nancy said, "and also thinks she'd get more money from the West. So she probably wants me to be in control and be responsible for the business end of things." Unable to take advantage of ethnic differences, and unwilling to be exploited herself, Songmo still hoped to profit from uneven exchange rates, but remained dependent on Western sympathy and expertise.

INTERETHNIC ROMANCES: CULTURAL MEETING OR MIRAGE?

Although tourism has often been touted as fostering cross-cultural understanding, conflict and misunderstanding are equally likely. As with economic relationships, personal relationships created by tourism are unequal for men and women. Because of different ideas about gender and sexuality, as well as inequalities in money, power, and mobility, local and foreign men and women have different options open to them, different access to each other, and different impacts. The social and health disasters created by the sex tourism industries in Thailand and the Philippines are relatively well-known. However, both male and female travelers create less obvious problems in their pursuit of romance and relationships abroad. The seemingly inconsequential actions of travelers often have long-lasting local impacts not apparent to those with the freedom to experience and move on.

The influence of outsiders on Tibetan youth is a growing concern for the refugee community. The influence of "freaky" Western tourists, particularly drug use, is widely considered a problem. Tibetan boys are much freer to experiment than girls who are given more and earlier household chores than boys. If not attending school, girls are likely to be helping in the home or in shops. By contrast, several informants told me that local Tibetan boys did not seem to become men until at least their mid-20s. Some Tibetan boys hang out idly on the steps of restaurants, strumming guitars with young travelers drifting through town. Many young men attend the video halls, while young women stay home watching Hindi movies on television. Women often seen in restaurants or with Westerners become the subject of gossip.

Relative to surrounding Asian societies, women in pre-occupation Tibet enjoyed a fair degree of sexual license. Divorce was possible, premarital sex largely tolerated, and illegitimacy did not cause tremendous scandal. In marriage, discretion was often more important than fidelity (Aziz 1978). But in Dharamsala the presence of the Dalai Lama and the monasteries, as well as numbers of the old aristocratic elite, are partially responsible for a new decorum in female behavior. A further influence is the concern for the opinion of the Indians and visiting Westerners. "Modern" attitudes are encouraged, including modesty in behavior and dress, attention to manners, and cleanliness. Refugees newly arrived from Tibet, not yet accustomed to exile standards, are considered "raw" and unruly. New refugee women sometimes wear make-up and bright, tight-fitting clothes, whereas Indian-born Tibetan women generally wear modified Tibetan dresses or more modest Western and Indian clothes. A young Tibetan friend, a new arrival himself, told me he thought recently arrived women were "cheap." Because they had no relatives in Dharamsala, he complained, they "can do anything, and go wild." He saw no irony in his having participated in several "Full Moon parties" above town, staying up all night drumming and smoking hash with Westerners.

Most young India-born refugee women are shy with foreigners, and other than brief interactions in shops, have much fewer opportunities than their male counterparts to form intimate friendships with Westerners. Sexual relationships between Tibetan women and Western men in

Dharamsala are relatively uncommon. However many women travelers enjoy erotic encounters with the exotic and handsome young Tibetan men. Foreign women are able to take more risks than local women. They can enter into social arenas, such as bars, where local women may be "out of place." One American volunteer commented that "Western women are treated as Westerners first, women second."

Anonymity and mobility allow female travelers the chance to experiment with sex, drugs, and appearance. For many Indian visitors to Dharamsala, photographs of young female tourists, whose bizarre behavior and colorful, skimpy clothing can compete with exotics anywhere, are eagerly sought after. Some Western women complain that local men simply assume they are promiscuous, and that sexual harassment from Indian men is common. While this is true, Westerners adopt many of the anti-Indian prejudices held by Tibetans and Indian men are stereotyped and compared unfavorably with the Tibetans. Indian men are therefore less likely than Tibetan men to enjoy relationships with female travelers.

For Western women staying in Dharamsala for extended periods, having a Tibetan boyfriend may be something of a status symbol. Women volunteers from the West, working side by side with Tibetan men for the government-in-exile, are quite likely to form romantic relationships with their coworkers. Of nine female volunteers I interviewed, six had engaged in sexual relations with a Tibetan. Only one had sex with an Indian, one with another Westerner, and one had not engaged in sex at all while in Dharamsala. For Tibetan men, involvement with foreign women can provide sexual and social experiences unavailable with more socially restricted Tibetan women, and sometimes offers foreign money or travel.

Many among the older generation of Tibetan exiles disapprove of interethnic relationships. Romantic relationships with foreigners divide the community and "threaten the Tibetan race" already under assault from the Chinese. Many Tibetans claim that the "Tibetan mind" and the "Western mind" are too different for long-term relationships to work. Many interethnic marriages fail because of the extremely divergent expectations of the partners. Western women, I heard frequently from Tibetans, were too independent. "They think they are like a man, and can do anything a man can do!" complained one young Tibetan man. He claimed he would "rather marry an Indian girl," a very unlikely prospect given the level of tensions between the communities. In several relationships, strong, independent Western women tolerated behaviors from Tibetan partners that they would never accept in the West, including alcoholism, sexual selfishness, and the idea that wives are servants to their husbands. Several of these educated women rationalized their submission as a form of "cultural relativism." They continued to idealize Tibetan culture, and blamed their underlying feelings of resentment on Western biases. Despite gender inequality, the greater power and options these women enjoyed as relatively affluent Westerners remained.

Many foreigners are oblivious to long-term consequences of romantic relationships for their partners. A few take care that their relationships remain discreet, and some send money periodically to their partners when they leave. Most, however, get on with their own lives once they return to the West, sometimes leaving their partner in difficulty. This is particularly true for Tibetan women left by Western men. They may suffer from gossip and even harassment, and find it difficult to find a Tibetan partner. Because of men's greater status and social freedom in Tibetan society, marriages between Tibetan men and Western women meet with less overt disapproval, and are more common in Dharamsala. However, such marriages often do not live up to their promise, as the case of "Tashi" will illustrate.

Tashi was a twenty-six-year-old refugee from eastern Tibet. A bout of tuberculosis when he first came to India had left him very thin. Tall, enthusiastic, and sweet, he looked and acted like a Western teenager. Tashi had spent several years at a refugee school where he learned to read and write Tibetan and speak English. I agreed to tutor him privately, with an emphasis on American slang. Cracking jokes and always laughing, wearing his jeans and T-shirt, it was difficult to imagine Tashi looking as he did in an old photograph he carried: he and his friend on arrival, wearing Tibetan wool garments in the Indian heat, faces fat and rosy, staring unposed into the camera. I tried unsuccessfully to picture him riding a horse, a knife at his side, over the fields of eastern Tibet.

Tashi was not the studious type, and soon was transferred from school to train for a job in a medical dispensary run by the Tibetan administration. Unused to regular working hours or formal procedures, he nearly lost his position for tardiness and unexcused absences but soon became self-supporting. After Tashi fell in love with "Marian," an American woman, he quit his job and married her in order to gain permission to emigrate to the United States. He and his new wife rented rooms in Dharamsala while they ran from Tibetan office to Indian office to the American embassy and back again attempting to clear up the paperwork.

After a civil ceremony conducted by Indian officials, Tashi and Marian had a modified Tibetan wedding in McLeod Ganj. The Tibetan official in charge of the public hall was a bit embarrassed by it all because everything had been arranged by the bride, not by family and friends. Marian was clearly in charge, as she was in all the couple's affairs. Tashi was becoming increasingly dependent. The wedding was well-attended by Westerners and Tibetans, and even a few Indians. Tashi wore a fur-trimmed Tibetan shirt, colorful Tibetan boots, and a fox-pelt hat. Marian wore a silk Tibetan dress and blouse made for the occasion. After a presentation of gifts, everyone sat outside under the Tibetan canopy and ate Tibetan food and drank barley beer. One of Tashi's friends began playing a *damyen*, a Tibetan stringed instrument, and a few Westerners joined in a circle of Tibetan dancing. Suddenly, from inside the hall, rap music drowned out the *damyen*, and a number of young Tibetan men and Westerners rushed inside and starting dancing. After a while, some young Tibetan women joined in the fun. Outside, old men and women and several nuns pressed their noses to the windows and watched the gyrations inside. Marian was a bit disappointed at the disruption of her "traditional" celebration

The next day, Tashi and Marian received a blessing from the abbot of one of the Buddhist monasteries. He told them it was good for Westerners and Tibetans to come together and learn about one another. The couple continued the visa chase for a few months, until Marian's money ran low despite an infusion from Dad back home. Then she left, promising to send money, write consistently, and come back for him as soon as she had saved more money and he had a visa. I wondered what exactly Tashi would do in the United States. Could he find work there? How would he react to the gay and anarchist friends with whom Marian lived?

One morning Tashi told me that a Tibetan official had made a speech criticizing Tibetans who marry Westerners. The official did not say Westerners were bad, just that they were different, and that the refugees needed to preserve the race. It was shameful, the official said, that some Tibetans "deceived" Westerners. Tashi told me that while this was true, no one could accuse him of that. "If members of the government can marry Westerners, why can't we?" Tashi demanded.

Checks and letters from Marian came less and less frequently. Tashi moved out of his apartment and into the room of a friend. He attended the philosophy classes at the Tibetan Library, took English lessons with me, and slept a lot. Tashi confessed he felt aimless, but was helpless to do anything about it. If he returned to Tibet, he feared, the Chinese would put him in jail. Strangers stopped him in the streets and sarcastically asked: "Where's your wife? When is she taking you to America?" My wife and I worried about him and gave him some money when we left Dharamsala.

We sent him a letter and a check when we returned to the United States, but he never replied and the check was never cashed. Later we heard that his brother had come from Tibet and told him he was wasting his life in Dharamsala, that going to America was just a dream. Tashi returned to occupied Tibet with his brother, telling his Western friends they should not write.

TOURISM: PANACEA OR POISON?

Sweeping generalizations about the impacts of tourism are misguided. The growth of tourism has complex and contradictory effects specific to each locale, bringing both benefits and social and cultural changes that cannot be anticipated or controlled by the local community.

Dependent on the interest of outsiders, communities subject to tourism become highly image conscious. The idealized image many travelers hold of traditional societies—like the Shangri-la myth—contrasts with the reality of the contemporary transnational world, and the problems and conflicts that new interethnic relationships create. However, despite the critique of essentialist myths about indigenous peoples that is currently popular among Western academics, such myths are often tightly embraced by Third-World peoples themselves and used to unify them internally and elicit support externally. Tourism both promotes and challenges these illusions.

Despite the growing significance of the travel industry, tourism is but one variable of economic development, the most important of which remains the continued dominance of the global powers and the expansion of capitalism, the uneven concentration of land ownership, and increasing pressure on resources by population growth. It is clear, though, that the impacts of tourism on the lives of indigenous and refugee communities are significant and uneven. Traditional artistic and cultural expressions become bound to the demands of an international market in which Third-World communities are in a subordinate position. Class, ethnic, and gender relations are inevitably impacted by tourism and community divisions may be exploited by the industry.

Both the frivolous and considered actions of temporary visitors have serious consequences on the society, culture, and lives of Third-World communities. Both hosts and guests would do well to keep their eyes open.

REFERENCES

Aziz, Barbara
    1978   Tibetan Frontier Families. New Delhi: Vikas.

Bell, Charles
    1968   [1928]. The People of Tibet. Oxford: Clarendon Press.

Bishop, Peter
    1989   The Myth of Shangri-la: Tibet, Travel Writing, and the Western Creation of Sacred Landscape. Berkeley: University of California Press.

Sloan, Gene
    1995   International Travel Reaches Record Levels. USA TODAY. Jan. 25, 1995, Section D: 1.

Turner, J. and L. Ash
    1975   The Golden Hordes: International Tourism and the Pleasure Periphery. Constable, London.

INDIAN OR WHITE?

*Racial Identities in the
British Columbian Fishing Industry*[1]

Charles R. Menzies

INTRODUCTION

It's late in the evening and the five-man fishing crew has just crowded
into the boat's small galley. Everyone is tired but jubilant. The boat is
nearly full of salmon and by early tomorrow morning should be headed
to town fully loaded. It has been the kind of a day fishermen dream of.

After a hurried meal the men begin to relax. A bottle of liquor is
brought to the table. Each man pours himself a drink. Talk of the day's
fishing turns to remembrances of the past. I sip my drink and listen as the
skipper begins to tell a story.

"It was the end of August, 1953," says Robert Bruce. "I was up at John
McNab's place. Evert Jones from Canadian Fish—he was the fleet manager—asked McNab if he wanted a job running a company seine boat. We
were between things right then. What with the fishing shut down up
north we had nothing to do. 'If yah got a place for Bob here,' McNab said,
'I'll do it.' "

---

1. My thanks to Anthony Marcus—friend, colleague, and comrade in arms—for
his ongoing commentary on my work and for the hours of discussions we have
engaged in. Thanks is also due to Dr. Gerald M. Sider for his continued support
and advice. A special thanks to "Robert Bruce" and "Scott Mills" for being patient
storytellers and considerate sources throughout my ongoing work on the pressing
problems of the First Nations people. An earlier version of this paper was
presented at the Canadian Anthropological Society meeting in Vancouver, B. C.
in 1994.

The three men passed a half empty rum bottle around and the deal was done: "All you gotta do," Jones told the two men "is go out to Port Edward [a small town a few miles from Prince Rupert] and pick up a seiner. Get it all rigged, pick up a crew, and I want you boys to go down to the Straights for the fall dogs."[2]

At the boat Bruce and McNab found a family from a nearby Indian village living on the boat. The man and his family had fished the boat for close to ten years. They didn't own the boat but when the company had first hired him it had been accepted practice to allow a skipper and his family to live on the boat in the off season. But now, because of a decision made over a bottle of rum, Bruce was carrying the man and his family's belongings off the boat.

"That Indian guy just stood watching, crying. He tried to get us to leave everything on the boat, to go away. He told us that he needed a place to live. McNab told him 'It's just a job.' "

As the skipper talked he refilled our glasses. He paused, took a sip and continued his story:

"It was a hard thing to do. The old man could have been my grandfather, an uncle. Times change. Fishing changes and the company didn't want the boat tied up to the dock rotting away. They wanted the boat out fishing. That Indian guy didn't want to leave the north. But he didn't own the boat. It wasn't his decision to make and once he refused to take the boat south the company gave McNab a chance to run it. That's it. You either work or you lose out. I wanted to work."[3]

Robert Bruce's grandfather, Jonah Mills, a named hereditary chief from a north coast Tsimshian village, was in fact related to the family thrown off the fishing boat that night. In the space created by the passage of time Robert Bruce remembers the event with sadness. I have heard this story told many times and in several variations. Yet the fundamental moral remains: the "Indian" fisher was unwilling to adapt, he was an anachro-

---

2. The Straights is a reference to the long channel between Vancouver Island and the mainland called Johnston Straights that runs from Campbell River on the south to Alert Bay on the north. Fall dogs refers to Chum salmon caught in the months of September and November.

3. The man evicted by McNab and Bruce was caught by the changes then occurring in the industry. Up until then most of the fishing was regionally based. The companies owned boats which fished in set areas and when the local salmon runs were over the boats were tied to the dock until the next fishing season. In many cases, as in this example, the skipper and his family would be allowed a limited use of the vessel in the off season. However, as corporate control became more and more centralized redundant vessels were scrapped and the existing fleet was redeployed to take advantage of as much fishing time as possible. Skippers who didn't want to change their fishing styles were unceremoniously dumped.

nism in a modern world. Robert Bruce desperately wanted to move into that modern world and in so doing became "white."

Since its inception in the late 1880s, the commercial fishery in British Columbia has been characterized by myriad ethnic, racial, and regional divisions and alliances. Out of this cauldron of ethnic diversity the racial identities "white" and "Indian" emerged. Being "Indian," "white," "Asian," man or women continues to play a determining role in individual experiences and life opportunities; roles are not as firmly fixed as one might assume. The following illustration is as much a history of how a family has been cut apart by capital as it is a story about the creation and reproduction of race. This story focuses on two cousins: one, Robert Bruce, white; the other, Scott Mills, Indian. The life histories of these two men were collected in the course of fieldwork on the interaction between First Nation and Euro-Canadian fishers within the highly charged context of First Nations land claims (Menzies 1994). Their history simultaneously unites them as kin while segregating them by race. My aim in recounting their story is to highlight the historical processes that create such racial-ethnic identities.[4]

THE DEVELOPMENT OF THE
RESOURCE EXTRACTION INDUSTRIES

Underlying many analyses of ethnicity or race is an essentialist assumption: ethnic groups are static and unchanging. Once created, they are always there until the homogenizing force of state power erases their uniqueness. In practice the expansion and consolidation of state power both destroys and creates ethnic variation (Sider 1993).[5] The origins of ethnic groups are often found in brief moments of demographic dislocation or conquest. Their historical trajectory is not determined at the moment of their creation. Rather, it is shaped by the enduring day-to-day struggle over the changing ways in which ethnic identity is used to structure, limit, or privilege access to resources at the local level.

On the northwest coast of British Columbia, Canada, people of European and First Nations descent have come together and separated over

4. In this analysis I focus on a decidedly male point of view. Historically, anthropologists did not consider the implications of the gender of their respondents when writing about the fieldwork experience. For the most part, both anthropologist and respondent were male. Today it is widely acknowledged that gender plays an important role in shaping our lives and structuring our experiences (see, for example, Moore 1988).
5. The creation of the Métis on the Canadian prairies is a case in point. The Métis emerged as a people at the point of contact between the indigenous peoples and the incoming Europeans during the early fur trading period (see, Wolf 1982).

the years as the result of the historical movement of capital. Initial contact revolved around the "cash nexus," the exchange of commodities such as fur, iron, beads, or other trade goods. As European settlement extended into First Nations territories, marriages between Euro-Canadian business-men and First Nations women became increasingly common. According to several commentators, these early marriages followed customary First Nations practices and were ostensibly designed to facilitate trade and cooperation between groups (Fisher 1977).

The extension of industrial capitalism into this region fundamentally altered the basis of alliance. No longer valued as trading partners, First Nations were slotted into the developing resource economy as a subordi-nate part of the growing industrial labor force in which workers were segregated by race and gender. Union organizers and social activists have attempted with little success to overcome these structural divisions.

In British Columbia, a maritime-based fur trade structured the early con-tacts between Europeans and First Nations (1774–1858). In this period a European-based mercantile capitalism articulated with an indigenous kin-ordered mode of production,[6] in which the control of labor power and the production of trade goods remained under the control of the native American traders who were for the most part "chiefs." They "mobilized their followers and personal contacts to deliver . . . otter skins, and [their] power grew concomitantly with the development of the trade" (Wolf 1982:185). The merging of these two modes of production—one based on the family and one based on European capitalism—produced new wealth and intense inflation for both First Nations and Europeans (Fisher 1977: 18–20, Codere 1961:443–467, Wolf 1982:186–192). However, as Europeans prospered from this fur trade and developed modern industry, First Na-tions people lost control over trade and were displaced by a settler-based industrial capitalism.

Vancouver Island and British Columbia began the change from colo-nies in which Europeans exploited indigenous manpower to colonies of settlement in the 1850s following the discovery of gold in the interior of the province. With the exception of the fishing industry, First Nations labor power "was only of marginal significance in the economic concerns of the Europeans" (Fisher 1977:96, 109). Mining, forestry, and fishing sup-planted the fur trade and became the backbone of British Columbia's economy. By the mid-1880s indigenous control of land and resources was almost completely destroyed. At the same time First Nations people be-came integrated "into virtually every major resource industry in [British

---

6. The kin-ordered mode of production is one in which access to and control of labor power is mediated by relations of kinship. For an elaboration of this concept see Wolf (1982:88–96).

Columbia] as workers and owner-operators" (Knight 1978:10). Throughout the period of industrialization and until the early 1970s they were workers on fishing boats, and in fishplants, mills, and logging camps. Consequently, First Nations and non-aboriginal people were allies throughout most of the early twentieth century in class politics such as trade unionism that de-emphasized tribal allegiances.

Alliances between First Nations and non-aboriginal fishers have played a major role in shaping British Columbia's union movement in the fishing industry (Knight 1978:78). On the north coast First Nations fishers and cannery workers supplied the bulk of the early labor force. In 1896, 1897, and again in 1899, they played a prominent role in central and north coast fish strikes (Knight 1978:96–97). First Nations people were also decisive in turning the tide in favor of the Fishermen's Union in a critical strike on the Fraser River in 1900.

That Fraser River strike was important for two major reasons: it demonstrated that a multi-racial (ethnic) labor force could work together toward a common goal, and "for the first time, the canners had been forced to concede a share of their economic wealth to their employees" (Meggs 1991:66). After nearly thirty years of expansion, the industrial canning industry was an almost invincible force. Until the 1900 strike the large processing firms had dictated nearly all terms of employment, prices of fish, and conditions of work. Following the strike, however, the canning industry was confronted by a union movement that had transcended racial, gender, and regional bounds to act collectively in their own interests as workers.

This early example of multi-racial union building was part of an overall mobilization sweeping across the Pacific northwest. Swirling within this new unionism were tendencies as diverse as the syndicalism of the "Wobblies," the social fabianism of the traditional labor movement, and the more radical revolutionary socialism of the Second International Socialist Parties of Canada, British Columbia, and the United States. As opposed to the earlier craft unionism in which workers would join unions or guilds that only represented one particular craft (such as teamsters, carpenters, or masons), these new unions aimed to organize the entire working class under the umbrella of "One Big Union" whose ultimate goal was to overthrow their capitalist bosses and introduce workers' control. From our vantage point today such a goal may appear utopian. In the early decades of the twentieth century, however, the possibility of working-class revolution was not an idle dream. In the general strikes in Seattle, Winnipeg, and Toronto, the workers uprisings in Germany, Hungary, and Italy, and the revolution in Russia, open class warfare was the order of the day.

Union building in the fishing industry was most intense in the 1890s–1910s (led by the Second International Socialist Party of Canada) and in

1925–45 (led by the Communist Party of Canada). Organizers worked hard at building labor unions that included both First Nations and non-aboriginal. Although they were accepting of First Nations self-organization, most union organizers believed that First Nations people's interests were with the working class in general. In fact, from the 1890s until the depression of the 1930s First Nations fishers opted to join the unions rather than organizing separately (Knight 1978:96–97, Meggs 1991:41– 42, 62–70, Pinkerton 1987:262, and Clement 1986:38). They did not begin to organize separately until the mid-1930s. An important "turning point was the 1936 Rivers Inlet strike, viewed by white union fishermen as a major advance but recalled to this day in native communities as a serious betrayal" (Meggs 1991:155; see also Clement 1986:38, and Gladstone 1953:32).

The conflict between Euro-Canadian and First Nations union members was in part a product of the respective fishers' home-ports and the differing extent to which their entire families were involved in the fishery. A great many of the Euro-Canadians fishers lived in Vancouver. Each season they would ready their boats, leave their families behind and set sail for fishing grounds spread along the coast. First Nations fishers, on the other hand, mostly fished in or close to their historic territories. More often than not their entire family labored in the fishery either as fishers or shoreworkers. In the Rivers Inlet strike, First Nations fishers were concerned about the well-being of their families locked away behind picket lines: "we weren't allowed to go up to Knight Inlet to see our wives and children and we wanted to know how they were getting along. They finally settled it but we didn't make hardly anything at all because we had been tied up nearly all season" (James Sewid, quoted in: Meggs 1991:155). Following this incident the Pacific Coast Native Fishermen's Association was formed at Alert Bay on the south coast which later amalgamated with the north coast Native Brotherhood of British Columbia to form one unified coast-wide organization (Clement 1986:95, Meggs 1991:154-5).

The social impetus that gave rise to the Native Brotherhood emerged out of the trade union movement's inability to deal effectively with the problem of racism. Though union organizers attempted to include them in pan-racial organizations, First Nations' fishers ultimately found themselves in conflict with many of their Euro-Canadian coworkers. The major point of contention between non-aboriginal and First Nations fishers was the issue of land claims. Despite their common confrontation with capital as workers, they never developed a united policy on redressing the theft of First Nations territories and Euro-centric attacks against First Nations social institutions. While unions addressed some aspects of First Nations experiences as workers, they seemed incapable of confronting the racism and segregation of the new industrial society that was emerging in British Columbia.

(RE)PRODUCING RACE IN THE
COLONIAL ENCOUNTER

The struggle of First Nations people to regain control of their traditional land and resources brings them into conflict with non-aboriginals employed in resource extraction industries such as fishing. Non-aboriginals anticipate the loss of their jobs and the end of their way of life. First Nations people look forward to a better tomorrow in which they again control their traditional territories. Although media and political attention given to First Nations land claims issues have increased, "public understanding of these developments has lagged far behind the amount of information being disseminated" (Dyck 1986:32). These different expectations and understandings of the issues and the potential futures arise out of a particular socio-economic history in which "whites" and "Indians" have been functionally segregated according to the needs of capital.

Initially canneries relied upon an indigenous labor force, especially in the north of the province. Cannery managers would contract with local village or house leaders to hire entire families much in the same way as trading alliances had been organized during the fur trade period. This system quickly broke down in the south of the province under the onslaught of Euro-Canadian-American settlement. It remained the dominant mode of labor recruitment in the north and central coast, however, until the 1950s when "changes in labour supply, in markets for fish, in technology, and in government regulation rendered Indians less central to fishing and eventually to fish processing" (Newell 1993:206).

In their role as labor brokers for the canneries some First Nations leaders became part of a system of social differentiation in which they were able to accumulate wealth and assume names of higher rank. On the north coast, for example, motorized boats were not allowed in the gillnet fishery until 1923: "With the restrictions removed, the leading Indians purchased their own boats, often using their control of the labour supply in the competitive market to extract loans for the purpose from the cannery owners" (Tennant 1990:73).

Though some aboriginal "chiefs" thereby raised sufficient capital to purchase their own boats and then break free from the companies, most First Nations fishers could not. The reasons for this reflect the colonial relationship between the Canadian state and First Nations. Legal restrictions prevented First Nations fishers from borrowing money from banks, keeping them tied to the processing companies through debt. Changing fisheries management regulations and technological innovation combined, moreover, to push up the cost of operation, driving First Nations fishers out of the fishery (see, for example, McDonald 1994).

Fishers of European descent faced an entirely different set of conditions. While there were no legal barriers designed to prevent them from securing a loan to buy a fishing boat, the fish companies were able to maintain effective control over the Euro-Canadian fishers through a monopoly-like control of fish prices. As opposed to their First Nations brethren, Euro-Canadian fishers could not fall back upon subsistence base or home village in times of need. Most resource workers of European descent circulated between jobs in forestry, fishing, construction, or other semi-skilled industrial jobs. Their only effective resistance against exploitation within the market economy was collective organization, as in trade unions, co-operatives, or credit unions.

A vital co-operative and credit union movement in the Euro-Canadian communities following the Second World War created an avenue of escape for white fishers. Once out from under the economic control of the companies, an independent boat-owning class of predominately Euro-Canadian fishers developed. The longest lasting of these was the Prince Rupert Fishermen's Co-operative Association which in its heyday had a membership of more than 2,000 fishers and employed 500 workers in its Prince Rupert processing plant.

The fish canning industry in British Columbia has always relied upon a racially segregated workforce. While this produced immediate and pronounced benefits for the companies and their distant shareholders, it has not been in the best interests of either the First Nations or Euro-Canadian communities. The different historical links of Euro-Canadian and First Nations to the fishing industry has led to the current segregation of the fleet. First Nations fishers are more highly concentrated in the north and among the gillnet fleet. White fishers, though by no means absent in the gillnet fleet, predominate in the more capital intensive seine and offshore troll fleets. It is against this backdrop that the family history of Robert Bruce and Scott Mills must be read.

THE FAMILY CONNECTION

The two main characters in this illustration are related as family through one man: Jonah Mills, a named hereditary Tsimshian chief.[7] Jonah Mills' own life reflects many of the changes occurring in the aboriginal world in his time. Born in the early 1860s, he was orphaned at an early age during

---

7. Among the Coast Tsimshian people traditional property ownership is vested in "names" which are theoretically passed down matrilineally. Actual practice can be very different. Especially during the early part of this century the succession of names did not necessarily follow previous practice (see, for example: Garfield 1939 were she talks about the conflicts between Euro-Canadian inheritance laws and local laws and the problems of finding heirs). The importance of names reside in the fact that they actually embody a form of legal entitlement to real resources and their utilization.

one of the last battles within First Nations. In his early adolescence he went to live with a kinswoman and her Irish common-law husband in an Euro-Canadian settlement on the Skeena River. For most of his working life (approximately 1880 to 1920), Jonah Mills worked as a wage laborer in the northern sawmill industry. During this period he accumulated sufficient capital to purchase a gas-powered boat which he used to transport trading goods and supplies between north coast First Nations villages.

Robert Bruce, born in 1929, is Jonah Mills' grandson. Bruce's mother was one of four daughters from Mills' first marriage in 1894 to a Tsimshian woman called Sarah. All four daughters married Euro-Canadian men and subsequently were "de-registered" and lost their status as "Indians" as defined by the then existing Indian Act of the federal government. Scott Mills, born in 1923, is Jonah Mills' son from his second marriage to a Tlingit woman in the 1920s.

By aboriginal custom of the time, all of Mills' children and grandchildren from both marriages would have had rights to membership in a specific house and clan (Garfield 1939) and potentially rights to a named position. Under Canadian law, however, only the children of the second marriage were granted Indian status. As a result the grandchildren from Mills' first family were legally non-Indian though their cultural identity was somewhat more ambiguous.

Though Robert Bruce and Scott Mills are closely related, they are essentially members of two separate communities segregated by racial identity. Robert Bruce is tied to the circuits of exchange and social networks that socially and economically define him as "white." He owns a modern seiner/longliner; for the most part he employs white crewmen; and he fishes for an organization opposed to First Nations' land claims and a separate aboriginal fishery. Scott Mills is firmly entrenched in the "Indian" sector of the fishery. He mobilizes support and labor from within the First Nations community for his projects but lacks the individual capital required to gain access to the "white" business world.

This is not to say that the two men do not interact, share friends, or have business associates in common; they do. But, irrespective of their ancestry, one is part of the "Indian" world and the other the "white" world. Bruce's and Mills' cultural identities imply more than simply degrees of membership in "racially" defined communities. They reflect and have implications for the ways in which "Indian" and "white" families have become involved in the fishing industry.

While a few First Nations people are involved as owner-operators of the larger fishing vessels (see, for example, Knight 1978, Spradly/Sewid 1969, and Inglis/Assu 1969), in identity and how it is played out in the shape and reproduction of the fishery, "white" fishers behave in certain ways and "Indian" fishers in different ways. This division is reinforced (if not created) by federal government licensing policies that once excluded First Nations fishers by creating the food fish category in the late 1800s and then in recent years by creating special native licenses (see, for example, Newell 1993). There are broad class differences as well.

ROBERT BRUCE

Robert Bruce was surprised by the number of First Nations people at his mother's funeral in 1942. He knew his grandfather Jonah was "Indian" but had a poor understanding of his First Nations heritage. As an adult looking back on his mother's funeral he speaks in wonderment: "They came from all over to pay their respects to her and my grandfather. At the time all I could think was all these Indians. They all came up to me at the end of the funeral and shook my hand. My grandfather had wanted an Indian funeral. He wanted to take her and bury her in his village. My father said 'no, no way.' He didn't want none of that. 'She didn't marry an Indian,' my father told Jonah Mills, 'she married me.' "

A few days after the funeral Jonah Mills approached his white son-in-law and asked for permission to take Robert Bruce to live with him in the village, so that he could be groomed as Mills' heir; but his white son-in-law refused.

Robert Bruce had one other opportunity to live with his grandfather. A few years after the funeral Robert Bruce left school to work in a northern fishplant. At that time Jonah Mills invited Bruce to come live with him and work on the family beach seine, located about seventy miles out of Prince Rupert in Jonah Mills' hereditary territory. In an interview Bruce said: "I wish I'd have gone. It'd have been good experience but I had a job that paid good money and I didn't want to lose it."

Robert Bruce's life in the 1950s and 1960s was like many other Euro-Canadian men in the resource industries: he moved from job to job as the need arose. He skippered a seine boat in 1955, and in 1957 he was hired to run a halibut schooner owned by his father's boss, a local ship-chandler and fish broker. In a fashion typical to many of his colleagues he settled down after his marriage to a Euro-Canadian woman in the early 1960s and took a deck-job on a high earning combination halibut-herring fish-boat.

He bought his first boat, a fifty-five foot combination halibut longliner-salmon seiner, in 1967 with a loan from the local credit union. For the most part he has only hired crewmen of European origins. The few First Nations fishers who have worked for him were relatives. As a boat owner he became involved in a local fishermen's organization best know for its hardline stance against land claims and for its refusal to recognize union-called fish strikes.

Though he has lived for most of his life in the Prince Rupert region, he sees little of his "cousin" Scott Mills. The two men will on occasion meet each other on the street or in a cafe but for the most part they live in social worlds that do not overlap in any meaningful way.

SCOTT MILLS

Scott Mills' life, though parallel to his cousin's, reflects the differences of his "Indian" identity. Scott's childhood and early adulthood was structured by life in his father's village, by customs that limited his choice of wife, and by the legal restrictions that inhibited his ability to own real estate, raise a loan from a chartered bank, or vote. However, as Jonah Mills' heir he held a name of power in his community.

Scott Mills operated his father's beach seine until the depletion of the local salmon run caused the federal Department of Fisheries and Oceans to close it down in the 1950s. He then ran a company-owned gillnetter on the Skeena River during the summer sockeye season. When the company sold its gillnet fleet in the early 1980s he purchased the boat he was then running.

His marriage to a Tsimshian woman from a nearby village followed the protocols of an historic treaty between their respective "houses."[8] When Scott Mills inherited his father's name he assumed the paramount position both in his house and in his village. As a hereditary chief he rose to prominence in the local Native Brotherhood and worked toward establishing a council of hereditary chiefs.

CIRCUITS OF CAPITAL AND RACIAL IDENTITY

Over the course of the last century and a half industrial capitalism has become the defining system of global production. In its wake local cultures have been destroyed and re-created. In the Americas racial and ethnic identities (such as "Indian," "White," "Black," and "Chicano") have emerged out of a colonial encounter that threw together Africans, Europeans, and First Nations.

On a macro-scale the form of political organization and the creation and reproduction of racial identities have been shaped by the colonial process and the development of capitalism. We may speak with ease and familiarity of the colonial process and the manner by which Spanish,

---

8. The house is the basic unit of kinship and political and economic activity amongst the Tsimshian. In terms of kinship a house is a matrilineage of people so closely related that the members know how they are related. It is the house that owns property and access to this property is determined through a ranked system of hereditary names distributed through the feast or potlatch system.

British, French, American, Canadian, and other Euro-centric regimes wrongfully expropriated First Nations land. However, the brute economic reality of this picture leaves aside the trickier and touchier questions of how cultural identities were reshaped, transformed, and re-created in the colonial process.

Along the borderlands of the North American settler society capitalism has been engaged in a spatial and cultural restructuring of racial, ethnic, and local identities. In this processes identities have not simply been imposed. They arise in a context of resistance and accommodation.

European merchants in the fur trade grafted their own capitalist economic system onto the indigenous kinship based system of labor control and surplus extraction. In the transition to industrial capitalism these prior relations allowed for the creation of a divided industrial workforce, with important consequences for both "white" and "Indian" kin-networks.

Robert Bruce and Scott Mills' family histories outline how two men of essentially similar origins have been socially assigned different racial identities. These identities were not set at birth. Many factors intervened to shape and structure who became "white" and who became "Indian." Both men made choices within the social bounds established by a system of production that relies to this day upon a racially segregated workforce. Their choices are limited and the penalties for transgression are severe. For Bruce the assimilationist policies of the Canadian state denied him the legal status of "Indian" while simultaneously denying Scott Mills the right to vote or borrow money from a bank.

In his act of throwing his "Indian" kin off the seine boat, Bruce participates in a system that relies upon racial segregation to function and in so doing becomes irrevocably "white." At one point in his life he had an opportunity to chose a different path, to join his grandfather and live with him. Bruce chooses to be "white," to be modern and take a job in the cash economy. To do otherwise would be to turn his back on what he saw as the "the modern world." The dehumanizing logic of capital forced and manipulated Bruce into a position in which he threw his kinfolk off a boat and out of work. In "becoming white" he became part of the shock troops of capital and implicated himself in the European appropriation of this land.

Scott Mills also made choices within the social limits of his life. He accepted the customs of his house and honored their past treaties through his marriage. He would not have been alone if he had refused to follow custom. Many First Nations people have selected spouses who would have traditionally been considered either a brother or a sister. In accepting his past, Scott Mills also becomes subject to the humiliating and at times debilitating institutional racism of the Canadian state.

The stories of these two men are by no means unique. Their personal life stories illuminate a process in which industrial capitalism restructured kin-systems creating a social category "white" against which was posited a category "Indian." The dehumanizing and expropriating processes of colonial and capitalist development create the need and despite themselves open the space for the emergence of collective identities which may be class, ethnic, racial, or regional.

In British Columbia, despite attempts to build universalist working-class organizations, the dominant cleavages in the fishing industry have almost always been expressed in racial or ethnic terms (even in the context of labor organization itself). As the first step in shaking the beast of capital from our backs, local, ethnic, or racial identities may be useful. Ultimately, however, such identities only serve to shackle us to the divisions created by capital and turn us away from the fundamental sameness of our different lives, cultures, and identities and our common experience as workers in a capitalist society.

REFERENCES

Clement, Wallace
    1986   The Struggle to Organize: Resistance in Canada's Fishery. Toronto: McClelland and Stewart.

Codere, Helen
    1961   Fighting with Property: A Study of Kwakuitl Potlatching and Warfare, 1792–1930. American Ethnological Society Monograph #18, New York: J.J. Augustin.

Dyck, Noel
    1986   Negotiating the Indian Problem. Culture 6 no.1: 31–41.

Fisher, Robin
    1977   Contact and Conflict: Indian-European Relations in British Columbia, 1774–1890. Vancouver: University of British Columbia Press.

Garfield, Viola Edmundson
    1939   Tsimshian Clan and Society. University of Washington Publications in Anthropology 7 #3: 167–340.

Gladstone, Percy
    1953   Native Indians and the Fishing Industry of British Columbia. Canadian Journal of Economics and Political Science Vol. 19:1.

Inglis, Joy and Harry Assu
    1969   Assu of Cape Mudge: Recollections of a Coastal Indian Chief. Vancouver: University of British Columbia Press.

Knight, Rolf
    1978   Indians at Work: An Informal History of Native Indian Labour in British Columbia, 1858–1930. Vancouver: New Star Books.

McDonald, James A.
    1994   Social Change and the Creation of Underdevelopment: A Northwest Coast Case. American Ethnologist 21 (1): 152, 175.

Meggs, Geoff
  1991   Salmon: The Decline of the British Columbia Fishery.
          Vancouver/Toronto: Douglas & McIntyre.
Menzies, Charles Robert
  1994   Stories From Home: First Nations, Land Claims, and
          Euro-Canadians. American Ethnologist 21 (4): 776–791.
Moore, Henrietta L.
  1988   Feminism and Anthropology. Cambridge: Polity Press.
Newell, Diane
  1993   Tangled Webs of History: Indians and the Law in Canada's Pacific
          Coast Fisheries. Toronto: University of Toronto Press.
Pinkerton, Evelyn
  1987   Competition Among B.C. Fish-Processing Firms. *In* Marchak et al.,
          eds. Uncommon Property: The Fishing and Fish Processing
          Industries in British Columbia. Toronto: Methuen, pp. 66–91.
Sider, Gerald M.
  1993   Lumbee Indian Histories: Race, Ethnicity, and Indian Identity in the
          Southern States. Cambridge: Cambridge University Press.
Spradley, James and James Sewid
  1969   Guests Never Leave Hungry: The Autobiography of James Sewid,
          Kwakiutl Man. New Haven: Yale University Press.
Tennant, Paul
  1990   Aboriginal People and Politics: The Indian Land Question in British
          Columbia, 1849–1989. Vancouver: University of British Columbia
          Press.
Wolf, Eric
  1982   Europe and the People Without History. Berkeley: University of
          California Press.

PART
III

Identity and Consumer Culture

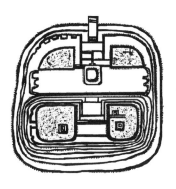

CONSUMPTION AND MIDDLE-CLASS IDENTITY

Shopping During Brazil's Economic Crisis

Maureen O'Dougherty

INTRODUCTION

In 1991, checking in at JFK airport on a flight to Rio de Janeiro, the middle-aged Brazilian man in front of me tried, unsuccessfully, to get the airline agent to dispense with the excess baggage charge—or perhaps it was excess weight, as the item in question was a microwave oven. Later, in São Paulo, I recounted the incident to a Brazilian friend. I noted that the man had tried everyone's patience with his erroneous assumption that he could talk his way out of the charges. The friend did not react until I derided the troops of Brazilians who return from the United States with mountains of merchandise. Then it was my friend's turn to become impatient. I later realized the North American arrogance of my position: after all, we are faced with the option of buying a readily available, reasonably priced microwave oven, or not, but in any case, we do not have to carry our houses on our backs intercontinentally.

The microwave incident was critical for me, as the confrontation made me start to think seriously about the relationship of middle- and upper-middle-class Brazilians to global goods and experiences.[1] Countless re-

---

1. This paper is part of my dissertation entitled "Middle Classes, Ltd.: Consumption and Middle Class Identity during Brazil's Economic Crisis." The dissertation documents the ways that middle-class Brazilians have engaged in defining and representing their class identity in an unstable context of chronically high inflation and recession. I would like to thank Francisco Alembert, Cristiana Bastos, Hélio Belik (deceased), Arlene Davila, Esther Império Hamburger, Yvonne Lassalle, Shirley Lindenbaum, and Lys France Portella for their stimulating comments and criticisms of this paper, and Gay Wilgus and Anthony Marcus for editorial assistance.

quests come to mind (for example, on one trip for high-top Converse All Stars and a hand vacuum cleaner), and I will recount a few incidents in order to consider what greater acquaintance with the "First World" and its goods during this past decade has entailed for Brazilians wanting that world for their country and themselves.

A decade of chronically high inflation (ranging from 100 percent in 1981 to the record of 2,700 percent in 1993) and recession made Brazil one of the most severe cases of the world economic crisis.[2] During the "lost decade" of the 80s and into the 90s, it fell from being the world's eighth to tenth largest economy. Periodically the government had to adjust to the accumulated inflation by decreeing "maxi" devaluations; this usually meant dropping off three zeroes, for instance, turning a 5,000 note into five. A given sum of money in 1967 (that is, before the crisis) was worth 80 percent less in 1992. So what to do to protect income and buying power? One strategy was to press for salary raises to accompany inflation. This met with differing success for workers of different categories. Another strategy was austerity. Indeed middle-class Brazilians did economize and work more to offset the salary erosions. At least one practice, however, was the reverse. In a country where few could invest in real estate owing to lack of housing financing, where savings accounts paid interest rates below inflation, and where many durable goods do not depreciate, a "strategy" of spending developed. In economists' terms, flight into consumer goods reveals avoidance of money. This fever to consume (as Brazilians put it less rationalistically and more judgmentally) extended to the international sphere. For despite inflation, recession, and salary devaluations on the one hand and governmental restrictions against, and heavy taxation on, imported goods, on the other, Brazilians have been increasingly pulled into the expanding transnational consumer market even during the crisis.

One question guides this discussion of the global dimension of the shopping system of middle- and upper-middle-class Brazilians: What is at stake in the consumption of transnationally obtained goods and experiences? I will argue that the stake is attaining social distinction through acquisition of goods associated with modern life (Bourdieu 1984, McCracken 1988, Friedman 1989, Wilk 1994). These consumption practices to attain social distinction and modernity are central to the realization of Brazilian middle-class identity, not only as symbolic means of presenting and proving status outwardly, but as the material means of securing and living it at home (see Frykman and Lofgren 1987, Wilk 1994, Rutz and Orlove 1989). This pursuit has a long history. Foreign goods and experience were significant to bourgeois-styled social reproduction in pre-

---

2. The Latin American average was 100% inflation in 1980 and over 1000% in 1989 (Nash 1994:12).

vious eras. Writing of Brazilian consumption of European goods at the turn of the century, the historian Needell (1987) reports that elites wore woolen suits in steamy tropical Rio de Janeiro. This striking example of status emulation reveals the importance of making symbolic class distinctions regardless of rationality. Our task is to consider the current relevance of international things for Brazilian middle classes.[3]

Continually encountering instances of transnationally-obtained goods, I found it reasonable to infer that nonlocal, nonnational elements are vital to contemporary Brazilian middle-class identity. At the same time, I checked local sources for emerging attitudes and practices relating to this consumption. As I will report, considering the expense and multiple risks of buying in Brazil and the continuing poverty there, the United States has become both a playground for leisure and a giant bargain basement for shopping. The material to be presented here counters the perspectives of some globalization theories which argue that new transnational forms of consumption will override influences on identity stemming from the local context. I will show instead that the terms or urgings for the transnational consumption, as well as the conflicts and significance, are in good part homemade.

EPISODE #1: CHRISTMAS SHOPPING

I was invited to spend Christmas 1993 with a family at their country home (*sítio*) outside of Embú, a town adjacent to São Paulo. Reiko [all names have been changed], daughter of Japanese immigrants,[4] social worker, mother of three, and married to a medical doctor, Ricardo, picked me up around noon of Christmas Eve day. We stopped by her parents' house to pick up the pork tenderloin (*leitão*) and visit for a bit. There in one of the daily newspapers, I noticed an article about a credit card company which had just held a number of raffles at the many shopping centers of the city.[5] The winners were to go the very next day to New York City to spend $4,000 in American dollars in one day's shopping. The news pointed out that this meant the winners had to spend 240 dollars per hour (in a sixteen-hour day) to avoid suffering any loss. This dramatic calculation struck me as particularly funny. On the TV report, one winner, a delighted

---

3. While I am sure that these practices to obtain foreign goods have parallels around the world, the particularities are of interest for understanding the phenomenon.
4. Thirteen percent of São Paulo's population is of Japanese descent; it is the world's largest urban center of Japanese emigration.
5. Brazil's first shopping center was built in São Paulo, and it dates from 1966. A shopping center boom in the 1980s brought the number in São Paulo to sixteen. These complexes themselves embody modern, First-World living.

teacher, was shown at the Shopping Center Norte, which is the most "popular" (that is, of the people) center in São Paulo's north zone. On the way to Embú, I discussed the raffle with Reiko. She said doing the trip for herself would be fun, but she would have her children in mind.

After dinner on Christmas Eve, Reiko casually passed her sixteen-year-old daughter Fabiana a gift: the perfume Volupté. Later she told me that it had cost seventy American dollars, and that she had ordered it from a *muambeira*. A *muambeiro/a* is the person who carries *muamba*. These are the quainter, lighter terms for contrabandist and contraband used preferentially for such cases. (*Muamba* is a Brazilianism, probably of African origin.) Reiko explained to her daughter that she had asked the *muambeira* to open it because she had heard of a case of someone buying perfume only to find a candle inside the box. Reiko had also ordered CDs from the *muambeira* from a list from her two sons. After the gift openings, Fabiana and her grandmother rewrapped the presents. I saw something similar at an Italian family's house: the European glass coffee pot (the push-down kind) was carefully put back into its original case after each use.

* * *

Let us consider first the presentation of international shopping practices in advertising, and then the middle-class means of obtaining foreign goods in Brazil. The intent of the Christmas promotional trip to New York City was to boost both credit card and shopping center usage. The $240 per hour calculation seemed designed to encourage viewers and readers to imagine concretely what their shopping strategies and buys would be in a more risk-free state than Brazil. In Brazil during the last decade buying anything, especially consumer durables, became complicated. In the United States people have the option of buying large appliances on a layaway plan or through a credit card loan. Precisely these purchasing methods were the most risky during the 80s and 90s in Brazil. Another informant, a bank administrator, described this extremely expensive method there: "For example a tape deck for the car. It costs 200 dollars if you buy it outright; if not, you pay in three installments of 90 dollars." Installment or layaway plans could also include interest applied as well as the store's reckoning of future inflation. In an economy of high and wildly fluctuating inflation, the smart shopper would have to have more than a calculating mind; she would have to be clairvoyant. The Brazilian news magazine *Veja* reported a man having bought a carburetor piece in 1988 for 900 cruzeiros. Fourteen months later he paid 72,000 for it—a 7,900% increase versus an inflation rate of 800% during that period (*Veja*, January 2, 1992). Such prices illustrate how merchants came to price their wares "defensively"; that is, they overpriced them to guard against future inflation losses. In Brazil, much as with the weather, an accurate forecast of future inflation was best made after the fact.

Besides rising with the fluctuating inflation rates, prices also varied from place to place. One day Ricardo arrived announcing to Reiko that prices for tires at three locations were CR$150,000, 75,000 and 60,000. In U.S. dollars, the price range was roughly from $40–$100. This variance demonstrates the logic of prices being raised "de acordo como as lojas quisessem," a friend explained wryly, that is, "according to the store's wishes"—in other words, any which way. As she put it, "let's say you go once and spend ten dollars on groceries. Another time you have no idea what you will be able to buy with that amount." Another informant said, "now when I stop at a newsstand to buy a chocolate bar and the guy says '200,' I have no idea whether 200 is a lot, a little, free, or very expensive. You lose sense of it."

Thus it seemed that even for the most common transactions one easily lost a sense of whether something was cheap, a good buy, or quite expensive. It was simply hard to tell: it was difficult unless one had reference to prices in a non-inflationary economy. Having come from an economy of low inflation, my reactions were different. When shopping for some innocuously simple item, I would often be quoted what seemed a jarringly high price, due to my reference to relatively stable prices. Brazilian informants from the younger generation (about thirty years old) often said they had only experienced adult life with high inflation; this unstable way of life with wildly rising prices was the rule. An informant of this generation (former secretary, now in sales) told me of a friend living in Switzerland who had made the following astonishing report: a can of mushrooms had cost 75 cents both ten years ago and today. Her husband (small business owner) added for emphasis: "not ten days ago, ten years." In the chronically inflationary economy, the question became not the "true" cash value of the item or even a reasonable price, but the price *today* ("Como é o preco hoje?").

Given the risks of buying through a layaway plan, the exorbitant interest rates (38 percent each month in 1991 and 20 percent in 1995), and the increasingly high cost of living, and finally, the risks of assault associated with being out on the streets of Brazil, the United States has come to offer bargain conditions as well as a playground of sorts. These conditions conspired to prompt middle-class people to become "international bargain shoppers." Hence the Christmas promotional scheme.

In sum, that advertising campaign served best, I would say, in inciting desires for shopping sprees in the United States, rather than the narrower intention of encouraging credit card usage. The advertising hype fit the Brazilian context in other ways as well. To buy frenetically, as the winner would have to do, was compatible with the "strategy" that expanded during the crisis known as immediatism in buying—that is, to buy when one had the rare, serendipitous combination of the money and a good deal. One final point: as is often the case with Brazil's media, it simultaneously acknowledged and abolished class barriers. The TV presentation of the winner was felicitous: what could be more (lower) middle-class than a school teacher, for whom the possibility of a trip to New York City is remote?

Those not able to travel can obtain imports, albeit illegally, either from *muambeiros* or, for a limited set of goods, from employees affiliated with the airport duty free shop. Such was the way another couple in the study bought a microwave. Reiko's Christmas presents and other instances I continually encountered during fieldwork attest to how routine the contraband practice has become, contributing to a burgeoning informal sector catering to the transnational tastes of Brazilians. But why the illegality?

Brazil has long had protectionist policies against imports, notably since the 1930s, in order to promote national industry. Only since 1990 has the government begun "opening" the market to foreign goods. Up until this time, imports of goods that were also produced locally were liable to such heavy duties at customs (as much as a 100 percent surcharge) as to effectively prohibit legal entry.

By these restrictions, Brazil was adopting an import substitution policy common in Third-World countries. Such development plans aimed to substitute for imported goods comparable ones made by fledgling home industries. In order to ensure that the population would buy these products rather than foreign made goods, governments often taxed the imports, or forbade their entry into the country altogether. Uninhibited by local or international competition, Brazilian industries gained a monopoly on their markets and could set prices (Baer 1989).

Though popular sentiment is currently very favorable to the opening of the market to foreign goods at international prices, industrialists and unions still exert pressures against it. An opinion poll of the *Estado de São Paulo* dated April 1, 1995, found a majority opposed restrictions on imports. A few months later, the metallurgy union of São Paulo staged a protest against car imports (*Estado de São Paulo*, July 31, 1995). In October 1995, front page headlines reported that products from the "Asiatic tigers," including domestic appliances, textiles, shoes, and rubber are held from the domestic market—which produces all these items—unless their prices are equal to or higher than domestic ones (*Estado de São Paulo*, October 2, 1995). With their characteristically satirical bent, the Brazilian newspapers called this practice "Operation Back Drawer." This news undoubtedly fueled popular sentiment against Brazilian businesses that are perceived as shielded by the government from foreign competition, guaranteeing exorbitant profits. In local understanding, imported goods would challenge the national monopolies and bring competitive pricing to the market.

Imported goods now sold legally in the country since 1990 are still taxed. In 1991 there was an 85 percent tax on stereos and beer; foreign made appliances were taxed at 42 percent in 1995, lowered from 72. In contrast taxes on imported cars were initially lowered to 32 percent but raised to 70 soon thereafter because of pressures from the car industry and unions (*Folha de São Paulo*, April 29, 1995). So even after the opening of the economy, imports of goods produced locally remain liable to such heavy duties at customs as effectively to discourage legal entry and purchase.

Customs currently allows Brazilians to bring in, tax free, up to the equivalent of 500 dollars worth of goods. Those returning with an excess of that sum may attempt informal, extralegal transactions with customs agents. There are two gambles at customs: one is to get the green light in the nothing to declare line. If the red light situation occurs, the gamble then depends on working with the official inspecting all baggage in order to get off free or with a pay-off, rather than pay a tax which would effectively wipe out the savings originally accrued. The safest bet is to have previously arranged with an official to go through customs without inspection. Agents even have a catalogue from a Miami publication with prices on relevant merchandise to consult for accuracy in verifying retail values.

Like the man with the microwave, Brazilians returning from U.S. travels typically have impressive amounts of baggage. Arriving at São Paulo's international airport to do fieldwork in 1993, I noted many travelers who, remaining undaunted at this last phase (after nine hours in flight), entered the duty free shop, later emerging with a case or more of Scotch (the prestige drink in this social sector).

Illegality at the airport borders has generally gone unchecked. Two incidents in the last years, however, have made front page headlines. Brazil's soccer team returned in July 1994 triumphant winners of the world cup; they also attempted to sneak in twelve tons of imported goods, and in fact filled five moving trucks with items including a refrigerator, washing machine, and gas BBQ range. President Itamar Franco wished to waive the duties (later estimated at one million dollars) for the national heroes, a position that further disgusted the public. In July 1995, the São Paulo newspapers reported that two sisters returning from shopping in the U.S. were pressured to pay the equivalent of 1,000 dollars to receive their bags from customs. Ensuing investigations at São Paulo's and Rio's international airports estimated that the customs racket afforded one million dollars in profit per day (*Estado de São Paulo*, June 26 and 27, 1995).

This fairly elaborate system of obtaining imported goods at international prices has a long history, making it perhaps not so troublesome to those long familiar with it as it may seem to outsiders. But there are novelties of scale and of the people involved. Brazil's middle and upper-middle classes have entered full scale into consumption of transnationally offered goods, engaging in what had been an elite practice originating in Europe. Why all this trouble? What is at stake?

It is curious that bringing these goods home for private use has entailed what is technically "white-collar" crime. For Brazilian travelers
themselves become *muambeiros* when traveling. I dwell on customs because it is the site where the class-directed tactic, one conflicting with state
policy, is exposed. Acquisition of these things is central for claims to a
class identity at or above the level of the individual or family in question.
The great and at times extralegal efforts of middle-class travelers testify
that imported goods and travel remain critical to the local status hierarchy
today. An additional sign of their ever increasing importance is shown by
the obvious increase in the occupation of contrabandist. This includes
both those who travel overland to Paraguay to buy goods in duty free
areas and then re-enter (without paying taxes on them) to supply merchants or resell directly, and those who travel by air to the United States
for the same purpose.

We must also consider why these particular goods. Observations from
various trips to and from Brazil, photographic evidence at airports, visits
to 47th Street Photo in New York City and downtown Miami, and fieldwork (including an interview with a *muambeira*) show that these are now
the favorite items: large screen TVs, VCRs, personal computers, camcor-
ders, FAX machines, cordless phones, cellular phones, microwaves, stereos, CD players and CDs, clothes, tennis, and more tennis shoes, toys,
and everything for beauty, hygiene, and health from drugstores.[6] These
goods can be categorized as the latest in fashion for the body and the
latest in hi-tech home appliances. As for the appliances, anyone can tell
you that the brands available nationally are considered inferior, or the
range too limited, or the specific item is not made; or again if the imports
are now available locally, that their prices are prohibitive. Given the circumstances of attainment and the national context, these might well be
called modern luxury goods.

Appadurai proposes that these goods are of note mainly for what they
communicate socially. He suggests that "we regard luxury goods not so
much in contrast to necessity . . . but as goods whose principal use is
rhetorical and *social*, goods that are simply *incarnated signs*" (1986:38). It is
interesting that the luxury-need distinction and the symbolic-material one
collapse so perfectly with consumer durables. At a popular level, brand-
name tennis shoes have become obligatory and attainable, as have theme-
park tee shirts; at the other end of the spectrum, are imported cars, an
unrealizable desire for most, yet so incessantly debated in the Brazilian
media one would imagine otherwise. Besides things presented on the
street which support claims to social distinction through goods associated

---

6. Some of these imports are targets for theft, especially tennis shoes and cellular
phones. More than one informant told of a child returning home from school
barefoot after a tennis shoe assault.

with ("first world") modern life, there are those which stay at home, another central arena for working out middle-class identity.

These foreign goods are not only arguments of status in public; they are important in private home consumption. Analysis of the impact of the introduction of such goods in Brazilian households is outside the scope of this article. Suffice it to note here two issues. One is their value as miniature investments in a period when real estate investment was out of reach and car prices exorbitant. I would also point out the very different function of such items in a home in which a domestic servant works. Issues arise since the items do not "replace" the maid, as the modernist aim might be, but coexist uneasily. For instance, the middle-class owner of an appliance such as a Cuisinart often fears the maid will lack the knowledge to use it or be careless and break it. This special attention calls to mind the preciousness of such goods.

Consider briefly the practice of keeping imported goods—examples are perfume and a coffee maker—in their original packaging for some period of time. Such care as given to the rare and exotic makes it seem as if they are sacred, in a way not usually associated with mass-produced goods. The efforts to keep the appliances in unworn, new condition oddly recalls the care given to antiques. It may be that through this practice owners are making the goods somehow nonconsumables, turning them into quasi-permanent objects of value. The special value of the imported becomes even more obvious when the price is low and rarity lacking. Note the preference for Crest when Brazil makes Kolynos, "basically" the same thing. In short, the consumption of these goods is an index of the very strong desire to live with, or better, to incorporate modernity on an intimate daily basis.

At another level, these shopping practices raise questions concerning the impact of globalized consumption on those world areas importing the goods. Consensus would now have us go beyond perspectives of Third-World countries that see them either as traditional, hence resistant to modernization, or as victims of "first world" exploitation. Both these views only allot the active and historical role of change to the "first world," leaving the rest passive (see for example, Nash 1981, Hannerz 1989, and Appadurai 1990). Yet power differentials between the regions remain. We must await economists' determinations about the impact of foreign goods on national business and employment.[7] But the people in question, Brazilian middle- and upper-middle-class consumers, have not

7. The trends seem familiar, especially with regard to hi-tech goods, as the magazine *Veja* (April 28, 1993) reports: "Until 1989, 95% of Gradiente TV parts were made in Brazil. In 1993, 80% are now imported. Production costs lowered, quality went up and prices went down. [. . .] Gradiente once had 9,000 employees. Today it has 2,700."

only been incorporated but have jumped headfirst into the "global flows." Let us consider one more brief episode in order to reflect further on the place of international things in this society and culture.

EPISODE #2: VELVET FLORIDA ROADS

After finishing high school, Marcos, a twenty-year-old engineering student at the University of São Paulo (USP), went to the U.S. with his cousin, a travel agent. He claimed they had driven from Miami to Orlando (a 230 mile drive) in just 2.5 hours. Waving his arm out to span the horizon, he recalled fondly, "The roads there are like velvet." After this warm recollection he remembered with annoyance that he had spent an entire day of his week trip looking for a 27-inch-screen TV. Including tax it cost less than $400 but in Brazil, he said, it would have cost $1,200. His plane ticket was only $400, so, as he put it, the trip was free.

* * *

The best way I can emphasize how great is the desire to travel internationally is to point out that besides Florida, which has the complicating, perhaps overriding draw of Disney World, Cancún has recently become a target vacation spot. Brazil has more than 7,500 kilometer miles of coastline, most of it breathtaking and diversely so. Famed for bathing, boating, and body watching, the beaches draw international visitors. Brazilians often told me with indignation that a trip to the northeast coast would run higher than an international package deal to Florida or Cancún. In fact, the airfares are comparable: round trip from São Paulo to northeast cities runs $500. Flights to Miami or Orlando often advertise that rate. People are aware that their nation's leisure spots are more accessible to foreigners than to themselves. Yet on the other hand, as Marcos's discussion indicates, Brazilian travelers frequently rationalize travel expenses abroad as absorbed in the low costs of items bought in the United States portion of a trip. Indeed such was increasingly the case as Brazil's inflation developed. By the time a successful plan ending inflation had finally come into effect (as of July 1994), domestic prices were so high and the dollar so low that travel to and shopping in the United States became even more accessible and no less "necessary."

Just as with goods, the international travel experience is also a critical milestone for middle-class social identity. As usual, the TV program "Cassetta e Planeta" (roughly comparable to "Saturday Night Live") looked satirically at this trend by comparing it to military service. It said in November 1994: "A trip to Miami—not even military service is as obligatory." ("Viagem a Miami que nem servico militar: é obrigatório.")[8] Nearly 335,000 Brazilians did travel to Florida in 1995 (Florida State Division of Tourism). Also instructive was a comment of a Brazilian friend who came to the U.S. that year. She said: "well, now I will no longer have to put up with people saying, 'when I was in New York. . .', or 'when I was in. . . .' " The verbal display of international experience and knowledge is perhaps as operative as goods for claims to social distinction.

There is a hierarchy of distinctions with respect to travel. While Europe remains the ultimate cultural experience, New York is now surpassing it in popularity. Ostensibly, one goes to these places for cultural pursuits, and to Orlando-Miami for theme parks and shopping. A friend called those who travel to the United States for consumer rather than touristic purposes "sacoleiros do ar." The translation I offer, "international bargain shoppers," gives an equivalent meaning, but it loses two local references. The government-subsidized discount warehouses for fresh fruits and vegetables, called "Sacolão" (literally big bag), are outlets where shoppers fill their bags and buy according to total weight, obtaining a better bargain than in the supermarkets for selected items. "Sacoleiros" are those who come with bags to these bare warehouses. The phrase "do ar," "by air," recalls lower-middle-class people and informal sector merchants noted earlier who go by bus to buy duty free goods in Paraguay. This expression teases the (upper) middle classes by likening their air travel to these cruder images. Such scoffing, some of it self-directed, has become a favorite pastime of self-conscious sophisticated Brazil.

Yet it seems to me that what is desired by the Cancún travelers is not solely economizing while gaining social distinction, but rather the First-Worldly, out-of-Brazil experience (Campbell 1994). By going to Cancún or to Florida, one may miss the untouched beauty of the deserted beaches of Brazil's northeast, but at the same time avoid the deep poverty of this less developed part of the country.

CONCLUSIONS

The continuing expansion of modern consumer goods to all parts of the globe has spurred various predictions. Some have celebrated the spread of goods and styles as a way of breaking down older status markers relating to class. The great quantity and worldwide circulation of goods and consumption experiences led the sociologist Featherstone to envision a blurring of distinctions and the "deconstruction of symbolic hierarchies" (1990:18). I argue on the contrary that Brazilians have long been adept at

---

8. By law military service is required in Brazil for all men. In practice most middle- and upper-class men manage an exemption; the poor men who usually serve often have willingly chosen to do so as it does provide paid employment.

adjusting international goods and travel experiences to local hierarchical classifications. Rather than effecting a departure from these classifications, the goods continue to mark class and status differences. Implicit in this perspective, moreover, is a notion of an increasing consumer democracy, goods entering more and more households. At least the desire for them has increased if not the means for mass acquisition.

Others have insisted that the spread of goods is leading to an internationalization of culture overriding national boundaries. A recent analysis finds that the dominant transnational businesses are encouraging consumerism by inculcating a sense that one's worth is related to engaging in particular forms of consumption,[9] including new global experiences. Certainly Brazilians are responding to the expanded consumers' market and its media, which engage an imaginary worldwide standard about what grounds the middle class, what special experiences it should have. It has been suggested that these trends in transnational business reveal the declining importance of the nation. Yet it is clear from the Brazilian case that the demand for foreign goods and travel, their impact and meaning, derive in good part from the national context.

In a nation where stability is out of the picture, where Brazilians have lost faith in an increasingly internalized daily life and, specifically, were blocked from consumption practices so central to the realization of their class identity, one means of bypassing national blockages has been through the circuitous, informal attainment of international goods through international travel. Latin American theorists have argued that consumption entails social conflict over the products of a society (see, for example, García Canclini 1995)—to which I would add that it also generates conflict over that which the society does not produce or provide access to for all citizens.

This discussion has emphasized both class and transnational differences for the simple reason that the nation-state is pivotal with respect to the means of appropriation of these goods; as to class, their acquisition both depends on and reinforces these differences. Furthermore, I find that the tactics as well as the intensity of the significance attached to these goods and experiences relates both to class and to the nation. For again it seems that middle-class Brazilians have become especially attached to "things international" in part to compensate for or even to surpass the nation-in-crisis. The decade-long crisis kept them grimly facing a Third World at home that constrained their ability to achieve First-World modernity but fanned their desires for it. This dilemma defines the First

---

9. As Rouse puts it: "an extension and intensification of a general ethos of consumerism, an attempt to persuade more people in more profound ways that their worth as persons is intimately linked to their capacity to acquire and consume particular kinds of goods" (1995:365).

World–Third World hierarchy as acknowledged by middle-class Brazilians. Indeed, these international goods and experiences prompt the Brazilians who have them to revalidate these terms.

REFERENCES

Appadurai, Arjun
    1990   Disjuncture and Difference in the Global Cultural Economy. Public Culture 2(2):1–24.
    1986   The Social Life of Things: Commodities in Cultural Perspective. New York: Cambridge University Press.

Baer, Werner
    1989   The Brazilian Economy: Growth and Development. New York: Praeger.

Bourdieu, Pierre
    1984   Distinction: A Social Critique of the Judgement of Taste. London: Routledge, Kegan Paul. [1979]

Campbell, Colin
    1994   Capitalism, Consumption and the Problem of Motives. In Consumption and Identity. J. Friedman, ed. Chur, Switzerland: Harwood Academic Publishers, pp. 23–46.

Featherstone, Mike
    1990   Perspectives on Consumer Culture. Soviology 24(1):5–19.

Friedman, Jonathon
    1989   The Consumption of Modernity. Culture and History 4:117–130.

Frykman, J. and O. Lofgren
    1987   Culture Builders: A Historical Anthropology of Middle-Class Life. New Brunswick: Rutgers University Press.

García Canclini, Néstor
    1995   Consumidores y Ciudadanos: Conflictos multiculturales de la Globalización. Mexico: Grijalbo.

Hannerz, Ulf
    1989   Notes on the Global Ecumene. Public Culture 1(2):66–75.

McCracken, Grant
    1988   Culture and Consumption. Bloomington: Indiana University Press.

Nash, June
    1994   Global Integration and Subsistence Insecurity. American Anthropologist 96(1):30.
    1981   Ethnographic Aspects of the World Capitalist System. Annual Review of Anthropology 10:393–423.

Needell, Jeffrey
    1987   A Tropical "Belle Epoque": Elite Culture and Society in Turn-of-the-Century Rio de Janeiro. Cambridge: Cambridge University Press.

Rouse, Roger
    1995   Thinking Through Transnationalism: Notes on the Cultural Politics of Class Relations in the Contemporary United States. Public Culture 7:353–402.

Rutz, Henry and B. Orlove, eds.
   1989   The Social Economy of Consumption. Lanham, MD: University
           Press of America.
Wilk, Richard
   1994   Consumer Goods as Dialogue about Development: Colonial Time
           and Television Time in Belize. In Consumption and Identity.
           J. Friedman, ed. Chur, Switzerland: Harwood Academic Publishers,
           pp. 97–118.

MI GENTE

Economies of Space, Identity, and Labor among Youth in Andalusia

Yvonne M. Lassalle

I learned about young people while sitting in a plaza in Córdoba, a city of about 200,000 people located in Andalusia, the southern-most region in Spain. This particular plaza, the *la Plaza del Museo*, got its name from its proximity to the Archeological Museum, located within the city's historical section. Youth from various parts of Córdoba gathered in the plaza all year round, but on spring afternoons and summer evenings it would be particularly crowded. Young people would cluster at *"el Museo"* just before or right after lunch and dinner to meet with friends. They would bring their bicycles and motorcycles, their musical instruments and their favorite pets, but most importantly their liters of beer—which they bought at nearby candy stores—and change to buy hash. With all "necessities" at their reach, they would sit with their *"gente"*—their "people," their clique—or talk to other friends and acquaintances for hours on the park's many bleacher-like steps and benches. They would talk about their lives, share jokes, make plans for the coming evening or for the future: taking a bicycle ride to the countryside, a camping trip, setting up a band or opening a small business.

The large number of unemployed and underemployed working-class youth who spent their leisure at *"el Museo"* reflects the lack of employment in Andalusia. This situation is not new. Steady economic decline since at least the nineteenth century left what was once one of the richest regions in Spain one of the poorest in Spain and in Europe. In 1936, a dictator, Francisco Franco, led a successful military takeover then won a brutal civil war that lasted until 1939. The war left the country terribly impoverished. The dictatorship instituted some programs of economic growth, but they had little impact in Andalusia, where there was little industry and most people worked as laborers on large agricultural estates. During the 1960s, meager wages drove over two million Andalusians out of the region. The situation changed somewhat after the dictator's death in 1975. A democratic government came into power and attempted to improve both the political and economic situation of Andalusians. Spanish society changed dramatically. The Spanish economy grew in the 1980s, standards of living increased, and democratization granted citizens civil liberties and freedoms which had been denied for over thirty-five years. Spanish society was dramatically transformed.

Nowhere was this transformation more visible than in youth culture. One person I interviewed remembered that in 1973 he was harassed by a police officer for discreetly kissing his girlfriend at a bus stop. Yet a friend who had just turned fifteen in 1982 described his adolescence: "It was a wild time. The streets reeked of pot, and everywhere people were making out, doing all kinds of drugs, shooting up in all kinds of places. If you walked on the streets, you could get mugged by gypsies,[1] by junkies, or by the police." Heavy metal and punk filled the streets, their lyrics giving voice to the chaotic experience of many youths as old ways of behavior became obsolete with little to replace them. Even Andalusia, where the transition seems to have been somewhat less chaotic and traumatic than in other places in Spain, felt the impact. Young Andalusians speak of "a generation lost to heroin," people but five to seven years older than themselves.

When I lived in Córdoba in the early nineties, the economy had declined. Unemployment was over 30%, even higher among the young. The youth culture was much calmer, yet people from all social sectors and political persuasions still condemned youth leisure practices. Conservative Andalusian discourse was predictable: today's youth are lazy; they do not want to work; drugs have destroyed their minds. However, I found much the same moralistic discourse in many who considered themselves progressives and had been deeply involved in the youth scene of the late 1970s and 1980s. The plaza was seen as the crystallizing of everything that had gone wrong, personifying the evils of democracy. The youth, hanging out for hours on end, smoking and drinking, were con-

---

1. Gypsies are an extremely underprivileged group in Spain. For centuries they have been victims of prejudice and discrimination. Racist comments such as this one are not uncommon.

tinuously described to me as *despreocupados* [careless] or even *inconcientes* [unaware, lacking consciousness]. These young people were squandering the democracy for which their elders had fought so hard. Of course there were no jobs and no prospects, but what were these young people doing about it? Nothing, I was continually told. They were just "dead weight," or else "driftwood being carried back and forth by the tides." Nothing good would come from my associating with them. I was wasting my time with completely uninteresting people.

I also was uneasy about these young people's use of their leisure time for, as with many stereotypes, the "outsiders'" perception of the plaza's denizens was pretty true. The plaza atmosphere was indeed oppressive, heavy with social deviancy and defeat. On Sunday mornings, when *el Museo* was deserted except for the older, poorer, and more marginalized, this sense of social defeat was painfully evident. However, outsiders were not acknowledging how much of this leisure time was enforced, created in fact by dismal employment opportunities and an educational system severely out of step with the needs and wants of these young people. Furthermore, youths often used their time in creative ways, given their meager circumstances and prospects. Few of those congregating in the plaza drew continuous and unambiguous satisfaction from the daily lazy routine hopelessly repeated, sunny day after sunny day. Most of these young people had plans for their lives which they knew required more than just hanging out. Nor were they impervious to social expectations that they become independent, establish a household, and even help in the support of their parents, all of which required employment. The alcohol and hash, which these young people used to blot out the immediate reality and its dismal prospects, only momentarily slowed them down.

These young people were actively and creatively seeking employment and remuneration, even if time and time again most of their job searches and money-making schemes fell flat. And as they grew older, they went to the plaza less and less, seeking more established, agreeable, and respectable places to hang out. All in all, the image of the *Museo* as a "dead end" street oversimplifies, even misunderstands, the young people at *el Museo*. In the pages that follow, I will describe how young people attempt to use their enforced leisure creatively, how they used their time in spaces like *el Museo* as well as outside of it: going to school, working, looking for formal work, or making a living outside the formal labor market. I believe, however, that spaces such as *el Museo* define even as they are defined by, the social position, values, and worldview of those who use them. Such spaces are integral to how young people see themselves and how they portray those they would distinguish themselves from or associate with. The activities that take place within them are also central in social and media representations of youth's everyday life.

El MUSEO

Young people hung out in the *"Museo"* for well over ten years. They shared it with a smaller group of older men, usually addicts or other petty criminals, who came to the plaza either to sell the youths drugs or to vicariously enjoy the *"vidilla"*—the life, the excitement—that young people brought to the park. Although the plaza had an eerie timeless sense, it had seen dramatic transformations during the last decade. Young people remembered fondly when *la Plaza del Museo* was a charming, typical Andalusian garden with a beautiful small spring rising slightly above the floor, its water flowing in four directions. Barely landscaped shrubs and foliage trees made the park a cozy and welcoming place. Back then the historic district where *la Plaza del Museo* is located had been abandoned, and most of the surrounding buildings were dilapidated. Poor and working-class men frequented the many bars and taverns to socialize, eat, drink, and according to my friends, listen to flamenco music. Youths in the late 1970s and early 1980s, attracted to this seamier side of life, became avid patrons. Democracy brought public funds and a local government determined to rescue the historic district from what it considered ruin. Gentrification rapidly made the neighborhood one of the most expensive real estate locations in the city.

The houses surrounding the plaza were sold and renovated and the archeological museum was refurbished and reopened. But authorities remained preoccupied with the plaza, viewing it as a foci of delinquency. So, like many other spaces in Córdoba and throughout Andalusia, it fell victim to postmodern design. The charming garden my friends described became an open space of gray granite, roughly divided into two sections. To the south, was an open area surrounded by bleacher-like steps. Beyond was a more clearly defined square where large individual trees stood as islands of nature amid the granite. At the center of this square stood a three-tiered fountain. Overturned and broken columns and pieces of stone such as are found in a collapsed Roman construction, hot in the summer and cold in the winter, served as benches. The overall impression was of a fluid if somewhat lunar landscape, a place to be admired from afar, certainly not to welcome human use and interaction. To the young people's credit they transformed this sterile and inhospitable place into a home of sorts.

El Museo once attracted a heterogeneous crowd, but it always seemed divided into zones clearly marked by the practices of their "regulars."

When I first knew *"el Museo"* it was divided into two "user areas." Youths and those who hung around with them occupied the largest area which was loosely subdivided into smaller sections where different groups of friends regularly congregated. This was less a matter of territoriality than of custom, and people would often congregate in different spaces, for various reasons: inclement weather, time of arrival, desire to speak to or avoid another group or person, the cleanliness of the plaza that particular day. A local bar had carved out the second smaller "user area," marked by plastic chairs and tables. This attracted a slightly older, more established clientele of thirty-something couples often with their children, as well as tourists seeking out the shade of its large trees.

Users of these two areas rarely mixed. Bar customers would occasionally wander over to greet and chat with friends hanging out around *el Museo* and perhaps buy some hash; and sometimes, when the young people could afford to buy—and treat others—to beer and drinks, they would sit on the granite benches or overturned columns close to the bar (not on the chairs) and consume. This separation was partly self-imposed. The young people derided the atmosphere of family life and stability of the bar's terrace and the patrons looked down upon the marginality of many of the plaza's denizens. Nor were the bar owners shy—they could not be—about making the unseemly and nonconsuming unwelcome in their area. And many youth could ill afford the bar's prices, though they were extremely reasonable.

LA GENTE DE MI PANDA:
THE ORGANIZATION OF
FRIENDSHIP AND SOCIALITY

Early in my fieldwork, I became close friends with a *peña*, (*panda* for short) a close group of friends who frequented *el Museo*. As has been described for other regions of Spain (Hansen 1977, Kasmir 1993), social relations among young people tend to be organized into small, tightly knit nuclei. Often formed in the neighborhood, these cliques can be consolidated much later in junior high or high school. People in these *peñas* hang around with one another constantly, and while friendships and relations can be established outside the group, those within them tend to take precedence. Best-friend pairs, while common in a *peña*, can in fact be broken and reconstituted with other members. Members refer to those within the *panda* or *peña* as *mi gente*, or *la gente*, though *la gente* can also refer more generally to "people" as in the phrase, *"allí es donde va la gente"* (that is were people go).

The *gente* of the *panda* with whom I became friends were in their early twenties, though they interacted quite closely with some people in their early thirties. The group shared similar family backgrounds. Most came from upwardly mobile working-class homes.[2] Internally, the group separated itself into *las niñas*, the girls, and *los niños*, the boys or the guys. The girls themselves belonged to a *"peña"* in their neighborhood. I became friends with seven of them: Pilar, Puri, Carmen (these three were sisters), Rafi, Anabel, María the Tall, and María the Short. All except Anabel lived quite close to one another in a neighborhood of working- and middle-class families which had been built in the mid-sixties. Several of them chose to attend an experimental high school which combined technical training with the standard curriculum offered in high schools tracked for college preparation. The school was well-regarded for its training in visual and performing arts. The young women recalled it as a "bohemian" scene: a cult of "artistic creation and creativity"; a turn to drugs as protest and as source of inspiration; and a fair amount of political debate and awareness. Indeed, the most memorable political intervention for these young women was the high school students' strike in support of the general strike of 1988.

Here they met the other "half" of the group, "the boys." While some of the boys—Manolo and Sancho—had also been neighborhood friends, others began to hang out while at school. Dani, for example, after falling out with his previous *panda*, a much rougher and tougher crowd, sought out this new clique. Two brothers, Manolo and Paco Marco, joined the group in high school as did Yupi. The *peña* became consolidated when a couple of the boys become attracted to a couple of the girls. Shortly after the two couples started spending more time together, a wider group formed,

---

2. In 6 of 9 families, one or both parents had migrated to Catalunya during the early stages of their work life but had returned to Andalusia to marry and start families. (One of the *peña* had been born outside of Andalusia, and a couple of others had lived in other areas of Spain as children, but none claimed to be influenced by this.) During this time the parents had acquired training and other expertise which had facilitated their economic takeoff upon return. Three of the fathers were working or had retired as workers for the railroad company; one was working in construction as a master carpenter; three of them were involved in sales or other white-collar private-sector service jobs, and two otherwise employed supplemented their income with small businesses; one had died many years ago. Some of the mothers worked sporadically as cleaning women. Only in one family had both parents completed post-graduate education, and they worked as art instructors at the high school where the *peña* had met and come together.

which included some of the neighborhood girls who had not gone to this high school. The *peña* had seen several tempestuous relationships and break ups, one of which was a long-term homosexual relationship between two of the women, and numerous other inter-group flirtations.[3] Toward the end of my stay, the strains of growing up, the departure of some members for reasons of work or school, and unresolved tensions between group members had many of them lamenting that "*la gente está muy perdía*," meaning that our people don't hang out, don't socialize together anymore.

A friend whose sister's boyfriend belonged to this *panda* introduced me to it. At that time, the group preferred a cultural association named *Juan XIII* as a hang out space. *El Juan*, as they called it, was a site for underground and clandestine political activity during the dictatorship and, to a lesser degree, after democracy. The *panda*, who imagined themselves as "bohemians," artists, musicians, and writers who pursued their craft in marginal settings and in alternative ways found *el Juan* particularly well suited for all these activities. This young crowd associated the space with difference and to a certain degree exclusivity—even if it was political and not social. Furthermore, it was centrally located in a beautiful old house in an old neighborhood known as *San Francisco*, just as historic but less gentrified than the area around *el Museo*.

Here they would smoke hash and drink beer or wine, discuss the latest book they had been sharing and reading—Henry Miller and Paul Bowles were popular authors—stage impromptu jam sessions or work on a collaborative writing project. This project consisted of a series of notebooks that they were writing and illustrating. It contained short stories, poems, essays, jokes, veiled and open critiques of each other, and general information pieces. It was not a fanzine, for it did not circulate except among the group itself. Just as often my friends chose to hang about joking and playing cards and dominoes. While the boys did consume significant amounts of hash and beer, the girls sipped pacharán (a blackberry liqueur) and anise, occasionally asking for a puff. Anabel, capable of smoking and drinking any of the boys under the table, was an exception.

There were crucial gender differences in educational achievement, wage earning expectations and strategies, as well as in general attitudes about work. The primary nucleus of the group consisted of seven women and five men. Three of the girls had received scholarships, two in fine arts and one in theater, at highly competitive schools in Seville; three others

---

3. I found that it is quite common for members of such groups to behave rather "endogamically" in their early stages, although members increasingly seek partners outside of the group as they grow older. This is also a source for separation from and disintegration of the group, as we shall see later.

studied special education in Córdoba; the remaining one studied voice-over and dubbing in Madrid, but was also an accredited radiotherapy technician. The contrast with the young men was startling. Of the five, only three had finished high school and of those only one had passed the college preparatory course. One had gone off to study fine arts in Seville with his two women friends. Shortly before I returned to the United States, two other of the "boys" had begun to study at a local private music conservatory.

As a group, they embraced the identity that in youth culture is known as "bohemian." They considered themselves to be artists, intellectuals, clearly superior to other of their peers who had lesser minds and talents. They conspicuously borrowed from the style of the 1950s and 1960s counterculture, particularly what in the United States became called "the Beats." Most of their clothes as well as their instruments and books were purchased in flea markets and secondhand stores. But they defined themselves most clearly in opposition to a constellation of possible lifestyles and worldviews. They took great pains to distinguish themselves from those who they called *hipis*. This was curious since many young *hipis* I met seemed to share similar tastes in clothes, and many were also quite interested in music and performing. However, according to my friends and many others I spoke to, the *hipis* were unkempt and uncouth, and they often accompanied the term *hipi* with the adjective *asqueroso*, filthy. This was partly because many people they identified as *hipis* lived on the streets, and were indeed unbathed. However, I think just as important was that *hipis*, more or less of their same age and perhaps not from dissimilar class backgrounds, were a reminder of their dire employment perspectives and precarious social positions. Indeed, I heard people, only half-jokingly, despair: "*Aquí hay que dedicarse a hipis*" (here we become *hipis* to survive.) Not surprisingly, *hipis* were seen as somewhat dangerous and untrustworthy, always hoping to scam an unsuspecting victim. *Hipis* often slept and earned a living performing or begging in the spaces that my friends and others chose for leisure and relaxation. This also meant that outsiders would lump all users of *el Museo* together.

Hipi was also the name given to sellers of cheap crafts and trinkets in the streets and markets. Many of these itinerant vendors were in their late thirties and early forties, and had become small-scale entrepreneurs, making profits that seemed considerable in the eyes of many youths. This did not endear them to my friends, who purchased some of these wares but resented the profits made at their expense. This form of engagement with the market they claimed was beneath them. They defined themselves as strictly "mental" laborers, and fondly if humorously accepted my epithet of "street philosophers."

For these same reasons they also looked down upon many of their peers who settled for steady jobs, objecting to what they saw as their work ethic. "*Currante*" and "*currito*" were some of the labels they bestowed on their peers who held steady working-class jobs. Manolo, for example, once described himself to me as "*parado*," [unemployed, but also and perhaps more importantly in this context, idle] though he was working forty hours a week. He argued that being *parado* was an existential attitude; Andalusians these days, he asserted, had lost that sense of enjoying idleness which had characterized them. "You see," he told me as we were sitting in "el *Museo*" on a Tuesday afternoon, shortly before he had to return to work, "a *currante* would not be sitting here in the middle of the day sipping a *tinto de verano* (wine with ginger ale). He'd be home with his parents, or worse, his wife, taking a *siesta* after having eaten, or watching a soap or something equally deplorable." Manolo, just as working-class as the hypothetical "worker" he described, deplored how the "worker" allowed his job, his labor to regulate his life, reducing him to drudgery and alienation.

The plaza of *el Museo* also attracted *okupas*, a group of squatters who had taken over a building not far from *el Museo*. Perhaps the most openly anti-establishment youth, they actively cultivated an aggressive, anti-social aesthetic that was drawn partly from the British punk scene but more specifically from the particular interpretation this music and aesthetic received in northern Spain. They criticized the current state of politics in Spain as repressive and oppressive, economically and politically. Considering themselves anarchists, they believed in communitarian living enforced by a minimal, local consensus governance, not elections. They openly displayed anarchist symbols and icons on their clothes and made constant reference to the anarchist resistance during and immediately after the Civil War. Like the Civil War era anarchists, they offered free housing to whomever needed it. They also provided an open space for young people to gather, socialize, and learn a wide variety of crafts and skills such as puppeteering and other "circus arts," as they called them, leather work, English, and playing the guitar, electric bass, or drums. These skills were meant to provide means for young people to support themselves with some independence from the capitalist market economy, which the *okupas* strongly opposed.

My friends, the "bohemians" from *el Museo*, had a very uneasy relationship with the *okupas*, viewing them as too aggressive and violent. I was often told that you never knew when "one of those *punkis*" (as the *okupas* were also called) was going to pick a fight or go off on a destructive frenzy. Indeed, my friends saw the *okupa*'s anti-establishment rhetoric as no more than a justification for their violent and destructive behavior. They shared neither the *okupa*'s interest in history nor their passion for politics and had radically different outlooks about work and leisure. While both refused to define themselves by the labor they performed, the *punkis* did not object to manual labor, rejecting only the conditions under which it usually took place: in a factory, or for an independent contractor. Indeed, the *okupas* were attracted to the circus in part by their desire to find a space that would challenge the standard separations between work and leisure, and so prove that work need not be drudgery.

Next to *el Museo*, in fact, directly behind the archeological museum, was another popular spot, *la Plaza del Séneca* or simply *el Séneca* named for the headless statue of the philosopher that occupied a pedestal over the plaza. Located on a steep incline in the outskirts of the historic section, *el Séneca* was made up of three open squares joined by steps and flanked by benches and hedges at either side. It was considerably smaller than *el Museo*, and used almost exclusively at night, as a place were the clientele from a nearby a bar, known as *Plateros*, would spill over. Despite their proximity the atmosphere was markedly different at each plaza. For one, the *Séneca* was rarely used during the day. When I asked people in the *Museo* about this, they would argue that *el Museo* was more hospitable than *el Séneca*: it was bigger, had more trees and fountains. I believe that equally important was that the *Museo* was further away from the street. But there were other differences: of class, work, politics, and worldview.

People who frequented other plazas disputed the boundaries drawn by the "bohemians" of *el Museo*. Some who hung out at *el Séneca*, even those friendly with "bohemians," viewed *el Museo* mostly with distaste. To them, it was dirty, dark, and there were too many *tiraos*, outcasts, marginalized unkempt people such as *hipis* and drug peddlers. They might occasionally purchase drugs from the outcasts, but the frequenters of *el Séneca* wanted to uphold boundaries of class, values, and morals.

Those of *el Museo* did not have any specific label for the people of *el Séneca* and did on occasion spend time there. They prefered *el Museo*, they said, because *el Séneca* was too crowded, and that those who went there were *"más pijos."* To be *pijo* meant to be wealthy, to be children of good families, very much *"niños (as) de papi y mami,"* that is, daddy's and mommy's little girls or boys. In fact, the crowd at *el Séneca* was not a wealthy crowd, but working- and middle-class young people who were slightly more conforming to social norms and did not identify with the quest for marginality that many of the youths who hung out at the museum embraced. The true *pijos* preferred the terrazas and the club scene near their neighborhoods, which was at some distance from this area.

My friends also spoke of another identity which was very distinct in their minds, that of *modernos*, or modern. While the "bohemian" emphasis on contemplation demanded an aesthetic of disinterest and passivity, the *modernos* pursued a very fast lifestyle of late night partying, often turning into weekend-long marathons of intense dancing, drinking, drugs, and revelry. If one takes seriously the youths' equation of modernity with the lifestyle of this group, then modernity for youths implies immediate gratification, conspicuous consumption, stark individualism and, most clearly, an enormous importance placed on appearance.

The *modernos* spend a considerable amount of money, whether their own income or their parents', on clothes and leisure.[4] Seeing this, my friends debated about the class background of the *modernos*. Some argued, they were not always *pijos*, born wealthy. Many held nine to five jobs, but in their consumption habits they appeared as people who had no worries about money. Furthermore, there were plenty of *pijos* who were *horteras* (tacky). But there was no denying how expensive the *moderno* lifestyle was. *Modernos* seemed to do most of their socializing in clubs, where drinks were considerably more costly than in terrazas. Furthermore, they often took part in the coastal club scene, which involved very expensive weekend-long binges of drugs and alcohol.[5] Considering that some did this once or twice a month, it became clear to me that the *modernos* possessed considerable disposable income.

BUSCANDOSE LA VIDA:
WAGE EARNING STRATEGIES

While in other countries in Europe, much of what has been called "subcultural innovation" (Hebdige 1977) relied financially on individual wages or on the support of the welfare state, in Córdoba few youths were fully independent economically or were able to live off state assistance. Among my friends, the "girls" were more active participants in the job market, willing to accept a wide variety of jobs. This work was part of the underground economy that included cleaning private homes, piece-work in the jewelry industry, temporary secretarial and other office work, and part-time positions at campgrounds during the summer. Not one was

4. It is widely held, and supported by statistical evidence, that youth in Spain spend over two-thirds of their resources in clothes and leisure activities. However, among the groups of young people I frequented this was certainly not the case. They were avid shoppers, but of the secondhand stores and *mercadillos* and had highly developed standards for what was expensive and what was not. In my experience these statistics were skewed toward middle- and upper-class consumption habits.
5. On two separate occasions I accompanied some young people in these weekend sojourns. On one of such weekends, the average amount of money spent by the young men was around 300 dollars, which included $50 for accommodations and about $10 in gas. The rest was spent on food and beer, though they only ate one full meal a day, and it was never over $5. Clubs sometimes had door fees, but most did not. Thus, they spent close to $200 in drinks and drugs in two-and-a-half days. Women spent somewhat less, for they were treated more often.

able to find fully regulated and compensated employment. The "boys" did not fare much better. Among those who had not finished high school, one worked selling ceramic flutes at the entrance to the Cathedral mosque for a local manufacturer. He was only paid after selling a specified number of flutes. His earnings were highly irregular, and a police crackdown on itinerant vendors further damaged his business. His friend who also had not finished high school sometimes sold flutes for him, but was basically dependent on his parents. He had on occasion supplemented his income as did two other of the "boys" by work as a migrant farmworker in France during the apple picking season.

Indeed, the government, through the state employment office and local programs, was looked upon as the primary source of employment. Both my female and male friends relied on the temporary employment lotteries, known as *bolsas de trabajo,* held periodically by the municipal and provincial governments in which they could look for unskilled clerical and menial labor such as gardeners, nurse's aids, and sanitation and public works jobs. Chances of obtaining employment in such lotteries was slim. However, registering for a government sponsored lottery made one eligible for a paid worker re-education program. Young people were very ambivalent about such programs. While participants received a minimal salary and the possibility of a job, the instructors were often considered incompetent and intolerably boring. Although technically people could indicate which programs they desired, in reality jobs were assigned through another lottery system. My friends and many of their friends saw these courses more as punishment than as leading to potential wage earning opportunities. Many people I spoke to agreed that the more selective worker retraining programs sponsored by the Unions were consistently better. But Union members had precedence here, and remaining spaces usually went to children or friends of Union members.

Parental neighborhood or workforce networks provided important sources of employment information and opportunities for young people. Neighbors who knew of friends with unemployed children often came knocking at the family's door with news about possible jobs or the latest deadline for employment lotteries. I saw this network at work on several occasions. In one instance, my friend Celia's mother came looking for her at the neighborhood bar where she knew we were having coffee. A friend of her neighbor had just seen a "Help Wanted" sign at a local boutique. She insisted Celia change her clothing and present herself immediately. My friend grudgingly followed her mother and, through a glowing recommendation of another neighbor who knew the owner, got the job. It lasted until her predecessor returned five months later. This was not uncommon. These jobs invariably were either short-term or very poorly remunerated, and young people saw them as less appetizing than the possibility of landing a full-term government job, which until quite recently came with guarantees of tenure.

Of the entire group, only one of the "boys" had work that was on the books offering full work benefits. He worked as a radio dispatcher at the headquarters of a tow truck company. However, his hours, from noon to 8:00 p.m., were highly undesirable and his job some distance outside the city often forced him to walk there or pay for a taxi. He had been hired through a government program whose stated purpose was to provide on-the-job training for youths. Such programs usually amount to a government subsidy for private enterprise or a cheap source of service and clerical personnel for the government. This was made amply clear with the *contratos de aprendizaje*, the apprenticeship contracts instituted in 1994. In the name of job creation, the government allowed business to pay people from the ages of sixteen to twenty-five less than the minimum wage and reimbursed the businesses for half the wages of every employee hired under this program. In common parlance, these jobs were called *contratos basura*, junk contracts.

Given the dire prospects of employment, my friends and their peers came up with a variety of strategies to supplement parental support. A common one was selling crafts. The "girls" experimented with this strategy one winter, deciding to sell jewelry made out of beads. So they pooled their resources, set out to Seville and purchased all the necessary equipment. Some of them even made their own beads out of papier-mâché. All fall they made earrings, bracelets, and necklaces. As the time grew nearer, some problems and debates emerged. Some argued that prices should be calculated by adding an agreed upon percentage to the cost of the materials, others felt that it should be calculated on the basis of labor. A very interesting debate emerged about what would be "fair" earnings, and what was a "reasonable wage." Those who opposed the idea of calculating a wage argued that it would be difficult to gauge what wage they should have been paid per hour; some were much more productive and skilled than others. Should they then be paid more? What were fair earnings? How were they to be distributed?

With all these questions unsettled, the time came to set up their stand at the arts and crafts fair sponsored by the city in one of the main pedestrian malls. Disappointment was immediate. Interest was high; sales were meager. They discovered that in another fair similar jewelry was being sold for less. Competition and consumer conservatism were not the only problems they faced. The stand was not officially authorized, for the price of renting out a space was way beyond their means. The owners of stores in the area complained bitterly that the arts and crafts fairs were hurting their business. A local weekly publication ran an article arguing that Córdoba was beginning to resemble a Third-World city because of all the street vendors. Police increased their vigilance in the market area, confiscating their goods several times.

The last day of the market I stopped by to offer moral support and warm beverages. But I could not find them. Fearing the worst, I ran to the police precinct. Seeing that they were not there, I called one of their homes, where they were hanging out. They informed me that they had decided to quit the business. When I saw them later that day, they said it had been too hard, and it wasn't worth it. They were barely making anything and had started fighting among themselves. Furthermore, one of them had been grounded when her parents found out what she was doing. Apparently, a neighbor had seen her selling jewelry at the stalls and had asked within her mother's hearing what kind of a person goes to sell junk at a stall? "Gypsies, Moors, good for nothings."[6] The lady ended her tirade by saying that the girl needed a job. But that was precisely what she and her friends had wanted in the first place.

They were also tired of the "boys" mercilessly teasing them. Indeed, their male friends considered this kind of economic activity problematic at best. Part of their derision seemed to have to do with issues of respectability. For example, they rejected out of hand my suggestion that as a group they all get together and perform in the streets for money. As happened to my women friends, they might be seen by a neighbor or acquaintance and that person would then "forever look down upon you."

Given the meager prospects for employment, young people often remained for a long period of time under their parents' roof until they were ready to marry and set up an independent household. This was a burden to many households since most families I became acquainted with in my study were quite large by contemporary Spanish standards (the average size was six, but they ranged from five to nine). In some instances the continued stay of grown offspring was a strategy on the part of parents, who expected and often received some support from their working children. But this was by no means always the case. As one would expect, these working-class families exerted great pressure on youths to contribute to the general household income. In one particularly large household the eldest son, who was partners with his father in the family business, and the eldest daughter, who had recently completed the University with flying colors and was heading toward a highly paid teaching position, were both pressed to delay their marriages. The son's marriage would mean either increasing his salary or bringing at least one more into the household, both options beyond the family's means. In the case of the

---

6. Like gypsies, the *moros*, "moors," the name given to North African immigrants, mostly Moroccans, who have been arriving in Spain in increasing numbers, are subject to enormous social prejudice and discrimination.

daughter, the father insisted that after being put through school she had to repay the debts incurred by contributing to the education of the younger siblings.

Yet I also found just as many working-class parents who were not comfortable receiving help for household expenses from their unmarried children who remained at home. One parent said of his working daughters' continued insistence on contributing to general household expenses, "It just makes me angry. It is my responsibility to support this family. When I am old, decrepit, or dead, that will be something else then." Older siblings complained of just the opposite: that their younger siblings, now in their twenties, were spoiled and not pulling their weight in the family. Interestingly, many parents were far more lenient with their sons than with their daughters. Time and again many of my women acquaintances complained of their brothers contributing less or not at all to family subsistence. It seems that the traditional social expectation that women will be more involved in household activities has translated into a greater pressure to contribute to the family coffers. And yet, when I asked parents if they would take measures to force the offspring out of the household, they seemed absolutely appalled. And parents seemed keenly aware of the difficult economic situation their children faced.

At first glance, I thought that young people were not in much hurry to leave their parents' homes. Home life provided enormous advantages, and parents, however vocal about their opinions, quite often respected those of their children. Young people enjoyed considerable leeway in their everyday home life, and received enormous emotional and financial support from their mothers. Many of my young woman friends reported having "friendships" with their mothers, and often relied on her complicity when engaging in activities that the father might not approve, such as extended vacations, new clothing, even late nights out. Young men also relied on their mothers' support, though they usually had great freedom or were left to their own devices altogether. But even in the most lenient of families, privacy was rare, and young people deeply resented this. The search for a space of their own, which they could share with lovers and friends, drove many to seek separate living quarters. This did not always imply financial independence from parents, however. I noticed how some of the *okupas* and other young people would return to their parents' home for meals and even an occasional overnight stay.

Young people moved out of the parental residence for two principal reasons. One was going to college. This move was not always permanent, for after graduation the young person would more than likely move back in, unless he or she was ready to set up an independent household. A romantic attachment was the principal and most permanent form of independence. In this situation, most people waited until the chosen residence, invariably an apartment, had been totally furnished before moving in.

Setting up household together did not necessarily involve marriage, although it often did. If the young couple was purchasing the apartment, they often owned the actual space and took over a year to equip it before marrying or setting up residence. Otherwise, all the necessary equipment and furnishing would be purchased and then an apartment would be sought out to rent.

The inability to procure housing and private spaces for interaction was what made the plazas and open spaces so important. Youths claimed these spaces as theirs, and did things that in other contexts would have occurred in more private spaces. However, the powers that be—the state, local government, the mass media, neighbors, and even parents—often conspired to control even such spaces. In late 1993, a new local tax on terraces drove the owners of the bar to close down its open-air tables, making a dramatic difference in the plaza's ambiance. The young people took over most of the space, but in doing so made it a much less central part of neighborhood life. Toward the end of my stay in Córdoba, in the summer of 1994, constant police raids in an attempt to crack down on the sale of hash in the neighborhood had made the plaza undesirable, not only because it was "criminalized" as a space, but because it was no longer possible to purchase hash there. Thus, as fewer and fewer young people hung around *el Museo*, it became more and more marginalized, to the point were it in fact became an undesirable place to visit.

SOME FINAL THOUGHTS

I have attempted to offer a picture—more of a snapshot really—of how young people in Córdoba interpreted and acted upon the reality that shaped their everyday lives. The ways young people used space to define boundaries of friendship and to create identities for themselves and others offered a running commentary on their values, their life expectations, their views on work and even their class identities. These definitions of friendship, space, and identity were shaped by an implicit debate about the proper relations between work and leisure. These definitions were not always fixed or precise, but they helped locate a person or group within a broader constellation of hierarchical relations. How young people went about creating friendships, using public spaces, being at leisure, looking for work, and cultivating specific tastes and styles all pointed to the limits of their acceptance of prevailing definitions of reality in Spanish society. These practices also highlighted the ways in which young people challenged and conceived alternatives to the limits this reality imposed on their everyday practices and their expectations for the future. In other words, I argue that although the various aspects of youth culture I discussed might appear to be superficial and restricted to issues of "lifestyle" or "pure aesthetics," they reflect instead an incipient critique of the social and economic situation of Spanish society.

REFERENCES

Hansen, E.
    1977   Rural Catalonia under the Franco Regime. Cambridge: Cambridge University Press.

Hebdige, D.
    1977   Subculture: The Meaning of Style. London: Routledge.

Kasmir, S.
    1993   The Myth of Mondragon: Cooperatives, Politics and Working Class Life in a Basque Town. Ph.D. Dissertation. Graduate School and University Center, City University of New York.

MacLeod, J.
    1995   Ain't No Makin' It. Boulder: Westview Press.

Roszak, T.
    1969   The Making of a Counter Culture. Garden City: Doubleday.

Willis, P.
    1981   Learning to Labor. New York: Columbia University Press.
    1990   Common Culture. Boulder: Westview Press.

HEMMED IN AND SHUT OUT

Urban Minority Kids, Consumption, and Social Inequality in New Haven, Connecticut[1]

Elizabeth Chin

THE VIEW FROM THE 'VILLE

One summer afternoon during a rainstorm, Natalia and Asia sat on Natalia's stoop and talked about Barbie. It was a sultry afternoon in the Newhallville neighborhood of New Haven, Connecticut, the kind where the humid air hangs as wet and heavy as the rain itself. Often referred to as the "'Ville" by local kids, Newhallville is a neighborhood whose population is overwhelmingly black, with many poor, and a reputation for suffering the gamut of inner-city ills. Characterized by multiple forms of isolation—geographic, social, economic, and commercial—the inner city is an "other" place intimately tied to the rest of the nation, and the rest of the globe. Kids like Natalia and Asia are aware of these connections, but cognizant as well that the complex and contradictory circumstances of their lives often leave them at a disadvantage.

Newhallville residents have access to the same TV programs, the same stores, and the same goods that most other Americans do, but their re-

1. This work was generously funded by dissertation grants from the Wenner-Gren Foundation, the National Science Foundation, and the Graduate School and University Center of the City University of New York. Mary Weismantel has, as always, given critical feedback in both senses of the word. The children and families among whom I worked in New Haven have been my mentors in all that I do. Their patience and kindness have been limitless and my debt to them is limitless as well.

lationships to these consumer goods—and the process of consumption itself—is distinctive. Natalia and Asia's comments about Barbie keenly express these girls' own sense of where they are located in the world, and in relation to consumption:

> ASIA: You never see a fat Barbie. You never see a pregnant Barbie. What about those things? They should make a Barbie that can have a baby.

> NATALIA: Yeah . . . and make a fat Barbie. So when we play Barbie . . . you could be a fat Barbie.

> ASIA: OK. What I was saying that Barbie . . . how can I say this? They make her like a stereotype. Barbie is a stereotype. When you think of Barbie you don't think of fat Barbie . . . you don't think of pregnant Barbie. You never, ever . . . think of an abused Barbie.

As Asia and Natalia were talking about Barbie, they were holding my tape recorder. "I would like to say that Barbie is dope," Natalia said, "But y'all probably don't know what that means so I will say that Barbie is *nice!*" A few minutes later, Asia had taken on an Oprah-like persona and was pretending to address an invisible, nation-wide television audience. "The streets . . . of Newhallville . . . next on the Asia show," she intoned with the same sort of dramatic, overblown mock solemnity pioneered on daytime talk shows.

These girls' dialogue reveals their awareness that this imaginary audience knows little about the character of Newhallville or the people who live there. Asia's stance is critical, playful, and ironic all at once. She knows that the Oprah audience is not interested in "the streets of Newhallville," as they are and how she experiences them, but rather they want to see and hear about "The STREETS . . . of NEWHALLVILLE. . . ." Likewise, Natalia recognizes that such audiences literally do not speak her language, and she roughly translates the richly evocative "dope" as the equivalent of the nearly image-free word "nice." The girls' ability to play with important consumer media—television, for instance—while on home turf is important, particularly because they did not play with these media in other settings, specifically the mall. Similarly, while at home they do not play with themes of sex and romance which in the neighborhood are threatening, oppressive forces. However within the confines of the mall, their romantic flights of fancy are powerfully imagined and playfully pursued as they indulge in long boy-chasing episodes and richly imagined romantic fantasies.

The neighborhood influences in specific ways the nature of the girls' engagement with the consumer sphere. The girls' overt and often-discussed fear of rape made it evident that they feel vulnerable in Newhallville specifically because they are young and female. "Do you know why men rape little kids?" Tionna asked Natalia one afternoon. "Because they can't talk, they can't say anything." Natalia, after a moment's consideration, answered, "well they rape girls, and women, too." Newhallville children are hemmed in at home, interacting with a consumer culture that rarely acknowledges their existence. In their own neighborhoods, girls did not use consumer goods as a medium for either romantic fantasy or playful exploration of sexual themes. Rather, Barbie was invoked when girls gave voice to their sense of sexual danger and to their profound awareness of being disenfranchised from mainstream Euro-American culture.

At the mall, Newhallville kids are shut out in various ways. Here, the discomfort and threat experienced by these girls emanates not from men, but rather from the stores and employees. And yet, the open, airy, and generally controlled space of the enclosed mall seems to allow the girls a sense of physical safety they do not experience in their own neighborhood. It is this sense of safety, perhaps, that provides one impetus for their freewheeling romantic fantasies, and their extended boy-chasing escapades. This contrasts sharply with the tension and discomfort they generally feel when in stores or when shopping.

Newhallville children undertake consumption under the same circumstances that shape all other aspects of their lives: in the midst of wrenching economic change, rising social unrest, and in the continuing, and some would argue deepening, atmosphere of racism. Both New Haven's downtown mall and its troubled urban neighborhoods are the direct and indirect result of decades of federally funded urban renewal projects undertaken by city administrations. The effect of policies shaping the economic, geographic, social, and commercial context of New Haven has not been neutral. As money has poured into a struggling downtown, Newhallville and other areas have had to deal with shrinking school budgets, poorly maintained roads, and public libraries that hardly ever opened their doors. A changing economy, too, has left both New Haven and Newhallville short on jobs for the semi-skilled and unskilled workers who once filled factories and workshops. New Haven embodies many of the conflicts presently experienced in cities and towns that were once happily expanding at the forefront of the industrial revolution, boosted by two world wars. Few companies in New Haven make anything any more; its primary industries are the production and dissemination of knowledge—taking place at Yale University—and health care, which takes place in the city's hospitals. Though growing, neither of these employers is prepared to provide replacement jobs for those formerly employed in industry. The result has been a dramatic and precipitous rise in the unemployed and poor, most of whom are minorities.

The blame for the city's condition has most often been laid at the feet of minority community members, and nowhere is this more clear than in the conflicts taking place over the rehabilitation of the New Haven mall. Malls, as places specializing in the simulation of gracious civic life, are not often meant to include those from all socioeconomic levels, ethnic groups, or subcultures. The New Haven mall is, ideally, a place from which Newhallville's children are absent. As a result, a variety of strategies for maintaining the mall's atmosphere impinge directly on the lives of children like those from Newhallville. These include preventing public transportation access; regulating shoppers' style of dress; regulating access of youth; playing music certain groups are thought to dislike; closely following and watching youthful and minority shoppers as they browse in stores. All of these strategies make Newhallville children's experiences in the mall unlike those of their better off or lighter-skinned peers.

The growing social science literature on consumption often points out that "we think we are free when our choices have in fact been consciously constructed for us . . . this is a dangerous illusion of freedom" (Tomlinson 1990:13). Some see malls—the consumer meccas of our time—as presenting this "dangerous illusion" with particular effectiveness (Williams 1982). For Newhallville children, however, these places—particularly when compared to shopping in their own neighborhoods—actually *do* offer a great deal of choice, albeit choice that is at some level circumscribed and predetermined both by a corporate entity and capitalism at large. At the same time, such choice is, however, not to be confused with freedom. For these children (and their families) these stores offer often painful glimpses of what they might be able to get if they only had the money.

Based upon ethnographic research conducted among black and Hispanic ten-year-olds in the Newhallville neighborhood of New Haven, this essay details the ways in which local, city-wide and national conditions in economy, geography, and social conditions set the scene for children's consumption practices and experiences.

NEW HAVEN

Connecticut has the nation's highest per capita income, but the impressive concentration of wealth in the state is rivaled by oppressive concentrations of poverty. Housing, education, jobs, and commercial districts are unequally distributed as well. These inequalities are starkly evident in New Haven.

Located eighty miles northeast of New York City on the shore of Long Island Sound, New Haven is a medium-sized city with 130,000 residents. It is the seventh poorest city of its size in the United States; for cities over

100,000, New Haven ranks first in the nation in infant mortality (Reguero 1994).[2] At the same time, New Haven is home to one of the nation's wealthiest and most elite educational institutions, Yale University. The city also possesses a bustling drug trade, a bankrupt shopping mall, a struggling downtown area, and deeply troubled public schools. Once a manufacturing-based town producing tires, beer, paper, apparel, and bagels, New Haven's population has shrunk by over 20,000 since its peak in the 1950s and the primary employment sector is today service-based.

NEWHALLVILLE

With a reputation as one of the poorest and most troubled areas of the city, Newhallville's residents (91.7 percent of whom are minority) have a median household income in 1990 of $20,569; 26.6 percent of Newhallville residents live in poverty (U.S. Department of Commerce 1993).[3]

Sycamores and maples line the streets, their arching branches creating a tunnel-like effect. The two- and three-story woodframe clapboard houses and the occasional six- to ten-unit apartment building have small, grassy yards front and back where children play and where gardens of flowers or vegetables are planted. Newhallville has neither tenements nor housing projects. The poor live side by side with owners of homes and businesses; on occasion the poor are themselves owners of homes and businesses. After a property tax hike of about 40 percent in 1992 (the first step in a five-part tax increase due to raise payments a startling average of 238 percent), abandoned buildings—fallout from bacnkruptcies and the vagaries of absent landlords—have begun to multiply at an alarming rate and can be found on almost every block in the neighborhood (62.6 percent of Newhallville housing units are rentals: United States Department of Commerce 1993). Boarded up, covered in graffiti, used as crack houses, these buildings were one sign in the early 1990s that the troubles in

---

2. In New Haven there are 18.5 infant deaths per 1,000 live births. There are some who argue the infant mortality rate in the city is inflated because Yale-New Haven Hospital has one of the nation's premiere neonatal units, and thus a higher concentration than normal of women with high-risk pregnancies and seriously ill infants. However, with one New Haven neighborhood showing an infant mortality rate of 66.7 deaths per 1,000 live births [Reguero, 1994] there are strong indications that the city has deep problems in pre-natal and neonatal health.

3. In contrast, in 1960 the Newhallville poverty rate was 17.6 percent for all persons; Newhallville's ethnic mix was 18.2% white, 81.2% "Negro," and .6% other. Between 1960 and 1990, then, the poverty rate rose by half (51%), while the minority population increase was not commensurate, growing 12.9%. Newhallville's racial segregation does not appear to have a simple cause-and-effect relationship with the area's rapid rise in poverty.

Newhallville were more than an undercurrent. Most blocks have also at least one empty lot filling with trash and discarded household appliances. Gunshots are a common occurrence, street-dealing of drugs takes place at several well-known sites as well as many more clandestine ones. At night in Newhallville, police routinely stop cars driven by young, white men on the assumption that they have only entered the neighborhood to buy drugs.

When Newhallville is referred to as a ghetto or inner-city neighborhood, it is the large minority population, visible drug trade, deteriorating housing stock, and high poverty rate that are being indirectly referenced. Susan D. Greenbaum, writing about a similar neighborhood in Kansas City, Kansas, cautions that "Ghetto is a monolithic concept, describing districts that may be ethnically uniform but which reflect a large degree of variability, both internally and among different cities. . . . When folk categories like ghetto are reified and made respectable in the models and taxonomies of scholars and analysts, consequences and intentions become viciously intertwined" (Greenbaum 1993:140). If Newhallville, with its graceful trees and carefully painted frame houses does not appear to be a "typical" ghetto or inner-city community, it is because these terms assume a great deal, and like the term "underclass" are so poorly specified as to what, exactly, they refer, that they are nearly useless for the purposes of social science.

Avoiding the loaded terminology of "ghetto" or "inner city," I instead focus on characteristics that set Newhallville and neighborhoods like it apart from the cities in which they are located. Among the most important of these elements are geographic, social, economic, and commercial isolation. These overlapping forms of isolation are not solely the result of an inward-turning community but one from which much of the rest of the city has turned away.

GEOGRAPHIC ISOLATION

Newhallville is a neighborhood that most residents must leave in order to shop or work. Stepping over Newhallville borders is a charged activity, and many Newhallville residents—like the Sistah in "Free Your Mind"—do not feel welcome in other New Haven neighborhoods, or in the city's downtown. These tensions and conflicts imbue most everyday activities with their peculiar flavor; the consumer lives of Newhallville children, under these circumstances, are similarly seasoned with these tensions and conflicts.

Newhallville's northern edge is at the border of the suburban town of Hamden. Where Hamden begins the streets abruptly become better paved, and a sleek junior high school atop a grassy hill overlooks

Newhallville's increasingly decrepit Jackie Robinson Junior High. In contrast to Hamden's windowed, brick school, Jackie Robinson is bunker-like and largely subterranean. Dominated by an orange color scheme, Jackie Robinson resembles nothing so much as a surreal prison. Much of this border area on the Hamden side is buffered by a sizable but inconvenient, uninviting, and underdeveloped park covering an area equal to about four or five city blocks.

To the east lies Prospect Street, which winds its way along the ridge of a hill separating Newhallville from the affluent Prospect Hill and East Rock neighborhoods. Lined on both sides with old mansions of twenty or more rooms, Prospect Street is not a place that any Newhallville resident I knew ever approached on foot. One man referred to Prospect Street as the "DMZ," the demilitarized zone, a sort of dangerous and charged no-man's land to be avoided. The street itself is wide, an impression that is magnified by the expanses of lawn stretching out before houses set back well away from the street. In contrast to the stoops and front porches in Newhallville where people sit, observe the action, or keep tabs on their children, Prospect Street marks the transition into neighborhoods where people stay indoors or in backyards, minding their own business.

On Newhallville's southern edge, the site of the Winchester Repeating Arms plant occupies a space equivalent to perhaps half a dozen square blocks, creating a buffer—or bulwark—between Newhallville and the city beyond. Now only partially occupied by gun production facilities, the bulk of the former factory has been torn down or rehabbed for other uses. The largest project has been Science Park, a business development whose purpose was to attract scientific research and development companies. In the process of transforming the former site of the Winchester Repeating Arms factory into Science Park, a portion of Winchester Avenue—a main neighborhood thoroughfare—was closed to the public. Gates manned by twenty-four-hour guards now stand at corners that had once been bus stops. The message is clear: Newhallville residents literally have been shut out of their own neighborhood. That this has taken place on a site that once was the area's main employer has only added insult to injury.

Processes hemming in Newhallville residents work in reverse downtown: in the city's center people like those living in Newhallville are shut out. During the early 1990s the Yale campus, like the Winchester site, became progressively more enclosed by walls, gates, and guarded entrances. While town-gown relations have long been problematic, such visible efforts to shut residents out of the campus noticeable exacerbated tensions. The permanent closing of a block of Wall Street in the downtown area of the campus—for which Yale compensated the city with a one-time payment—fueled suspicions of many minority residents that city hall and the University are in cahoots to fence them out. These suspicions took shape in a rumor that the city and Yale have together cooked up a plan to up a plan to cut off water and electricity to selected parts of the city should there ever be a repeat of the riots in the black community that took place in 1967. As one young man said, "They'll starve us out!"

SOCIAL ISOLATION

Newhallville receives few visitors—unless they are from nearby Dixwell, another poor neighborhood, or have relatives there. Those outsiders who do regularly come are mostly educators, police officers, health care workers, social science and medical students. Most are white and middle-class, and a number of them are uniformed, and so their status as outsiders is visible and underscored in multiple ways—not the least of which is that most are there to mend or circumvent social problems. This visibility is often though not always characterized by tension. In particular, teachers at the elementary school (many of whom are black) are well-loved and respected. The city's police chief, Nick Pastore, can often be found in front of the Newhallville community police station—early in the morning, midday, and late at night, clad in a white shirt and tie, talking with neighborhood kids, teenagers and adults, and dispensing his signature hug to nearly everyone who comes within his reach.

Although New Haven's population is fifty-one percent minority, the city's diversity has not resulted in an integrated residential sector: 11 of New Haven's 28 census tracts had minority populations of 60% or more in 1990 (United States Department of Commerce 1993). With a long-standing presence in New Haven that stretches back nearly to the colonial period, the African-American population in New Haven grew significantly during these postwar boom years. Between 1950 and 1960 that population nearly doubled from 9,600 to 23,000 (Minerbrook 1992:37). More recently, immigrants from Central America and the Caribbean have increased the city's minority population. These immigrants have not settled in Newhallville, however, but in other neighborhoods such as "the Hill," or in nearby Fair Haven.

Residential segregation, already well under way in the first half of this century, was given a big boost in the years during which New Haven undertook extensive urban redevelopment. The social isolation of neighborhoods such as Newhallville may be seen as being primarily a product of urban redevelopment, not the result of social factors internal to the Newhallville community. Getting in on the bottom floor of the nation's urban revitalization efforts, New Haven emerged as the nation's model "model city" by the time the Great Society years were in full swing (Fainstein 1974).

From the late 1950s through the early 1970s, over half a billion federal dollars funded urban redevelopment projects. Urban revitalization ostensibly sought to wipe out blight but many so-called improvements had a debilitating impact on the black community. Urban renewal projects eventually displaced almost forty percent of New Haven's black population, leveling long-standing communities of houses and home owners to relocate residents in housing projects which were owned and administrated by city and federal agencies. Between 1950 and 1970 about 10,000 units of housing were destroyed (Minerbrook 1992); equivalent replacement housing never materialized, and most new units were intended for middle-class and elderly residents. New Haven's residential segregation, and hence its social isolation, is hardly the result of such processes as individual preference; rather, it can be seen as the not wholly surprising outcome of programmatic urban restructuring undertaken by successive New Haven political administrations and city agencies in conjunction with Federal programs.

ECONOMIC ISOLATION

The character and population of Newhallville has changed dramatically in forty years. From the time that the neighborhood's main employer was the carriage factory owned by George T. Newhall until the 1950s, the area had been occupied primarily by German and Irish and finally Italian immigrants of the working class. Then soon after the end of World War II, throughout New Haven, large industrial employers began downsizing and relocating. The changing fortunes of the Winchester Repeating Arms plant capture the upheavals that have faced New Haven and Newhallville residents in the past fifty years. From the turn of the century until the 1950s, Winchester was a major employer in New Haven and the focal center of Newhallville. During the years around World War II, Winchester employed 12,000 people, many of them from Newhallville. By the 1970s changing employment opportunities left a bleak vista. Winchester's roster, for example, had dropped over forty percent to 7,000 workers. By the 1990s, the *entire city* of New Haven had just over 7,000 manufacturing jobs and only 475 people worked at Winchester in 1992.

Like many other places nationwide, New Haven has made the transition from a manufacturing-based economy to one where service industries provide the lion's share of jobs. Today New Haven's largest employers are Yale University and the Yale-New Haven Hospital, together accounting for 14,979 jobs (New Haven Downtown Council, 1992). These jobs are, on the whole, not only less plentiful than their manufacturing counterparts once were; they are less secure, offer fewer benefits, lower pay, and often require higher degrees of literacy or special technical skills that necessitate secondary or vocational education. Given that the cumulative dropout rate for New Haven high schools is probably near forty percent,[4] there is a great probability that public school students, at least, are unlikely to acquire the needed skills and education to secure available jobs.

Employment is a primary problem in Newhallville. Efforts to develop unused portions of the Winchester plant into a business park have yielded little. Only a small portion of the old factory had been refurbished as a development for science-based businesses and renamed "Science Park." Most of this newly developed space remained unoccupied. The irony of the situation has only been intensified by one of the most visible occupants of Science Park, the New Haven Family Alliance, a non-profit organization devoted to helping dysfunctional families and troubled youth. Neighborhood residents must ask security guards for permission to enter the former site of their (or their parents') employment in order to visit an organization whose purpose is to help families deal with stress and behaviors brought on by their poverty and underemployment.

COMMERCIAL ISOLATION

In the 1950s, the area had developed a varied and lively commercial sphere and was home to a dry cleaners, at least two drug stores, one corporate supermarket and several small-to-medium sized groceries, a butcher, several luncheonettes, two laundromats, one (and possibly more) dentists' and doctors' offices, hardware stores, and auto repair shops. In addition, according to long-time residents, the neighborhood housed a dairy plant, the Winchester plant, a pharmaceutical distribution company, and a popcorn supply house.

Not only constituent elements of the consumer setting, these last establishments were large-scale employers of neighborhood residents. Many local businesses, moreover, provided crucial services—particularly medical care. Today, the only neighborhood medical care available is from the MotherCare van, a mobile facility parked in front of the local elementary school every Thursday.[5]

A series of incidents related to police clashes with local Black Panther leaders and the riots in 1967 in which the federal government deployed

4. Official figures are hard to obtain here. This figure was quoted to me by the head of the citywide PTA. I was also told by several school administrators that significant numbers of drop outs occur in the junior high school years. High school drop out rates, then, fail to account for those students who have dropped out before starting high school.

5. Funded and operated by the local Catholic hospital, the MotherCare van provides prenatal, pediatric, and general health care, but does not provide services or information related to birth control or abortion.

the National Guard drove some white business owners out of the neighborhood; other businesses were destroyed in the burning and looting that took place. Jackson Rollins, who took me on two walking tours of his childhood neighborhood, remembers the doctor, dentist, hardware store, and pharmacy all to have been white-owned. The black-owned enterprises that came in afterward did not replace these businesses in kind: as can be seen today, they are typically small groceries, barbershops, liquor stores, and bars. Further, as Winchester and other large employers closed, businesses (such as lunch counters) which catered to factory workers foundered. Finally, an urban revitalization plan—undertaken with limited community support according to some residents—razed a large stretch of shops in preparation for a modern, new shopping strip. This new commercial center was never built.

The main places that Newhallville children frequent are corner stores, such as Rabbit's grocery, where the owner dispenses as much advice as he does change. These stores are small, and typically carry perhaps five hundred different items, compared to the 25,000 items a large supermarket is likely to stock. Kids buy chips, gum, candy, and drinks before and after school, or stop in to play video games. In comparison to large supermarkets, small markets like Rabbit's offer little choice and high prices to boot. It is difficult for a family which does not own or have access to a car to provide nourishing meals if shopping only in the neighborhood, but the nearest supermarkets are nearly two miles away.

THE MALL

If kids—or their families—want any item such as clothing, housewares, or toys, they must go downtown to the mall, or drive even further to local suburban shopping areas. Going to the mall is at once exciting and frustrating for kids from Newhallville, who are often treated with suspicion. Children's experiences at the mall illustrate the ways in which consumption is entered into and experienced as a realm of inequality—one in which other forms of inequality come into play.

Late in April of 1992, it was announced that Macy's, the New Haven mall's anchor store, would close in June. Near bankruptcy, the mall was a sinking ship. On April 1 a *New Haven Register* headline read, "White Person Slips, Falls at Mall; Black Teenager Being Sought." It turned out the headline was an April Fool's day joke published by the *New Haven*, a local weekly tabloid that emulates the *Village Voice*. The headline condensed several prickly issues New Haven residents were mulling over: the widely held perception that the local newspaper is less than even-handed in how it reports on the black community; that the mall is an unsafe place for white shoppers; and that African-American kids are the reason why whites feel uncomfortable there. This tension between the middle class, predominantly white, and often suburban population and the poorer and darker New Haven residents is one that typifies malls throughout the country, particularly those located near urban areas (Everett 1994). Rather than braving the city, the logic went, suburban shoppers stayed closer to home, shopping at malls in the nearby towns of Milford and Hamden where the "inner-city ills" to which Everett alludes above are at least minimized.

Malls in Connecticut, including New Haven, have taken steps to reduce the presence of minority youth. After a protracted legal battle, one Connecticut mall, Trumbull Shopping Park, gained the right to ban public transit from making stops on its property on Friday and Saturday nights. The owners' express reason for making this decision was security problems arising from teenagers—most of whom were minority youth from Bridgeport. New Haven had employed a similar strategy, moving bus stops from directly in front of the mall to relocate them across the street on the town green. This move considerably increased discomfort for bus riders. The original bus stops, located in front of the mall, were placed on a covered walkway open to the street that provided at least some protection from rain and snow. Across the way on the green, two rather small bus shelters hardly provide the same amount of protection from harsh weather conditions.

Some malls have gone so far as to monitor kids' dress, and the Sunrise Mall in Corpus Christi, Texas, even instituted a policy banning backward-facing baseball caps (*New York Times* 1/9/95). As a result, fashion trends among poor and minority youth are branded as signaling trouble and are likely to be prohibited from the mall. Practices such as dressing alike—common among many minority youth and not just gangs—are increasingly likely to get kids ejected from malls on the grounds that dressing alike is in itself a marker of gang affiliation. This trend is significantly more troubling than the old "No shirt, no shoes, no service" policies that were at least usually clearly posted.

In most cases policies limiting kids' access to malls, their appearance, or their behavior have been spurred by violent incidents involving guns, and, in two cases, fatal shootings. Ironically, these much-feared kids often say themselves that they go to the mall in order to be safe. In New Haven, the neighborhoods these kids come from—Newhallville, The Hill, Dixwell—are widely held by residents and outsiders alike to be unpredictably dangerous.

The owners of the seventy shops in the Chapel Square Mall considered for a time a proposal to limit the hours during which unaccompanied young people could be on the premises. When word of the proposal reached the public, it was widely criticized as racist. The conflict was typical of those cropping up around the country on the nature of mall spaces: are they public or private? How do you define "security"? If the spaces were deemed public, shop owners hardly had the legal right to bar access to kids, although the management company that runs New Haven's mall already has an official policy of keeping school-age shoppers out of the mall during school hours. If the spaces were private, mall owners could legally be held accountable for thefts, robberies, and injuries suffered by visitors.

Regardless of the reasons for which consumers who are older, more affluent, or lighter-skinned have abandoned Chapel Square, youth and teens (mostly minority) now constitute the mall's most important market (*New York Times* 11/23/93). Shop owners have had to develop subtle means of discouraging young people from spending too much time in the mall's public spaces, while enticing them to continue to spend their money in its commercial venues. These strategies include an increasingly visible uniformed security force and the use of piped music featuring genres thought to be unappealing to undesirable youth. In a variation of what Russell Baker (*New York Times* 7/23/92) jokingly called "the Beethoven Defense," I found on one visit to the New Haven mall the building's hidden speakers filling the space with songs by Frank Sinatra.

Though the relatively large proportion of black shoppers in the New Haven mall might have had something to do with its economic decline, there nevertheless seem to be other factors at work. In comparison to larger, newer, and more architecturally and visually spectacular malls, the New Haven mall—which was built in the 1960s—is rundown, offers little variety, and in contradiction of a basic mall dictum the parking is not even free. Currently the mall houses no outlets of prominent chains such as Gap, Express, Banana Republic, Pottery Barn, Crate & Barrel; instead, discount enterprises—Sam's Dollar Store, and Payless Shoes, for example—are in the majority.

Development of nearby areas has encouraged the movement of moneyed shoppers away from the mall. A prominent local development company, Schiavone, has considerably perked up the Upper Chapel Street area that is located two blocks above the mall and directly across from part of the Yale Campus. This newly-renovated stretch of shops and restaurants is now distinctly upscale, housing downtown's priciest venues. Further up, the rundown Broadway area is currently being rehabbed with a $7.5 million federal grant and a $1.9 million contribution from Yale siphoning off whatever upscale business remains downtown and relocating it closer to the Yale campus.

Lower Chapel, which once housed a large Kresge's store (Kresge's is the predecessor of K-Mart), is now home to discount stores and jewelry shops. Nearly all those shopping on Lower Chapel are black and Hispanic; while shoppers on Upper Chapel and Broadway are racially and ethnically diverse, few are poor or working-class. As one person, who had grown up in Dixwell, which borders the Broadway shopping area, said "We used to go down there to look at the people walking funny!" This remark was accompanied by a raucous imitation of the stiff, uptight walk of the middle class, whites, or fearful Yale students.

In a city already starkly segregated in its residential areas, downtown is now headed toward a similar segregation. Lower and Upper Chapel streets house shopping areas that cater to starkly different clientele. The mall physically occupies the middle ground between the two, and though perceived to be used by an ever-poorer and darker population, people who go there remain relatively diverse in both race and social and economic level, especially when compared to the territories on either side. As the physical and perceptual middle ground downtown, the mall is a conflicted site. Many shopkeepers are caught between trying to appeal to all economic levels of customers while others have attempted to capitalize upon the mall's changing demographic mix and have opened stores carrying hip-hop fashions, African folklore and artisanry, or Afro-centric merchandise.

The Chapel Square mall is not unusual in its attempts to maintain a profile as a safe, communal space that exists in distinct opposition to the chaotic, violent city beyond. Such consumer community-building amounts to the proffering of togetherness through shopping. This effort is most evident in the yearly Christmas spree of conviviality and community events sponsored by the mall.

Halloween has more recently emerged as a time when the mall is offered as a healthy alternative to the New Haven streets and all its dangers. This effort is supported not only by its own publicity efforts but by institutions such as the public schools. Since the early 1990s, mall shopkeepers have distributed candy and Halloween balloons to hordes of costumed kids who trick-or-treat their way around the two-story concourse on a weekend near the 31st of October. Significantly, this event is designed to appeal to young children and their families, segments of the population mall management finds amenable, not problematic older children and teens. During my fieldwork, the principal of the Lincoln school, sent a note to each child's family that encouraged caretakers not to allow their children to trick-or-treat door to door, but instead advised them either to take children only to family members' homes, or to go trick-or-treating at the mall. While in this scary world you cannot be sure that your neighbors will not insert razor blades into the apples they put in your child's goodie bag, you can trust that local store owners are not so perverse as to harm their customers or their families.

Community, in this situation, is not based on the kinds of mutual obligation and civic commitment embodied in the notion of neighborliness, because you cannot trust those you know. Trick-or-treating is safer amidst the relative anonymity of the mall, where shopkeepers know better than to bite the hand that feeds them. While refraining from the bite, shopkeepers do bark, and it is at their young customers that they bark most often.

NEWHALLVILLE GIRLS GO TO THE MALL

From the time they are very small, Newhallville children accompany their families, whether parents or older siblings and cousins, on downtown shopping excursions. When children—especially girls—are about ten years old, many of their families begin allowing them to go downtown without the accompaniment of their elders. Among the children from the main study group, girls go downtown alone more often than do boys, who spend much of their unsupervised time riding bikes around the neighborhood—or farther afield.

For these girls, going to the mall without adults is often a thrilling experience, and one that allows them to be playful in ways that are impossible at home and in the neighborhood. Despite widespread feelings in New Haven that the mall is not a particularly safe or comfortable space to be, the statements and behavior of Newhallville children indicate that for them, the mall offers freedoms unavailable elsewhere, while also imposing particular forms of restraint.

SPATIAL FREEDOM

As mentioned earlier, some kids go to the mall because they feel safer there than they do on the street. "Kids come here to stay out of trouble and to shop," said sixteen-year-old Cherie Lee in an interview with the *New York Times* (11/23/93). Though none of the kids I knew stated this feeling quite so directly, I was struck by the changes in their demeanor when we went to the mall. Some of these changes had more to do with the social setting than with the spaces or architecture of the mall itself. While the spatial and social aspects of Newhallville kids' mall experiences are examined here separately, these are ultimately mutually determining.

Malls are often compared to theme parks such as Disneyland in part because like theme parks, malls feature controlled, utopian, yet carnival atmospheres. Several recent megamalls, such as the Mall of America in Minnesota or West Edmonton Mall in Canada (with 5.2 million square feet) actually *contain* theme parks, further eliding the two forms that are at once architectural, social, and economic. Tionna, Natalia, and Asia, when they went to the mall often used its spaces as their own kind of personal amusement center, going down the up escalators, and up the down ones, running through public spaces loudly laughing and shouting, and tailing cute boys like easy-to-spot, giggly spies. Before Macy's had closed, the second-floor breezeway connecting the mall to the department store was a glass-encased tunnel through which they could run, gallop, shuffle, or tumble. Macy's itself was a kind of playground, with its three floors, numerous escalators, and accessible displays of electronics, jewelry, and makeup. Excerpts of field notes from a shopping expedition taken shortly before Christmas in 1992 detail some of the typical activities in which kids engaged when visiting the mall:

> Asia and Natalia lean over the second floor railing throwing pennies into the fountain below on the mall's main floor. Bunches of poinsettia plants are set high upon wire pillars that rise up out of the fountain and the brilliant red flowers seem to float in the air. By the edge of the fountain is a cart whose proprietors are selling religious clocks and metal, laser-etched images of saints and reproductions of the Last Supper. Asia and Natalia decide to try to throw a coin down on top of someone's head. They drop some pennies down. The coins miss the unsuspecting person, who is minding the cart with the Last Supper reproductions. The girls come running up to me, jumping, hopping, vibrating with the excitement and danger of what they have done. Then they spot some cute boys and take off in close pursuit. I take off after them.
>
> They have lost the boys and decide to look for them in the Macy's game section one floor up. They go up there, pretending to shop, looking at electronic typewriters. The boys are not there. After a few minutes of playing and fiddling with electronic displays, Natalia says, "Now we got to go boy huntin' again." As we are walking, Asia says, "Miss Chin looks hype. All she got to do is lose the bags." Natalia, however, announces, "Miss Chin is bad luck." Meaning it's my fault they lost the boys. We are by the escalator and the girls consider going downstairs. "That's where the perfume is," Natalia says. We go up to the third floor again. No boys. "Miss Chin, you're making us lose men," Natalia wails. We go all the way to the first floor and the girls stop at the Clinique counter for a few minutes, playing with the facial "computer" there. We head back upstairs again, on an escalator, and on the way the girls place coins on the moving rubber rail, calling to me and saying, "We gave the coins a ride!"

In pursuing the boys the thrill is in the chase itself. Exploring different departments in Macy's, playing with electronic typewriters and children's toys, riding the escalators, fiddling with cosmetics displays are fun and exciting for these kids. These activities would be fun for any kids, but what was absent from the surface, at least, of these children's playful meandering, was any engagement with most spaces as consumers with money to spend. They played with the typewriters just to play with them, not so that they could think about buying them or even wish that they could have one of their own. The escalators were by far the most exciting and fascinating element, aside from a certain pleasure they seemed to take in knowing they were on the verge of wildness—all the roaming up and down and up and down again—and yet unlikely to suffer any painful consequences.

This was *their* mall: a large, open, interesting, exciting space, full of cute boys and girls and dotted with inconvenient security guards and disapproving grownups; lined with stores containing fascinating merchandise; punctuated by escalators that lifted them to the mysteries above or lowered them to the unknown below. They were not there only or even primarily to shop, but to explore, to go "boy huntin'" as Natalia said, and to generate a safe, yet thrilling, excitement. This is not the sort of use for which Macy's or the mall were designed or perhaps intended; like the amusement park, Macy's and the mall presented the kids with a closely monitored—and hence relatively safe—space.

SOCIAL FREEDOM

Being at the mall does not place kids in a field of unadulterated freedom, but it does allow some pressures and problems to recede from the forefront of their experiences. Tionna, Natalia, and Asia can revel in being girls while at the mall. At home, they worry that men might be after them; in the mall, they chase boys as if every day were Sadie Hawkins day. The following are portions of an interaction that took place in the mall's food court:

> Asia spies a boy she knows. With ten-year-old bravado, Natalia says that she's going to get up and go over to them. Asia tells her to go ahead. Overcome with the idea, Natalia suddenly decides she can't possibly do it. Asia gets up and goes over to the boys, tells one of them that Natalia likes him. Natalia squirms, moans, giggles, slides under the table and, emerging again, tries to bury herself inside her coat. Asia comes back. I drink my soda and they eat, glancing back at the boys who are sometimes looking our way. The taller boy comes over and says to Natalia that the other boy wants her to go over there. Now she's really dying. She's saying she's too shy and she can't talk to them.

The freedom might appear, from an adult point of view to be very childlike, even though much of it focuses on boy-girl interactions of a romantic nature. However, the girls, at least, think of these mall outings as a way to begin to explore growing up, not being kids. Tionna explained that at the mall "We try not to act like kids. When we're here, at home, then we act like kids, we play, we play with our dolls." Being able to explore the city and the mall on their own is thus a mark of maturity—one intrinsically opposed to the vulnerability of childhood and playing with dolls at home. Children often yearn to be grown-up for a whole host of reasons. For Tionna, Natalia, and Asia, one of these might be that feeling of freedom and safety they receive when roaming downtown.

CONSTRAINTS

Minority youth are well aware that they are at best only temporarily welcome—and then only under certain circumstances—in most mall spaces, and that they are almost if not literally unwelcome in others. The loud and often disruptive behavior of Newhallville kids in the mall can be seen in part as an assertion of their right not only to be where they are, but to be in the world.

The most obvious way that kids are made to feel self-conscious is when store employees or owners pointedly watch or follow them as they move through stores. Children are extremely sensitive to this. Asia, when preparing to enter Claire's, an inexpensive accessory store, recounted a recent experience in which she imagines being able to one-up a salesclerk whom she feels had mocked her on an earlier occasion because she was short of money:

> "Last time I was in there the lady was laughing because I didn't have enough money. The other day I went in and I bought all this stuff and the lady said, 'that will be forty dollars.' I pulled out a fifty dollar bill and said, 'Here.'" Asia demonstrated, and the look on her face was both self-satisfied and challenging. "I swear I was about to say 'keep the change' until my grandmother came up," she said.

Asia's story captures the pressures many Newhallville kids face in having to assert their right to be in the mall by demonstrating their ability to buy. In Asia's story, when she is at first unable to pay for what she wants, she is sure that the saleslady is laughing at her. The pleasure she took later in being able to present this woman with a fifty dollar bill was palpable, as was her frustration in not being able to add insult to injury by imperiously directing the woman to keep the change.

These kinds of interactions—where black shoppers are assumed to be unable to make purchases, where they are steered toward inferior merchandise, or where they are poorly treated as if giving them attention is a waste of time—are recounted often by young and old alike. These kinds of problems are one reason, for instance, why many Newhallville residents dress up when going downtown to shop: it is an effort to appear respectable to store personnel, and so to be treated with attention and respect.

Regardless of the impressions kids want to create, money is often an issue for them. Walking through Macy's one afternoon, Asia spotted an outfit she thought was "cute." After looking at the price tag, however, she said "Once you see the price of clothes it's not cute any more. It's expensive." Kid's experience of desire was circumscribed by their own sense of what was a good price for something—and, I suspect, by their keen knowledge of the limited nature of their own and their family's finances.

Two mothers told me why it is so important to rein in children's desires, and to require them to suppress those desires:

> "If you get them used to having all this stuff, when they get older and you say no, they get *real upset*," Diana said, explaining why she is so adamant now about saying "when I say no it means no," to the kids. "I don't promise them things," she said. "I say, 'we'll see.' " "What do you mean when you say they get upset?" I asked. "Well," said Yvonne, "if you buy them all these expensive things when they're little, they still expect you to buy it when they're older. My mother raised seven children alone and she worked three jobs. She always got us the best of everything. She went to the best stores, we always had nice clothes. Now I still get mad when I can't have things. I can act like a little kid, and I say 'I want that!' "

More than once I came across children in Newhallville with tear-stained faces, after they had been punished for being "bad" in the store, which usually meant asking one time too many for something. By the time kids are nine or ten, they seem to know better than to ask or pester. In the course of the research I took over twenty-five separate shopping trips with children, yet I only heard them say "I want that" once or twice. Only one child directly asked me to purchase anything. He later explained to me that he was purposely testing me and announced, "You weak!" Several refused my offers to buy them small things, such as a soda or ice cream cone, saying "I don't want to spend up all your money, Miss Chin!"

CONCLUSION

In the summer of 1992, music from the debut album of the 90s girl group En Vogue was a hit nationwide in the United States. All over Newhallville the song floated out of open windows, or erupted from the bass-heavy speakers of passing cars. Kids enthusiastically belted out words to one of the album's songs, "Free Your Mind":

So I'm a sistah
Buy things with cash
That really doesn't mean that all my credit is bad
So why dispute me and waste my time
Because you think that the price is too high for me
I can't look without being watched
You rang my buy before I made up my mind
Oh now attitude why even bother
I can't change your mind you can't change my color

In a song that criticizes and questions racism and sexism, an entire verse is dedicated to the experience of consumption. This song resonated strongly among Newhallville's children: for them—as for many African Americans, shopping is a consumer activity fraught with conflict and contradiction. "Free Your Mind" highlights a number of issues that New-hallville kids often confront: the assumptions made by salespeople that a "sistah" who pays with cash also has bad credit (and is therefore poor); of being watched while shopping (because they are potential shoplifters); of being treated with a lack of respect and politeness (because they are poor, potential shoplifters, and black). The final line in the verse pinpoints the problem as one of racism: "I can't change your mind, you can't change my color."

Popular stereotypes of African Americans often hinge on what is perceived to be their pathological involvement with consumption. From the image of the welfare queen—stereotypically an unwed teenage mother who has dropped out of school to live off the state while buying Nike sneakers for herself—to the gold-draped and logo-clad drug dealer who feels no remorse at committing random violence in the pursuit of territory or profits or debts, black consumers are viewed as being what have been described as "a nation of thieves" (Austin 1994). The En Vogue song, however, illuminates another point of view and instead describes the frustration, anger, and humiliation often felt by black shoppers whether at the supermarket or Saks Fifth Avenue.

Consumption is a complex process that involves not just shopping and buying but also thinking about, wishing for, and using commodities in a variety of settings and for a variety of purposes. Because consumption is fundamentally social, it is at once a sphere of inequality on its own and a medium through which other forms of inequality are perpetuated. As with other forms of structural inequality—such as class, race, and gender—the mechanisms perpetuating inequalities in the consumer sphere are subtly enforced in and through mundane activities: watching television, shopping, reading, playing. The children who are the subject of this work witness and experience themselves as situated in race, class, gender, and age as they see ads for things they know they cannot possess, as they are closely monitored when browsing in stores, as they play with toys whose fantasy lives they reject.

In Asia's critique of Barbie, she observes that there is no fat Barbie, no abused Barbie, a comment that directly addresses the doll's inability to speak to some of the central concerns of Asia's own life. In the neighborhood, where protecting oneself from sexual danger is part of the daily routine, it is striking that Asia does not even enter a playful mode when she discusses this issue as it relates to a toy. The incident did, however, contain some powerful aspects of playfulness—these related not to Barbie, but to consumer media themselves such as television, the narrative form of the talk show, and the consuming public. The clear and critical voice and eye that Asia applies to her view of Barbie while on a New-hallville stoop becomes a little shakier at the mall, when she cannot confront a store clerk who she believes has humiliated her, with the same directness. While she wants to humiliate the woman in return, she cannot while actually at the mall. She is able to recover some of her bravado as she relates the story when back in her own neighborhood, at a safe distance from the mall itself and the constraints it places upon her.

Surprisingly little research deals with the consumer lives of children and even less has directly addressed consumption in a nonwhite, non-middle-class setting (Honeycutt 1975 is one exception). This attention gap arises in part because the notion of the poor consumer is an apparent oxymoron: how can one be engaged with consumption without the means to consume? The common assumption is that those without economic resources who do consume do so dysfunctionally; poor consumers who are also black and young are portrayed not as being just dysfunctional but as being pathological in their patterns of consumption.

In a growing literary genre that seeks to portray life on the mean streets of big cities like Chicago, Los Angeles, and New York, out-of-control consumption is continually evoked to provide garish accent to descriptions of the grinding routine of living life in deep poverty. Liberal accounts such as *On the Edge* (Nightingale 1993) take the position that the pathology is not the fault, really, of any given individual, but is due to a faulty social system and the evils of consumption itself; conservative treatments of the issue see nothing much wrong with consumerism but rather bemoan the loss of family values, morals, and a lack of ability to delay gratification (Wilson 1987). My stance jibes with neither of these points of view. Consumption is much too pervasive to reject or wish away, and the issues presented by looking at consumption in communities like New-hallville must be understood not only as acts of individuals but as acts that also take place in a particular set of circumstances. What Newhallville kids do as they shop, try to earn money, or play with toys reflects, among other things, the fearsome struggles in which they must daily engage as they negotiate territories of race, class, gender, and age.

REFERENCES

Austin, Regina
    1994   "A Nation of Thieves": Consumption, Commerce, and the Black
          Public Sphere. Public Culture 7(1):225–248.
City of New Haven
    1982   Inside New Haven's Neighborhoods: A Guide to the City of New
          Haven. New Haven: New Haven Colony Historical Society.
Commission, City of New Haven Blue Ribbon
    1990   Final Report of the Blue Ribbon Commission Appointed by Mayor
          John C. Daniels. City of New Haven, 1990.
Everett, Peter S.
    1994   Violence Comes to the Mall. Trial 30:62–65.
Fainstein, Norman I. and Susan S. Fainstein
    1974   Urban Political Movements: The Search for Power by Minority
          Groups in American Cities. Englewood Cliffs: Prentice-Hall, Inc.
Greenbaum, Susan D.
    1993   Housing Abandonment in Inner-City Black Neighborhoods: A Case
          Study of the Effects of the Dual Housing Market. *In* The Cultural
          Meaning of Urban Space. Robert Rotenberg and Gary McDonogh,
          eds. pp. 139–156. Westport: Bergin and Garvey.
Honeycutt, Andrew
    1975   An Ethnographic Study of Low Income Consumer Behavior.
          Unpublished DBS Dissertation, Harvard University.
Minerbrook, Scott
    1992   Why A City Alone Cannot Save Itself: The Story of New Haven
          Shows How Big Social and Economic Forces Overwhelm Local
          Leaders. U.S. News and World Report, November 9, 1992:36–40.
New Haven Downtown Council
    1992   Major Employers in New Haven County. New Haven Downtown
          Council, 1992.
Nightingale, Carl
    1993   On the Edge: A History of Poor Black Children and their American
          Dreams. New York: Basic Books.
Reguero, Wilfred and Marilyn Crane
    1994   Project MotherCare: One Hospital's Response to the High
          Perinatal Death Rate in New Haven, CT. Public Health Reports
          109(5):647–652.
Sorkin, Michael, ed.
    1992   Variations on a Theme Park: The New American City and the End
          of Public Space. New York: Farrar, Straus and Giroux.

Tomlinson, Alan
    1990   Introduction: Consumer culture and the aura of the commodity.
            In Consumption, Identity, and Style: Marketing, Meanings and the
            Packaging of Pleasure. Alan Tomlinson, ed. pp. 1–40. London and
            New York: Routledge.

U.S. Department of Commerce
    1993   Detailed Housing Characteristics: Connecticut. Government
            Printing Office, 1993.

Williams, Rosalind H.
    1982   Dream Worlds: Mass Consumption in Late Nineteenth-Century
            France. Berkeley: University of California Press.

Wilson, William Julius
    1987   The Truly Disadvantaged: The Inner City, the Underclass, and
            Public Policy. Chicago: University of Chicago Press.